Francis T. Bassett

The Catholic Epistle of St. James

A Revised Text With Translation, Introduction, And Notes, Critical And Exegetical

Francis T. Bassett

The Catholic Epistle of St. James
A Revised Text With Translation, Introduction, And Notes, Critical And Exegetical

ISBN/EAN: 9783337840341

Printed in Europe, USA, Canada, Australia, Japan

Cover: Foto ©Lupo / pixelio.de

More available books at **www.hansebooks.com**

THE CATHOLIC
EPISTLE OF ST. JAMES.

A REVISED TEXT.

WITH TRANSLATION, INTRODUCTION, AND NOTES,
CRITICAL AND EXEGETICAL.

BY

FRANCIS TILNEY BASSETT, M.A.,

VICAR OF DULVERTON,

AUTHOR OF "TRANSLATION OF THE PROPHET HOSEA," ETC.

Multæ terricolis linguæ, cœlestibus una.

LONDON:
SAMUEL BAGSTER AND SONS,
15, PATERNOSTER ROW.
1876.

TO THE

Rev. THOMAS DEHANY BERNARD, M.A.,

CANON RESIDENTIARY OF WELLS, AND RECTOR OF WALCOT,

THE FOLLOWING PAGES ARE

INSCRIBED WITH GRATITUDE AND ESTEEM.

CONTENTS.

	PAGE
PREFACE	
Introduction	i.
Epistle of St. James	1
Excursus on the " Glory "	87

PREFACE.

In the midst of the multitude of commentaries, critical, exegetical, and homiletical, which swell our religious literature at the present day, an apology may seem to be the necessary prelude to introducing this small volume to the theological public.

The great uncertainty that hangs like a mist over the authorship of this Epistle, the long birth-struggle that preceded its affiliation among the canonical Scriptures, the peculiarity of its structural composition, the absence of Christian dogma, the confessed difficulty in harmonizing the treatise on justification with the doctrinal definitions of St. Paul, and other inspired writers on the same subject, may furnish sufficient ground for some further inquiry, especially as, to the writer's mind, the whole question has been treated in an unsatisfactory manner; the evidence of facts has not been fairly admitted, theories or guesses of by-gone days have been accepted without sifting their value, and these loose and unsupported conjectures of an uncritical period, leaning on the artificial aid of an unquestioning tradition, have come down to the church of our day, and been received as authoritative and reliable.

PREFACE.

The present work proposes a system which is based in the first place on external evidence and objective facts, the only sure foundation for the student of Scripture to build upon, and this in the second place is strengthened by internal evidence and undesigned coincidences, the screws and rivets which, though small and to many invisible, have no mean office in bracing and holding together the superstructure. This system, it is believed, will account for the various perplexing phenomena both in the history and the contents of the Epistle.

The pages have not been burdened with an ever-recurring and overwhelming reference to authorities, as is too frequent in theological works; it will be enough to say that solitude in opinion has not been regarded as strength, and above all the hope has been cherished that the Spirit of God may vouchsafe to employ the feeble ὀρμή of the pilot to guide the ship to the haven of truth, chap. iii. 4.

My thanks are due for many acts of courtesy and kindness to Professors Westcott, Lightfoot, Swainson, and Wright, of the University of Cambridge; and to the Rev. F. Field, late Fellow of Trinity College, and, through him, to Dr. Ceriani of the Ambrosian Library, Milan, and to Dr. Lange of the University of Bonn.

DULVERTON VICARAGE,
February 8th, 1876.

THE EPISTLE OF ST. JAMES.

INTRODUCTION.

THE AUTHORSHIP.

OPINION, almost universal, has excluded St. James, the son of Zebedee, from the authorship of this Epistle: the general verdict may be summed up in one word, "It is impossible." Whether this sentence is arrived at on enlightened and sufficient grounds is a grave question. However that may be, the honour of penning this Epistle has been conferred upon another James, who is called the brother of the Lord, and was the Bishop of Jerusalem, although no small controversy has arisen as to his identity with James the Less, or rather the Little, the son of Alphæus, one of the twelve Apostles.

It will be sufficient for us to distinguish him at present from James the Elder, as he has been called, the brother of John and the son of Zebedee, who was one of the first called among the Apostles and one of the favoured three among them.

In entering upon the question of the authorship of this Epistle, it is necessary to premise that the whole subject is exceedingly unsettled, and that the ordinary opinion rests on very weak and uncertain foundations; and further, that there is some evidence for believing that James, the son of Zebedee, was the writer of this Epistle. After a careful investigation of the question of authorship, this opinion has been forced upon the mind. External evidence on the whole subject is extremely vague and next to valueless; a decision of the question is on external grounds impossible; room is left only for opinion, which must be formed solely on the internal evidence furnished by the Epistle itself, and the undesigned coincidences which link it to the Gospel narrative.

The point at present submitted to our inquiry is to distinguish between the claims to the authorship, it will therefore be necessary to confine our remarks to this subject alone; we have nothing to do, consequently, with references in Patristic writings to this Epistle, real or supposed, unless those passages bear upon the question of *authorship*.

The first who quotes this Epistle with the addition of a name is Origen, who flourished in the middle of the third century. In his commentary on St. John he uses the words ἐν τῇ φερομένῃ Ἰακώβου ἐπιστολῇ, where it will be observed he does not say to which James he ascribed the Epistle. In Rufinus' Latin version of Origen's Homily, the eighth on Exodus we read, "Apostolus Jacobus dicit," but again he does not specify which one of that name. In one place he is called the "brother of the Lord," but it must be remembered that this was only in a translation made after the question was looked on as settled.

Eusebius, who lived in the early part of the fourth century, in his well known Ecclesiastical History, in speaking of this Epistle says, ἡ λεγομένη Ἰακώβου φέρεται ἐπιστολή., *H. E.*, iii. 25. And again, after quoting from the writings of Hegesippus an account of the martyrdom of James the Just, the Bishop of Jerusalem, he writes: "These accounts are given respecting James, whose the first of those called Catholic Epistles is said to be:" Οὐ ... εἶναι λέγεται, *H. E.*, ii. 23. See also iii. 25.

Jerome, who lived at the close of the same century, says, "James who is called the brother of the Lord, and surnamed the Just, wrote only one Epistle, which is one of the seven Catholic Epistles, though it is asserted to have been published by some one else, though by degrees, as time went on, it gained authority:" "Jacobus, qui appellatur frater Domini, cognomento Justus, unam tantum scripsit Epistolam, quæ de septem catholicis est, quæ et ipsa ab alio quodam sub nomine ejus edita asseritur, licet paullatim tempore procedente obtinuerit auctoritatem." The authority of the Syrian Church and of Ephrem Syrus has been cited in favour of the ordinary view, but it would appear that this is based upon the Greek version of his works only. See Westcott's *Canon of the New Testament*, p. 395.

Such is all the evidence to be gleaned from the ancient church in favour of the authorship by the Bishop of Jerusalem, and the sum total of that evidence does not go beyond the words λέγεσθαι and φέρεσθαι. Even in the judgment of Eusebius it was only a hear-say, a tradition more or less circumstanced in doubt. And Jerome, whose critical attainments were the highest in the Western Church, qualifies his former statement by throwing the gravest suspicions on the whole subject. However, it would seem that the impression that the Bishop of Jerusalem was the author gradually passed current, and when the Council of Carthage, A.D. 397, accepted the Epistle as canonical, all disputings were laid to rest. The Fathers of this period and their successors in after times ascribe the Epistle to the Lord's brother, but the strength of a chain is only the strength of its weakest point, and the abundant assertions of a late period will not compensate for the lack of testimony on the part of those who lived nearest to the date of the composition of the Epistle.

The internal evidence in favour of the authorship by the Bishop of Jerusalem may be summed up briefly. That there was not time before the date of the martyrdom of the son of Zebedee, which occurred A.D. 44, for so large a number of Jewish Christians to be found in the Dispersion; but this begs the question, a most important one as will be seen, whether the Epistle is addressed to believers in Christ only. The corrupt condition of the churches is also advanced, which could not have increased to such an extent at an early date; but this begs the same question. Various features in the graphic descriptions with which the Epistle abounds, serve to show that the author's residence was in Judæa, and that he had an intimate acquaintance with the characteristics of the Holy Land; but such evidence would be equally applicable to both, and therefore may be passed by as irrelevant to our question. Perhaps the only verbal coincidence that would furnish an argument for the authorship by the Bishop is the use of the verb $\chi\alpha i\rho\epsilon\iota\nu$, chap. i. 1, which reminds us forcibly of the superscription to the letter sent to the Gentiles containing the sentence of the Council of Jerusalem, Acts xv. 23, which was undoubtedly from the pen of the Bishop of Jerusalem.* The implied nearness of the destruction of Jerusalem has also been advanced, but this is a most uncertain basis: this portion of the Epistle will be found hereafter to furnish evidence in favour of the authorship by the son of Zebedee.

We now turn our attention to the arguments that may be adduced in support of the view that St. James the Elder was the author of this Epistle.

The superscriptions and subscriptions to the Epistle found in the most ancient uncial MSS. claim our attention in the first place; those that are affixed in later ones, necessarily in a case like this, are of little value, as opinions had settled down on the matter. There is no superscription in ℵ, A and C; B superscribes Ιακωβου επιστολη. In the subscription ℵ has επιστολη ιακωβου, B has Ιακωβου, and A Ιακωβου επιστολη.

It will be perceived that these, the most important MSS. we possess, state nothing beyond the name of James. There is no mark that would attribute the Epistle to any one of the three of that name.

We now turn to the ancient versions. There were but two made in the earliest days of the Christian era. For convenience sake we may mention first the old Italic Version, made most probably at the commencement of the second century in Africa. It is most probable that this version did not contain *originally* the Epistle of St. James; there is, however, a MS., Codex Corbeiensis *ff.*, which contains among other writings the Epistle of St. James in an *ante-Hieronymian* translation. This MS. itself is held to be of the ninth century. Martianay made an edition of St. James' from this at

* See note on chap. i. 1.

Paris, A.D. 1695, but it has since been conveyed to St. Petersburgh. This valuable MS. has definitely this subscription to our Epistle, "Explicit Epistola Jacobi filii Zebedæi."

There was only one other version of equally early date, the Peshito Syriac. The exact period at which it was executed cannot be determined, but it certainly existed in the second century, and was probably made at the close of the first century of Christianity. There are several points of interest in connection with this version that have a bearing on the Epistle of St. James. Syriac had become the vernacular dialect in Galilee. The Apostles spoke Syriac. A large number of early believers used this dialect also. It has even been held by some that this Epistle, as well as the Gospel of St. Matthew, and the Epistle to the Hebrews, was composed in Syriac and afterwards translated into Greek. The Syriac Version was undeniably made in the neighbourhood where the Epistle was written, and the task of translation must have been performed by one who was allied in tongue and thought with the highest authorities, the Apostles or their immediate successors. Now the oldest MSS. of this version have, either in the superscription or the subscription, or both: "The Epistle of James the Apostle." This brings in another point of evidence, and narrows the question in some degree. If the view enunciated by Jerome, that the son of Alphæus and the brother of the Lord are identical, is untenable; or if the opinion held by the ancient church that James the brother of the Lord was the son of Joseph by a former marriage, be true, then the Bishop of Jerusalem was not an Apostle; and consequently the author must either be the son of Zebedee, or the son of Alphæus; there is little that can be advanced, either from ancient testimony or internal evidence, in favour of the latter, if he is regarded as a distinct person from the Bishop; and but few modern critics who make this distinction support his pretensions to the honour.

But it has been long and freely asserted that the Peshito Syriac assigns this Epistle to James the son of Zebedee; this brings us to an interesting question in connection with the testimony of the printed editions of the Peshito Syriac Version. Grotius, in the *Critici Sacri*, writes, "Jacobum hunc Syrus, qui inscriptionem fecit ad has et sequentes Epistolas, putat fuisse Zebedaidem."

And Pole in his *Synopsis Criticorum* quotes and supports this: "Erat hic Jacobus Zebedæi, Ita putat Syrus, qui inscriptionem fecit ad has et sequentes Epistolas."

Hammond, in his paraphrase of the New Testament, bears a like testimony: "though the Syriac conceive it (the author of the Epistle) to be the son of Zebedee."

Michaelis, in his introduction, vol. iv. p. 277, says: "In the Syriac Version, into which the Epistle of St. James, the first of St. Peter, and the first of St. John have alone been admitted as canonical, these three Epistles have the following joint subscription, according to the edition of Widmanstadt: 'In the name of our Lord Jesus Christ we here close the three Epistles of James, Peter, and John, who were witnesses to the revelation from our Lord when He was transfigured on Mount Tabor, and who saw Moses and Elias speaking with him.'

"In the edition of the Syriac Version published by

Tremellius the subscription is to the same purport, but more concise: "The three Epistles of the blessed Apostles, before whose eyes our Lord was transfigured, namely James, Peter, and John." According to this subscription, then, the elder James, the son of Zebedee, was the author of the Epistle, for he, and not the younger James, the son of Alphæus, was present at the transfiguration."

Lange, in the introduction to his commentary on this Epistle (p. 10, Clark's translation), follows the same view: "the subscription in the Peshito and that in an old Latin translation ascribe without any reason the authorship to him" (that is, to James the son of Zebedee).

And the writer of the article on this Epistle in the *Bible Dictionary* repeats the assertion: "The author of the Epistle must be either James the son of Zebedee, according to the subscription of the Syriac Version; or James the son of Alphæus, according to Dr. Davidson's view; or James the brother of the Lord," etc.

After all this *catena* of authorities, it may be well to investigate on what ground the assertion rests. The MSS. of the Peshito Syriac in the British Museum, ranging from the fifth or sixth century to the eighth, have simply in the superscription of the Epistle, or in the subscription, or both, "The Epistle of James the Apostle," ܐܓܪܬܐ ܕܝܥܩܘܒ ܫܠܝܚܐ, but no further mark of identification is furnished.*

We now come to consider the printed editions of the

---

* A MS. in the Cambridge University Library has in the subscription, "Here ends the Catholic Epistle of James, chief of the Apostles and Bishop of Jerusalem." This MS., however, is not older than the eleventh or twelfth century, and therefore this testimony is almost valueless.

Peshito, to which reference has already been made in citing the remarks of Michaelis.

In the year 1555 the first printed edition of the Peshito was published at Vienna by Albert Widmanstadt, Chancellor of the Emperor Ferdinand I. Moses of Mardin, legate from the monophysite Patriarch Ignatius to Pope Julius III., seems to have supplied a MS. of the Jacobite family for the purpose. Widmanstadt contributed a second MS. of his own, and these two scholars, together with Portell, edited the work. It is in this edition of the Peshito that the title quoted by Michaelis is found: ܟܬܒܐ ܕܬܠܬ ܫܠܝܚܐ ܫܠܝܚܐ ܝܥܩܘܒ ܦܛܪܘܣ ܘܝܘܚܢܢ. . .

Tremellius published a second edition in 1569. This contained the New Testament in Hebrew characters, with a literal Latin version. Tremellius used several MSS. in preparing his work. It is from this edition that the second quotation in Michaelis is made: דְּיַתִיקָא חֲדָתָא הַגּוּדְרִין . . . וּתְלַת אִגְּרָן דִּתְלַת שְׁלִיחָא דְּאִשְׁתְּחַלַּף מָרָן לְעֵינַיְהוּן הַגּוּדְרִין דְּיַעֲקוֹב וְדְפָטְרוֹס וְדְיוֹחָנָן.

The assertion so freely made by Grotius and Pole and later writers that the Peshito Syriac assigns this Epistle expressly to James the son of Zebedee, appears to be without any foundation so far as the authority of MSS. is concerned, and must have been derived from this general title to the three Catholic Epistles in these early editions of the printed text. Then the question will arise, could Widmanstadt have found this title in either of the MSS. he used, or did he supply the title himself? Again, did Tremellius derive his general title from the MSS. he used, or did he take it from Widmanstadt? It has been suggested to me by a learned friend that the word ܚܬܡܢܢ, which Michaelis renders, "we close," signifies properly "we seal," and so might be understood of the "closing" of a book; but that this meaning is scarcely suitable for the title placed at the *beginning* of the three Epistles, for Widmanstadt prefixes it as an introductory note: hence he infers that the first editors of the printed Syriac copies adopted this verb as the nearest and best to express the newly discovered operation of *printing* in the same way that τυποῦν and *imprimere* were adopted in Greek and Latin for the same purpose.* This theory, if accepted, would prove that the title was inserted by Widmanstadt, as the mention of *printing* could have had no place in the MS. from which he framed his edition; it would also account for the mistranslation of Michaelis; but if not accepted, the origin of this title is left in mystery. Still it is a testimony of some importance, however it arose, that Widmanstadt and his co-adjutors held this view of the question of authorship, as it is well known Luther did at least at one period of his life, though it does not appear from what source their opinions on the subject were derived.

At all events we may come to the conclusion that from this insertion in the earliest printed editions of the Peshito, the impression was made on after critics that this ancient translation of the Scriptures contained a *direct* authority for assigning this Epistle to St. James the son of Zebedee, an assertion which is not supported by the facts of the case.

* This verb is used in this acceptation in the Syriac Bible edited by the late Professor Lee.

The external evidence thus being, as we have already observed, feeble on all sides, we must have recourse to internal evidence, as the only means left us of arriving at a conclusion; the attention of the reader is therefore solicited to the internal testimony and the undesigned coincidences furnished by the Epistle in favour of the authorship by the son of Zebedee.

(1) There were three Apostles who, if we may so express it, were in the first class of the Apostolic College. It is well known that Peter, James, and John were the favoured three, ἐκλεκτῶν ἐκλεκτότεροι, as Clemens Alexandrinus calls them; that they (with Andrew) were the first called both to discipleship and apostleship, and that these three had the privilege of being present on the most important occasions in our Lord's life and ministry: we may note especially their being witnesses of the transfiguration on the Mount, Matt. xvii. 1, and of the agony in the garden, Matt. xxvi. 37. The prominent position of the three is so patent that we need not press upon the reader the evidence furnished of the rivalry which existed in the prayer of the widow of Zebedee and her two sons, that they might sit on the right hand and on the left hand of the Lord in His kingdom. Neither is it necessary to urge the strong probability that at the last supper, in the upper room at Jerusalem, this prayer received a kind of answer which might be typical of their rank in the future kingdom, for St. John was on the right hand of Jesus, and as it is certain from St. Peter's making signs to him to ask Jesus who the traitor was, he could not have occupied the place on the left hand; it remains therefore almost proved that the second place of dignity was conferred

upon the other member of the favoured three, on St. James. It would appear strange that one who had so exalted a rank in the ministry during our Lord's life on earth, who had been an eyewitness of the most impressive scenes, and afterwards was honoured with the first crown of martyrdom among the apostolic band, should have come so far behind his compeers in the greatest privileges, St. Peter and St. John, in being excluded from the honour of leaving his testimony to others in the writings of the inspired Scriptures. St. Peter has bequeathed to the church his two Epistles and doubtless the Gospel which bears the name of St. Mark, and St. John has left behind him his Gospel, three Epistles, and the Apocalypse. It would seem, therefore, *a priori*, most probable that St. James, their fellow in previous honours, should also leave some like legacy of the wealth of grace he had received from his divine Master, some testimony of his own to the truth on the page of the inspired Word.

(2) Assuming for the instant that St. James the Elder did not only preach with his voice, but also pen some writing with his hand, we may fairly take this Epistle which has come down to us under the name of James, without allotment of that name, and subject it to examination with a view to discover whether there are any hints or undesigned coincidences which link together expressions in the Epistle with the history and experience of the son of Zebedee as narrated in the Gospel history.

No one can have read this Epistle with ordinary care without observing the close resemblance that exists between the teaching of the writer and the ministerial utterances of John the Baptist. The burden of the

Baptist's preaching was conviction of sin and the necessity of repentance. The same exhortations are echoed throughout this Epistle. The Gospel is not revealed in its full development as a system of reconciliation, pardon, and peace to the believer, but the pathway for its acceptance is being cut through the forest of opposing passions and prejudices with the axe of conviction, and the summons to the heart of the hardened Jew, "Thou art the man." The general parallel between the Baptist and the Apostle is so obvious that we need only point out a few passages, by way of example, where the correspondence is clearest. Compare Matt. iii. 8 with James i. 22, 27; Luke iii. 11 with chap. ii. 15, 16; Matt. iii. 9 with chap. ii. 19, 20; Matt. iii. 10, 12 with chap. v. 1-6. This similarity in the teaching leads us to enquire whether there was any acquaintance between the two; whether the son of Zebedee had come within ear-shot of the preaching of the Nazarite of the wilderness. We gather from Jno. i. 35, 42, that on one occasion when the Baptist was engaged in the great work of his mission, two of his disciples were with him, and when he uttered the memorable words, "Lo! the Lamb of God," they followed Jesus to whom their teacher directed them. One of the twain, we are told, was Andrew, himself an intimate companion of James, see Matt. iv. 18-22. And the other, there can be little doubt, was his brother John, who in his writings invariably conceals himself under the anonym of humility. Moreover, Andrew's first act after converse with the Lord is recorded. He went and found his brother Simon and brought him to Jesus, Jno. i. 42. It would be quite in keeping with the customary delicacy of St. John to suppress the fact that he did the same kind office to his own brother; but be this as it may, we have here in close connection with the Baptist, Andrew, a friend, and most probably John, the brother, and Peter, another friend, of James. It is most likely that all the party, the leading quaternion in the Christian army, were all disciples of John the Baptist before they enlisted under Jesus, the great Captain of Salvation; but it is quite sufficient for our purpose to show that James, the brother of John and intimate friend of Andrew and Peter, must have had either personal knowledge of the Baptist, or have heard immediately after he had delivered his startling discourses, graphic accounts of them from those that had heard them; and thus from his own hearing or from immediate information from those that had been present, a similarity in their mode of teaching arose, to say nothing of the special purpose which both had in their minds, a subject which will be treated of in another place. It is almost needless to remind the reader that James the son of Alphæus does not appear to have received his call to discipleship at this early period, as we find no mention of him till Matt. x. 3, and if we regard the brother of the Lord and subsequent Bishop of Jerusalem as distinct from him, it is evident from the testimony of St. John, chap. vii. 5, that at a period some time after this he was not reckoned amongst the disciples.

Another feature in this Epistle which has attracted universal notice is the striking similarity which is traceable between it and the sermon on the mount. The principal parallels, to quote the summary given of them

INTRODUCTION.

in the late Dean Alford's *Prolegomena* to this Epistle, are:

JAMES		MATT.
chap. i. 2	with	chap. v. 10-12.
i. 4		v. 48.
i. 5; v. 15		vii. 7 and foll.
i. 9		v. 3.
i. 20		v. 22.
ii. 13		vi. 14, 15; v. 7.
ii. 14 and foll.		vii. 21 and foll.
iii. 17, 18		v. 9.
iv. 4		vi. 24.
iv. 10		v. 3, 4.
iv. 11		vii. 1 and foll.
v. 2		vi. 19.
v. 10		v. 12.
v. 12		v. 33 and foll.

It is purposed to treat of the reason of this relationship between the sermon of the Master and the treatise of the servant in another place, but it will be sufficient for the argument we have in hand to emphasise the fact that James the son of Zebedee had received his call before the date of the preaching of the sermon on the mount, and that he was present when our Lord delivered that exposition of His doctrine, comp. Matt. iv. 21, 22 and v. 1, whereas the call of the son of Alphæus was posterior to this date,* and we have no hint given us of the presence of the future Bishop, if he were a distinct

* It will be gathered from this that the narrative in Luke vi. 20 and foll. is considered to be distinct from the sermon on the mount, Matt. v.-vii.

person. The reader may therefore be left to judge which author would be the more likely to have remembered those sayings, and to have woven them into the fabric of his own teaching; the one who had heard the sermon, or the one who had not.

The next occasion that the subject of our enquiry comes before our notice is connected with the special ordination by our Lord of twelve out of His most intimate friends and followers to be His apostles. The list is found in all three of the synoptic evangelists. All agree in recording the symbolic surname of Peter which was given to Simon, but St. Mark alone has preserved to us the information that a like honour was conferred on the two sons of Zebedee: the Lord "surnamed them Boanerges, which is, sons of thunder," chap. iii. 17. Whether we take this figurative *cognomen* as descriptive of the fiery zeal of the two brethren, or as prophetic of the power with which they should appeal to the ears of men's hearts, which is the more consistent interpretation, we might search far and wide throughout the writings of the New Testament to find a finer example of the zeal and force with which the ancient Hebrew prophets pealed forth their denunciations with the voice of thunder, and electrified the hearts of the sinful and the reprobate. And surely it were strange, if the younger brother penned the writings that go by his name, that like the wires of the telegraph have conveyed the spark of the grace given him, and the fire that dwelt on his tongue, to every portion and generation of the church, that the thunders of the elder brother's voice, though co-partner in this title, should so long since have ceased, and not a single syllable of his utterances been preserved as an echo of his preaching, that like an alarum from the skies bowed his hearers with awe, and aroused them with the "burning words" of zeal from the slumber of ignorance and sin.

The next incident in the life of this James that serves to supply a connecting link with this Epistle is found in his being selected, together with Peter and John, to be a witness of the transfiguration of the Lord. Only these three were present; the rest of the twelve were excluded from the sight. That the appearance of their Master "decked with light as with a garment" made an abiding impression on the minds of those who witnessed this epiphany is clear from St. Peter's well known reference to the scene, 2 Pet. i. 16-18. And St. John, though he has not in his writings categorically related this divine manifestation, yet most unmistakably refers to his being an "eye-witness of the majesty" in one of his most important paragraphs: "And the Word became flesh and tabernacled in us, and *we beheld his glory*," ἐθεασάμεθα τὴν δόξαν αὐτοῦ, Jno. i. 14. Compare also 1 Jno. i. 1, 2 with 5, 7. Now when we turn to our Epistle, chap. ii. 1, and find the writer entitling Jesus Christ as the "glory," the *Shechinah*, which was manifested at the transfiguration, there can be little doubt that he was the other eye-witness of that glory, and that the same indelible impression had been printed upon his memory as on that of the other two. The charge, moreover, of their Master at the time not to divulge the things they had seen till He were risen from the dead, and the questioning of these three brethren one with another what "the rising from the dead" meant, would serve to deepen the importance of the revelation, and to enhance the

c

necessity of making known afterwards this evidence of the Messiahship; hence can we most satisfactorily account for this reference to the transfiguration.* And we may fairly put the question to the unbiassed reader, which would be most likely to have introduced into his writings this allusion to the transfiguration, the son of Alphæus or the future Bishop, who were not present at the scene, or the Apostle who gazed upon the glory in the Holy Mount?

Another feature in the character of this Apostle is adverted to by the Evangelists, which at least seems to have suggested some lines of thought and warnings against like failings in the Epistle. I refer to the strife for supremacy among the disciples. The commencement of this rivalry first crops up soon after the three disciples Peter, James, and John had received the special honour of being selected as witnesses of the transfiguration: a most likely time, not only to assert their superiority over the rest, but also to discuss the primacy amongst themselves. We are told by St. Matthew, xviii. 1 and foll., that "the disciples came to Jesus, saying, who is the greatest in the kingdom of heaven?" It must be remembered that the transfiguration was a type of the full development of that kingdom, according to our Lord's own statement, Matt. xvi. 28. The controversy had evidently been engendered by the recent circumstances, as St. Mark tells us, chap. ix. 33, that the Lord enquired "What was it that ye disputed among yourselves by the way?" It is evident that although Jesus called the twelve to hear the rebuke He administered, yet the chief parties in the quarrel must almost necessarily have been the three who had been already pre-

* See on this subject the Excursus on the "Glory."

eminent in privilege. In the recent honour James and John had been preferred before Andrew, why should they not be above Peter his brother? why should not the sons of Zebedee be advanced before those of Jonas? It is to this, perhaps, that we are to attribute Peter's question to the Lord, which is found in proximity to the narrative of this dispute, " How oft shall my brother trespass against me, and I forgive him?" Matt. xviii. 21. But all uncertainty as to the individuals among the twelve who were ambitious of the highest rank is removed when we find James and John, with the aid and advocacy of their mother, desiring the greatest honours of the future kingdom, the seats on the right hand and the left hand of the Lord. The ten heard of the request that had been made, and " were moved with indignation against the two brethren. But Jesus called them unto him, and said, Ye know that the princes of the Gentiles exercise dominion over them, and they that are great exercise authority upon them. But it shall not be so among you: but whosoever will be great among you, let him be your minister; and whosoever will be chief among you, let him be your servant," Matt. xx. 24-27. But even this reproof did not suppress the emulation, for we learn from St. Luke's narrative that even after the last supper this strife again burst out, when a similar rebuke was given by the Lord, but with the addition of a remarkable promise, as if with the intent to pacify their minds and allay their jealousies: " Ye are they who have continued with me in my temptations: and I appoint, διατίθεμαι, to you a kingdom, as my Father hath appointed unto me; that ye may eat and drink at my table in my kingdom, and sit on thrones judging the twelve tribes of Israel," Luke xxii. 28-30. We have already called attention to the fact that St. John occupied the right hand of the Lord at the last supper, and the probability that St. James was on His left hand; hence it is natural to suppose that this new outburst of jealousy was connected with this arrangement, and that St. Peter was the one who felt dissatisfied, and that consequently the dispute originated on this occasion with him; and have we not a hint that such was the case in the solemn address the Lord made to Peter immediately after quelling this unseemly and ill-timed cavil: "Simon, Simon, Behold Satan desired you, ὑμᾶς, to sift as wheat; but I prayed for thee, περὶ σοῦ, that thy faith might not fail. And when thou art converted, strengthen thy brethren," Luke xxii. 31, 32. To say nothing more definite, may we not trace in the teaching of this Epistle passages that seem to be reflections of these scenes, and echoes of these rebukes? the very faults of the writer in his previous life furnishing the material for warnings to others. St. Peter's Epistles are full of such allusions to the past history of his experience. Is not St. James' Epistle also? The general character of the Epistle is a strong protest against pride, the prevalent self-exalting Jewish pride, the domineering of one over another. This natural tendency of the human heart had met with severe reproofs from our Lord's lips, and now the Apostle, humbled himself, preaches humility to others. A few passages may serve as the direct outcome of the scenes in the Apostle's life which have been referred to. In chap. i. 9-12 the lowly brother is exhorted to rejoice in his exaltation, and a gloomy picture is drawn of the doom of the opposite character. The subject was one calculated to awaken the remembrances of the past, and the language of v. 12 seems to recall the memories of the last scene in which the jealousy of the brethren manifested itself, when the Lord covenanted to give them a kingdom; for, writes St. James, " Blessed is the man that endureth temptation, because having become approved he shall receive the *crown of life which the Lord promised to those that love him.*" The caution against jealousy and selfishness in chap. iii. 14, 16, seems almost like an utterance prompted by a penitential remembrance of personal failings in former days, and comes most fittingly from the pen of one who had felt the evil of arousing such contentions among the brethren. Chap. iv. begins with a severe reprimand of those that manifested a quarrelsome and ambitious disposition, and the citation, probably from Prov. iii. 34, which, consistently with our argument, by the way, is also embodied in the writings of St. Peter, another of the great but litigious three, 1 Pet. v. 5, seems to be the categorical form of the lesson these Apostles had received under the tender illustration recorded by the Evangelist: " Jesus called a little child unto him, and set him in the midst of them, and said, Verily I say unto you, except ye be *converted* (mark the parallel use of this word to St. Peter on a like occasion, Luke xxii. 32), and become as little children, ye shall not enter into the *kingdom* of heaven. Whosoever, therefore, shall humble himself as this little child, the same is greatest in the kingdom of heaven," Matt. xviii. 2-4.

Remembrances of such scenes and exhortations might be stamped forcibly on the mind of the son of Alphæus, experiences of his own heart and life; or the need that others had of such instruction, might give birth to these monitions and reproofs, but surely they appear to be more consistently attributed to the Apostle who had been the cause of eliciting from the Great Teacher the same rebukes that, under His inspiration and the promptings of his own experience, he was now administering to others. And we may again remind the reader that there is no evidence that the future Bishop was present on the occasion referred to; and that it is almost certain that he was not.

Closely consequent upon the first instance of the outbreak of rivalry among the brethren is another incident in the life of James the son of Zebedee, which occurred in a village of the Samaritans, as the Teacher and the twelve were on their journey to Jerusalem. The link that ties together the exhibitions of ambitious and revengeful temper has been preserved to us in its proper place by St. Luke. See chap. ix. 46-56. It would seem that the three disciples after the transfiguration had become inflated with their supereminence over the residue, and were tempted to dispute between themselves for priority. This perversion of the privilege they had enjoyed together, the Lord, as we have seen, rebuked ; but thirst for dominion and narrow-mindedness go hand in hand. St. John, evidently with his spirit ruffled by the recent rebuke, put in the remark, full of the same inflated selfishness, " Master, we saw one casting out devils in thy name; and we forbad him, because he followeth not with us. And Jesus said unto him, Forbid him not; for he that is not against us is for us." Soon after this occurrence the journey to

Jerusalem commenced. The way lay through Samaria; they enter a village that belonged to that district. The inhabitants would not welcome the Lord and His followers: they perceived that the Lord, who made no secret of His Messiahship in Samaria, was going up to Jerusalem to keep the feast, and not to Mount Gerizim, and therefore they refused to acknowledge and entertain Him. Here then was another wound to pride, and the feelings of the two brethren, which had scarcely recovered from the former excitement, were again inflamed. The recent sight of Elijah on the mount, and the neighbourhood where he had called down vengeance on the foe, 2 Kings i. 10, 12, alike flash across their mind, and James and John said, "Lord, wilt thou that we command fire to come down from heaven and consume them, even as Elias did?* But he turned and rebuked them."

Two distinct references are to be found in this Epistle to this incident in the Apostle's life. In chap. i. 19, 20 he exhorts his brethren to be "slow to speak, slow to wrath," adding, "for the wrath of a man, ἀνδρός, does not work out the righteousness of God." What could reflect with greater exactitude the sin he had committed, or the lesson he had learnt in the village of Samaria? Again, the reference, in chap. v. 17, to Elijah has doubtless a twofold origin. As the transfiguration had made a deep impression on the minds of those that witnessed it, so must also the persons who were associated with the Lord in the glorious vision; chap. ii. 1 and this passage

* The words 'Ὡς καὶ 'Ηλίας ἐποίησεν are not found in א and B, although they are in A, C, D, etc.; but this does not in any way affect the argument, as the thought must have been suggested by what the prophet had done in that place, even though it might not be expressed in the text.

may therefore both be advanced in favour of the son of Zebedee being the author of this Epistle, but the epithet we find applied to Elijah in this place adds another strong link to our argument. James, when he mentioned Elijah, was reminded of his own faults and failings in connection with the abuse he had made of the great prophet's example, yet was Elijah one like himself, ὁμοιοπαθής, of like passions, feelings, experiences, infirmities, impulses. He, too, had lost his patience once on a time; see 1 Kings xix. 4, 10. Thus there was a parallel between the prophet and the Apostle both in their zeal and in their infirmities; and this epithet applied by the latter to the former seems almost intended to plead an apology for his failings, as well as to inspire confidence that the prayer of a just man, although subject to the weaknesses of humanity, would not be ineffectual in gaining the desired answer.

Once more, it is frequently advanced that the destruction of Jerusalem is spoken of as close at hand in this Epistle, and therefore it must have been written at a period later than A.D. 44, when James the Elder suffered martyrdom, and that thus we are compelled to assign it to the son of Alphæus or the Bishop of Jerusalem; but this is a slender foundation for the superstructure. The Bishop could not have penned the letter much after the year A.D. 60, which is the usual date fixed, as he was put to death at the passover A.D. 62, exactly eighteen years after the death of the elder James. In the fulfilment of a prophecy which the Apostles believed was imminent every day of their lives, would not sixteen or eighteen years be a vanishing fraction?

But there appears to be internal evidence even here

that the elder James was the writer. St. Mark tells us that when the Lord had left the temple for the last time, and his disciples had pointed out the magnitude and magnificence of the structure, and He told them that not one stone should be left upon another; after this, as He sat upon the Mount of Olives, " Peter, *James*, and John and Andrew asked him *privately*, Tell us when shall these things be; and what shall be the sign when all these things shall be fulfilled?" Our Lord's reply to the inquiring disciples embraces all the points found in the Epistle relative to the same subject; indeed, the warnings of the Apostle are but an epitome of the Divine predictions. Compare Mark xiii. 7 with James iv. 1; Mark xiii. 9 with James ii. 6, 7; Mark xiii. 32 with James iv. 13, 14; Mark xiii. 19 with James v. 1-3; Matt. xxiv. 27, 29 with James v. 3, 5. When we thus discover the chief particulars foretold by the Lord in the ears of this James, a privilege, be it remembered, not conferred upon the son of Alphæus, the wars and rumours of wars, the persecution of believers in the synagogues, the unexpected coming of the judgment, the general affliction and the princely luxury and carelessness of the period, all reflected on the pages of the Epistle, can we withhold our conviction that the Apostle who heard these prophecies from the mouth of the Lord in one of his last conversations with Him, and in answer to his own anxious inquiry, would be more likely to remember and record them than those who had not been privileged to hear those predictions; or in other words, that the son of Zebedee is the more likely to be the author of our Epistle than the son of Alphæus or the Bishop of Jerusalem.

There are, in addition to the foregoing arguments, certain verbal coincidences and other features that forbid formal classification, that may be adduced in support of our proposition.

No one when reading the Epistles of St. James and 1 Peter can fail to be struck with the correspondence that exists between them. Some of these parallels may be cited: Jas. i. 2 and foll. with 1 Pet. i. 6, 9; Jas. i. 10 and foll. with 1 Pet. i. 24; Jas. i. 21 with 1 Pet. ii. 1 and foll.; Jas. iv. 6, 10 with 1 Pet. v. 5 and foll.; Jas. v. 20 with 1 Pet. iv. 8.

Such a mutual reflection of kindred thoughts, doctrines, and expressions between the two writers naturally suggests which we know was the case, supposing our author to be the son of Zebedee, that the twain were closely allied in calling, training, experience, and work. Such an alliance, it is true, *might* exist between Peter and the son of Alphæus or the Bishop, but we know that such an intimacy did exist between Peter and the elder James, who were side by side throughout the ministry of our Lord, and were fellow class-men of the highest rank under His Divine tuition. We claim, therefore, this unison of sentiment as a strong internal evidence that the writer was none other than the near friend of Peter, James the son of Zebedee.

Further, we may mark some features among the illustrations contained in the Epistle which seem to corroborate our view. In chap. i. 6 we have a graphic sketch of the sea labouring under the influence of wind and storm, evidently drawn by an artist familiar with such a scene. And how fitly does all this fall in with the circumstances of the son of Zebedee, who had spent all his early life on those waters, and had so often seen them subject to violent disturbances. Again, in chap. iii. 4, the illustration borrowed from the *ship* and the helm, to show the influence and power of the tongue, cannot fail to remind us of the boat in which he had plied his trade and left to follow the Lord, or of that boat in which he had so often embarked with His Master on the Sea of Galilee, and "come to the land whither they went." It is quite conceded that both the son of Alphæus and the brother of the Lord were familiar with both the sea and the ships, but we have no authority for supposing either of them to have been fishermen, and as conversant with maritime matters as the son of Zebedee. Whatever view is taken of the relationship termed "brother," whether this James were the son of Joseph by a former marriage, or the son of Joseph and Mary after the birth of the Lord, the latter would more likely be of the same occupation as Joseph, as indeed our Lord himself is said to have been, Mark vi. 3. The figures of speech referred to above, will, with more consistency with known facts, harmonize with the antecedents of James the Elder.

The peculiar use of Δίκαιος, the just one, James v. 6, as not only an epithet but a synonym of the Messiah, is worthy of observation in connection with the similar use of the word in other writers; the nearest approach in the Epistles to this example is 1 Jno. ii. 1, "Jesus Christ the righteous," 'Ιησοῦν Χριστὸν δίκαιον: compare also v. 29. Very near to the same use is the language of St. Peter, Acts iii. 14, "But ye denied the holy one and just," τὸν ἅγιον καὶ δίκαιον: compare also 1 Pet. iii. 18. This title of the coming Messiah, the "just" or "righteous one," is frequent in the psalms and prophets. We know that at the time of His coming there was a wide-spread expectation that the Messiah was at hand, and many of the predictions on which the Jews rested their hopes had gained circulation. It is highly probable that this character of the great Deliverer was not unknown among the Gentiles, for it is significant that Pilate's wife employs this word in her message to her husband, Matt. xxvii. 19, and Pilate repeated it in his declaration of the innocence of Jesus before the people, v. 24. The centurion who was on guard at the cross reproduced it in his exclamation, when Jesus gave up the ghost, Luke xxiii. 47, to which confession perhaps Peter refers in his expostulation with the Jews already cited, Acts iii. 14. If we except these examples of Gentile use we find the epithet only in the mouth of Stephen when before the Sanhedrim, Acts vii. 52, and of Ananias at the baptism of St. Paul, Acts xxii. 14.

The growth of the word from an epithet to a synonym, traceable in the use of it by Peter, James, and John, hints at the same conclusion, that our author was James the Elder. It may be that this title was one to which they were specially attached, and they used it frequently in mutual conversation until the very familiarity rendered it equivalent to a proper name.

There is also a striking similarity to be traced between the composition of St. James and St. John in this particular, that both are in the habit of making a statement, and then, apparently for the sake of emphasis, denying the opposite, or *vice versâ*. This feature in St. John's style is so well known that one or two examples will be sufficient for us to refer to: Jno. i. 3, 5; xx. 7; 1 Jno.

i. 5, 6, 8; ii. 11, 15; v. 12. It would appear from many passages that this was a feature frequent in our Lord's discourses.

For examples in St. James' Epistle, see ch. i, 5, 17, 23; iii. 17. Perhaps we may venture to regard this as a family likeness between James and John in their style of address and composition; if so, it will serve as an additional link in our chain of evidence.

In the days of the Apostles there arose two distinct and opposite heresies: the Docetæ, who sprung from the false teaching of Simon Magus, taught that our Lord's body was an apparition only; and the Ebionites, who held the simple humanity of Christ, that He was born of Joseph and Mary. Against both these errors we find constant and undoubted protests in the writings of St. John. Tracing upward chronologically the later Epistles of St. Paul, the pastoral, and still further back, those of the earlier captivity, we find evidence that those errors which afterwards were systematized in Gnosticism were growing and diffusing with alarming rapidity; but even at a prior date, A.D. 57, in the first Epistle to the Corinthians, there are not wanting references, especially in the essay on the resurrection, to these errors, then perhaps, only emerging from an embryo state. This is a wide subject, which it would be out of place to pursue or enlarge upon here; all that is necessary for our argument is to remind the reader that the Ebionites were a sect of Jewish origin, and that the name is clearly derived from the Hebrew אביון, *poor*.* Two reasons may be assigned why the sect received this name; it may have

---

* The theory of Tertullian, *De Præscrip.*, chap. xxxiii., that it was the name of a man who formed the sect, is unfounded.

been imposed on them by the Jews as a name of contempt, or, which is far more likely, they assumed it themselves, as a title of honour, seeing that throughout the psalms and prophets the word was used almost as an equivalent for *pious*, and that in the sermon on the mount the Lord had employed it in the same manner; hence "with a pride that apes humility" they distinguished themselves by so goodly a name: but throughout our Epistle we find the "poor" equivalent to the believing, humble Christian, in contradistinction to the "rich," who oppresses, defrauds, and despises him, in exact accordance with the usage of the Old Testament and the sermon on the mount. Hence it is evident, for this is the point we have to insist upon, that if our Epistle were written at the date generally assigned, A.D. 60, we should see St. Paul deep in his labours to arrest the spread of a system of error, whose advocates prided themselves on a title which they had arrogated to themselves in a self-righteous and complacent spirit, and St. James complimenting the really pious and humble among the Jews by the very same title which was being perverted by the heretics; this could scarcely have happened. The history of the church has constantly shown that words and terms, orthodox at one period, have necessarily been laid aside at a subsequent one, when the meaning has changed, or the application been abused, and such doubtless was the history of this word.

But if the Epistle was written by the son of Zebedee, we gain at least thirteen or fourteen years before the first references are made to these false teachings by St. Paul. Before the martyrdom of St. James, A.D. 44, the error, to say the utmost, could only have existed in the very earliest germ, and scarcely have been in a nascent state, much less could the system have been distinguished by the holy name which was afterwards depraved by heretical assumption : we contend that this is another argument in favour of the authorship by the son of Zebedee.

The chief objections to this view we have already dealt with, such as the implied nearness of the destruction of Jerusalem, and the generally received opinion that the Epistle was the work of one of the other two who bore the same name. There is none other worth naming except, perhaps, the omission of the title *Apostle* in the preface of the Epistle. This would be equally fatal to those who hold that the Epistle was penned by the son of Alphæus, who was one of the twelve, but St. John, the brother of James the Elder, never adopts this title in any of his introductory addresses, probably from motives of humility; why should there not be a family likeness in this lowly grace, and the brethren who sought the highest places of honour in the kingdom become content to be followers of the "holy and humble men of heart ?"

The preceding arguments, though far from being conclusive, are still very potent, especially so when the weakness of the testimony is considered that is brought forward to prove the authorship of another James ; the tradition of a "hear-say," and that only partially received by the reporter, is but scanty evidence; but when we turn to the second James, we are met with another difficulty, which it seems never has been, and probably never will be, removed. Is James the son of Alphæus identical with another James, called the brother of our

Lord, and generally known as the Bishop of Jerusalem, or are they distinct individuals? This question again involves another of equal difficulty: What relationship are we to understand by "the brethren of the Lord?" This subject has been several times referred to already, and although a solution of the difficulty has nothing to do with the views entertained in these pages, yet the Introduction to the Epistle would be imperfect without some reference to the identity or non-identity of James the Less, or rather the "Little," with James the Just, the brother of the Lord and Bishop of Jerusalem, and to the relationship which is implied in the term, "the brother of the Lord." On both these subjects much has been written, both in days ancient and modern; every commentary more or less touches upon them; and of late years some very valuable treatises, from the pens of both continental and English theologians, have appeared, yet neither of the questions has received a satisfactory and certain solution; all the testimony that can be scraped together has been sifted, and ingenuity in framing theories, we may hope, has been exhausted; any addition that would be likely to bring these doubtful points to a conclusion is impossible, unless further evidence should spring up by the discovery of some more archives of an early date, a boon not likely to fall to our lot.

There are three distinct opinions on the subject of the "brethren of the Lord," all of early date, which claim our adoption and adhesion, and it is a strange coincidence that the three commentaries which most deserve our respect, and are in most frequent use by students of Holy Scripture, severally advocate each of these three proposed solutions of the difficulty, a fact which is the best evidence of the impossibility of settling the question. It would be quite beyond the limits of our Introduction, already too long, to enter into all these theories, and cross-examine their testimony, balancing the weak points of each against the strong points of the others; it will be enough to direct the reader to the commentaries of Bishop Wordsworth and the late lamented Dean Alford in their Introductions to this Epistle, and in their notes on Matt. i. 25 and xiii. 55, and to Professor Lightfoot's admirable essay on "the brethren of the Lord," in his commentary on the Epistle to the Galatians. A brief sketch of the outline of the three theories will serve our purpose in showing the uncertainty that hangs over the whole question.

(1) The ancient Ante-Nicene Church held, with the exception of Tertullian,* and the reference of his remarks is not altogether clear, that the so called brethren of the Lord were the offspring of Joseph by a former marriage, that Joseph was an aged man when he took Mary, whom he treated as a ward rather than a wife. Joseph died not long after our Lord reached His twelfth year, so that the Virgin Mary and her step-children remained together with her divine son as members of one household. This view is entertained by the apocryphal Gospels, which probably retained the tradition of truth in this matter, by Clement of Alexandria, Origen, Eusebius, Gregory of Nissa, Epiphanius, and other fathers, and by the ancient services of the Eastern church.

* The passage which is quoted in almost all commentaries from Papias, as supporting the views of Jerome, has been proved by Professor Lightfoot (see *Commentary on Galatians*, p. 259, note) to have been penned by another Papias, a writer of the eleventh century.

d

In the fourth century a strong tide in favour of celibacy over the marriage state set in. Helvidius, a disciple of Auxentius, an Arian, who lived at Rome, attacked this school and its teachings, and asserted that the Virgin Mary bore children to her husband Joseph. Bonosus, probably Bishop of Sardica, and Jovinian, an Italian monk in the same century, held the same view; which has been endorsed by Strauss, Herder, Davidson, and most rationalistic critics, and by Dean Alford in his well known commentary. The leading arguments advanced are the natural impression that would be made on the general reader of the narratives of the early portion of the Gospels of St. Matthew and St. Luke, though the actual expression, πρωτότοκος υἱός, Luke ii. 7, and the ἕως οὗ ἔτεκε, Matt. i. 25, are not pressed so urgently as formerly, as the "first-born," in the Jewish mind, did not involve the thought of a *second-born*, and the latter passage refers rather to the miracle of our Lord's birth than to any subsequent circumstances.

Jerome, when a young man, opposed the view propounded by Helvidius, and wrote a treatise against him; and at that time originated the solution of the question which from his day has been almost universally received in the Western Church, and till quite recently may be said to have been the accepted theory of the leading theologians of our own Church. The explanation given by Jerome was that the "brethren" of our Lord were not, as Helvidius taught, the sons of Mary the Virgin, but were the *cousins* of our Lord, being the offspring of Mary, the sister of the Virgin and wife of Alphæus. The followers of this theory have identified Alphæus with Clopas, these two names being different forms of the Aramaic חלב. This mode of explaining the relationship was new at the time, as Jerome cites no ancient authority in support of his views, and he did not press his opinion in after years. It involves a great number of difficulties, and postulates many concessions.

There are also several other hypotheses of later date on this subject, but they are all entirely unsupported by external evidence.

Hence it will appear from an inspection of these three theories, that if the last-named is accepted, James the son of Alphæus and the Bishop of Jerusalem were identical, but if either of the other two furnishes the solution, then James, the Bishop of Jerusalem, was not the son of Alphæus, and consequently not an Apostle. The statement of St. John, chap. vii. 5, is very conclusive on this point, and all the evasions that have been fabricated to escape from the plain and literal meaning of the words only serve to strengthen their testimony. To enter into this part of the question would be quite beside our purpose. The discussion has occupied the attention of most modern theologians and divided their conclusions. The view respecting the authorship maintained in this work is quite distinct, and the only object in making reference to these questions is to show the doubts that have been entertained concerning both the person and the office of the generally reputed author of the Epistle. Some have regarded this difficulty as so insuperable and the testimony so entangled and conflicting that they have taken refuge in a theory still more desperate, that the Epistle was written by a different James altogether.

We conclude, therefore, that external evidence on the

whole question is weak on all sides; too weak, indeed, to settle the dispute with any degree of certainty. There is more than a doubt concerning the identity of the son of Alphæus and the Bishop of Jerusalem. The testimony to the authorship by the latter is very indefinite in ancient authorities, and if stated qualified and all but cancelled, and those that support this view unreservedly are too late to be of any critical value. The direct external evidence also for the authorship of the elder James is but small, and only reaches probability. It may be summed up thus: the most ancient MSS. of the Peshito Syriac Version call the author an apostle, which title in its full and proper sense would eliminate James the Bishop; and as the son of Alphæus, considered distinct from him, has little or no claim to the authorship, the title of *apostle* would most fitly describe St. James the Elder.

Again, it would appear that some tradition had come down with this ancient version, from the fact that the first editor of the printed text in the sixteenth century, together with those that assisted him in his work, held the opinion that the son of Zebedee was the writer.

Further, only one MS. is extant of this Epistle, in an ante-Hieronymian Latin version; this in its subscription attributes the Epistle to the son of Zebedee; we may thus fairly claim the two earliest versions on our side. But on turning to the evidence afforded by internal marks and undesigned coincidences, the verdict is strongly in favour of the opinion that the Epistle was written by St. James the Elder, the brother of John and the son of Zebedee.

This will be further corroborated when we examine

the question, To whom, and for what purpose, was the Epistle written?

TO WHOM WRITTEN.

It is a matter of the greatest importance when we investigate any subject in connection with divine revelation to strip our minds of all subjective and self-spun theories and inclinations, and to yield ourselves up willingly to the guidance of the objective facts placed before us. Evidence, not invention, should shape our decisions; facts, not fancies, should rule our verdict. Perhaps there is no writing in the New Testament that has suffered so much as this Epistle from neglecting the broadest hints and the plainest statements on the one hand, and inventing hypotheses with an exuberant imagination on the other. The whole question, To whom is this Epistle written? is settled for us without any inquiry being necessary, in the fewest words, " To the twelve tribes." It is really painful, as being utterly obstructive to the discovery of truth, after reading this address with which the letter is inscribed, to find critics, like postmen who are ill-skilled in deciphering handwriting, conveying the letter to every house except that of the person whose name is specified on the envelope. Thus De Wette, Kern, and others, hand over the Epistle to Jewish Christians and Gentile Christians as though the "twelve tribes" were synonymous with the Catholic Church, or the phrase were a symbolical designation of Christendom. Neander, Alford, and others, to Jewish Christians, as though Christianity had already embraced the twelve tribes and all Israel were converted! Huther, to the twelve tribes, interpreting the phrase to mean true Jews, those worthy of the name, but where is this phrase found as equivalent to the "remnant according to the election of grace?" And Lange appropriates "the poor man with a vile raiment" to the *Gentile* Christian; the Gentile Christian in a synagogue! It is true that such critics find a difculty when they come to the alarming denunciations found in the fourth and fifth chapters, but the difficulty is slurred over with an easy evasion: they were unworthy members of the churches, the state of things was unsatisfactory, Jewish errors had been imported, and such like. But where, at any period before A.D. 60, adopting the date of our critics, could such a picture as that painted by St. James be found as a faithful *fac-simile* of the church? Surely if any church had deserved the caricature, it would speedily have been disestablished from the Apostolic communion. The church of Corinth, it is true, has been cited as parallel, but though they had been gross sinners before they joined the church, this was now a thing of the past, so that St. Paul wrote to them in this wise: "such were some of you; but ye are washed, but ye are sanctified, but ye are justified in the name of the Lord Jesus, and by the Spirit of our God," 1 Cor. vi. 11. And as to the delinquents referred to in the eleventh chapter, the cases compared do not admit of comparison; for the Corinthians just redeemed from Gentile idolatry had confounded the great Christian rite with their former idol feasts, and had acted at the former as they had done at the latter, and they were rebuked by divine chastisements in order that they might not be condemned with the world; but the sinners referred to in the Epistle of St. James are denounced as those on whom the divine judgment, like a ripe thunderbolt, was just about to fall irremediably.

But "*to the twelve tribes*" is not the whole of the superscription, particulars are given which are of a distinguishing character, serving to fix both upon the parties addressed and the localities where they would be found. "To the twelve tribes *that are in the dispersion,*" ταῖς ἐν τῇ διασπορᾷ. It is evident that this section of the Israelitish people was in the author's view, and this is rendered even more clear by the fact that the letter was beyond all doubt penned and posted at Jerusalem, yet with a strange perversity we find critics of very high character holding that the designation of the dispersion does not necessarily limit the readers to the Jewish churches *out of* Palestine. Thus the portion of the family abroad is the same as the portion at home; but surely the Jews of the dispersion known as ʽΕλληνισταί were considered a distinct section of the Hebrew race ever since the Babylonish captivity. The Jews who did not return to their native land after that great crisis in their history, the בני הגולה, were the ancestors of that widespread distribution of the Jewish people over the then known world, the διασπορά. These sojourners amongst the Gentiles were known also by the name Hellenists, ʽΕλληνισταί, from their having adopted the customs, and manners, and language of the Greeks among whom they dwelt. Of necessity their religious privileges must have been considerably less than those of their brethren who lived in the land near their temple and under the regimen of the ceremonial law; the chief tie that linked them to their brethren at home was the payment of the half-shekel to the temple service. Representatives of the various settlements, it would also appear, went to Jerusalem to keep the chief feasts. See Acts ii. 5-11. But that they were distinguished and had feelings of jealousy against their more favoured brethren, is seen by the "·murmuring of the Grecians against the Hebrews, because their widows were neglected in the daily ministration," Acts vi. 1.

It was to the Jews of the dispersion, to the Hellenists, beyond all dispute that St. James addressed this Epistle; to those who were non-resident in the land of Judæa, as distinct from those who were resident there; to Grecising Jews as distinct from Hebrews. And if any doubt could exist on this point, it is removed by St. Peter's testimony. It has been remarked that a strong relationship is visible between these Epistles, and in his superscription the Apostle of the circumcision addresses his letter to the "sojourners of the dispersion ($\pi\alpha\rho\epsilon\pi\iota\delta\dot{\eta}\mu o\iota\varsigma\ \delta\iota\alpha\sigma\pi o\rho\hat{\alpha}\varsigma$) at Pontus, Galatia, Cappadocia, Asia, and Bithynia," 1 Pet. i. 1. The *dispersion* is therefore specified to be the Jews who were scattered up and down the Gentile world. But further, it would appear that the letter was addressed to them as *Jews*. The difference between the superscription of this Epistle and that of 1 Peter is very suggestive: there the sojourners of the dispersion are "elect according to the foreknowledge of God the Father, in sanctification of the Spirit unto obedience and sprinkling of the blood of Jesus Christ." They are expressly defined first to be Jews, secondly to be Christians, Jewish Christians; but St. James defines his readers simply as the " twelve tribes in the dispersion." This marked dissimilitude between the two Apostles in their description of their readers is a strong argument against the date ordinarily assigned to this Epistle, which would make the two Epistles to have been written almost at the same time, whereas it is barely credible that two inspired writers could have addressed the same people, at the same period, in terms so widely discrepant. In brief, we can but hold that St. James wrote to *the Jews of the dispersion, as such;* but they were at this time a mixed assembly in a religious point of view, as a large infusion of Christianity had spread among these scattered communities of Israel through the information brought to the various centres of their sojournings by the visitors who came up to Jerusalem at that memorable Pentecost, when the Holy Spirit was poured out upon the Apostles, and from other sources. St. James makes reference to these believers as the poor, humble, tempted, beloved brethren. The sharp line of distinction between the synagogue and the church had not yet been drawn: the Christian Jew, at Jerusalem attended the services at the temple, and those of the dispersion worshipped in the synagogues holding, it is most probable, a gathering or after-meeting of their own body at a different hour. To this custom, it is likely, St. Paul refers in Heb. x. 25, "Not forsaking the assembling of yourselves together," τὴν ἐπισυναγωγήν. Thus our Epistle when read, would be read in the synagogue where all met together, and thus be heard of all, both Jewish non-Christians and Jewish Christians: the former were to appropriate the rebukes, the latter the consolations of the Epistle. With this view all the parts of the Epistle are consistent with each other, and the extremes of praise and invective, in themselves so irreconcilable, each receive their own allotment and proper direction. The general tone of the letter is decidedly one of severe reproof, at times rising to prophetic denunciation, relieved by tender utterances of love and whispers of consolation: the former adapted to the majority of the attendants at the synagogue, who were non-Christians, and the latter to the minority, who had in different degrees of light received the doctrine that Jesus of Nazareth was the Messiah.

In proof of this position, the reader may be reminded that the standpoint of this Epistle is essentially Jewish: the address, as we have seen, is to the twelve tribes; the terms "rich" and "poor" are distributed after the manner of the Old Testament writers; the place of worship is the synagogue, chap. ii. 2; the definition of the faith they possessed is the Jewish creed, the *Sh'ma Israel*, that "God is one," chap. ii. 19; the oaths prohibited are Jewish, chap. v. 12, etc.; the sins denounced are those to which the Jews were addicted, pride, self-conceit, ostentation, over-bearing, fraud. Commentators who insist upon the Christian character of these Jewish churches, as they call them, may well find a grave difficulty when they come to chap. iii. 9, and read of the members of these churches cursing one another; or to chap. iv. with its charges of lust, and murder, and envy, of evil speaking and godless boasting; and to chap. v. with its withering denunciations of judgment upon ungodly hoarders, and pleasure-seeking wantons, and murderers of the Messiah. Strange features, truly, to be found in a Christian church immediately after its foundation! But when we remember that the persons addressed are the twelve tribes, Jews not Christians, the characteristics all hold good: the invectives of the Apostle fit in with the well known features of the condition of the Jewish people at this period of their history, when they were ripening for the divine judgments. The dispersion as well as the people of the land were similar in their sinful thoughts and habits, and the presence of a large deputation of the dispersion at the Passover feast when Christ was crucified, who doubtless co-operated in raising the cry, " Crucify him," and who by their continued unbelief still echoed that cry, would bring them under the ban of that awful charge, " Ye condemned and murdered the just One," chap. v. 6.

On the other hand, the arguments in support of the Epistle being addressed to *Christians, as such*, are easily disposed of: they either place a too strong emphasis on those passages which relate to the Christian converts, who were undeniably included in the dispersion, as though those passages formed the general tenor and tone of the Epistle, or they do not prove the point which they are cited to establish. For instance, the title by which St. James opens his Epistle, "James, a servant of God, and of the Lord Jesus Christ," is advanced as evidence that the Apostle was addressing *Christians*, but it is one thing for the writer, himself a converted Jew, to confess his faith, and another to imply that all his readers must be fellow-believers with him in the Gospel, especially when we remember that he immediately adds, " to the twelve tribes that are in the dispersion," among whom Christianity could not have been the prevalent religion. Again, the frequent use of " brethren," " my brethren," is supposed to involve a brotherhood in the Christian faith; but the writer and his readers were alike descendants of the Jewish race, and therefore the name of *brother*, so familiar among the Hebrews, would not be out of place on the ground of national unity, whereas the two places where "my beloved brethren" is found, chap. i. 16 and chap. ii. 5, very probably express a double and a closer relationship, a tie both in the flesh and in the spirit.

In chap. i. 18 "the firstfruits of his creatures" is a term applicable to the Jewish race, and does not necessitate a Christian interpretation. See note *in loc*.

Chap. ii. 1, "do not hold the faith of our Lord Jesus Christ, the Shechinah, with respectings of persons," can only prove at the utmost a fact which we admit, the mixture of believers with unbelievers in the synagogue, the place where the fault reprobated was committed, see note *in loc*. And for the argument based on καλὸν ὄνομα, chap. ii. 7, we may also refer the reader to the note *in loc*. The exhortation to patience in suffering, and the injunctions concerning confession and prayer, in the fifth chapter are beyond controversy addressed to the believing section of the dispersion. Our argument, it must be remembered, does not exclude "the remnant according to the election of grace," but holds that the majority of the twelve tribes in the dispersion were, as we know they must have been, unbelievers, and as this Epistle was addressed to the twelve tribes in the dispersion, it must necessarily have been addressed to a body of Jewish people, the majority of whom were unbelievers in the Messiahship of Jesus of Nazareth.

Consistently with this we find in the preface of the Epistle no salutation of "saints," "elect," "called," "church," or the like; there is no mention made of the distinctive doctrines of the Gospel; the blood of Jesus is not preached in its atoning power, as by St. Paul; the unction from above is not insisted on, as by his brother St. John in his Epistles; Passover and Pentecost are not celebrated, and the name of Jesus Christ is only found twice throughout the whole Epistle. There must be some real and fundamental reason for this singularity and exceptional peculiarity. To say that the writer was enforcing practical religion, or removing impressions that had been erroneously arrived at through a misunderstanding of the writings of St. Paul, only evades the difficulty without explaining it, or even proving the existence of the difficulty which commentators have invented in order to combat. Such a shift is alike unworthy of the critic and the Christian, and more so of the grave subject over which they deliberate. This will become more plain when we consider the *Object in view*, which the author of our Epistle had. This may be briefly stated.

THE OBJECT IN VIEW.

We have already called attention to the similarity between this Epistle and the preaching of John the Baptist, and to the still closer relationship both in doctrine and form of expression that exists between it and the sermon on the mount. Where such a resemblance is found, both in the matter and the manner of distinct discourses, it may with safety be concluded that the purpose of those discourses is also similar, and that the object their several authors had in view would be nearly related, if not absolutely identical; and this inference gathers strength when we remember that the Baptist and our Lord uttered their appeals to Jews, and that St. James wrote his Epistle to Jews, to people of the same race and religious antecedents. The question now arises, What was the purpose of the Baptist's teaching? and the reply, it may be presumed, is ready on the lip of a general confession, that the great prophet of the wilderness preached the gospel of repentance and conviction of sin; that his mission was to excite in the hearts of his hearers a sense of their sinfulness and unworthiness, to break down the wall of carnal security and reliance on external privileges. Hence the desert rang with the cry, "Repent ye," and the stream of Jordan conveyed the echoes of warning, "Flee from the wrath to come." To be a descendant of Abraham involved no merit in the sight of God. Bring forth fruits meet for repentance; the fan of judgment shall sever the chaff, and the fire consume it; and the axe of retribution shall lay low every evil tree and every unproductive tree; God can raise up children to Abraham out of these stones; trust not in the mere accident of a pious pedigree.

And what was the object that the "greater than John" had in the ever memorable sermon preached on the mountain? It was an unfolding of the true meaning and intent of the law, a lifting up of its teaching above the mere external letter and bare outside obedience to its precepts to the higher platform of loving self-dedication and spiritual service. He told the Jew, inflated with his privileges and boasting in the law, that the evil thought was equivalent to the evil deed, the evil look to the evil act, the inner surgings of anger and malice were the same in God's sight as the outburst of passion and the perpetration of murder; that almsgiving might go hand in hand with sin, and prayer itself involve a penalty; a great show of religion might cover a nest of abominations, the sheep's clothing of a prophet might robe a ravening wolf; fasting disfigure the face of a hypocrite, and hands lifted to heaven in the sight of men betray a heart bowed down and enslaved to the things of earth. What was all this but the same teaching as the Baptist's? conviction of sin, based upon the requirements of the law. It forestalled the language of St. Paul: "the law is holy, and just, and good," "by the law is the knowledge of sin," "by the deeds of the law no flesh shall be justified." We need not, after having pointed out the parallels between our Epistle and the preaching of the Baptist and the sermon on the mount, stop to remind the reader that the teaching of St. James is precisely parallel, the doctrine the same, the very language often the same, and the illustrations also. But, further, this doctrine of conviction of sin was the necessary preface to the preaching the Gospel of grace and pardon and acceptance in the merits of Another; the Jews of that day needed to be led, like their forefathers, to the foot of Sinai before they were in a condition to appreciate the milk and honey of the Gospel Canaan; the conviction of our needs must go before the supply of those needs, and this system of education, both in the case of communities and individuals, is everywhere traceable in the school of our great Father. But to apply the foregoing remarks to the Epistle before us, the Baptist preached repentance and conviction of sin to the *Jews that were in the land:* " There went out to him Jerusalem and all Judæa, and all the region round about Jordan," Matt. iii. 5. Our Lord also preached the sermon on the mount dealing with the same subject at the commencement of His ministry to the *Jews that were in the land:* " There followed him great multitudes of people from Galilee, and from Decapolis, and from Jerusalem, and from Judæa, and from beyond Jordan," Matt. iv. 25. Now if there was a necessity to enforce this special doctrine of conviction of sin on that branch of the Jewish people that resided in the land, the same doctrine would be necessary also for the dispersion; the ancestry of both was the same, the trust in the righteousness of Abraham the same, their self-righteousness was the same, and therefore their needs were the same. It was therefore consistent with the harmony of the Divine proceedings that the dispersion should have the same training for the Gospel as their brethren at home, and St. James the Great, we believe, was selected for this service; hence we can account for the varieties found in this Epistle. He is the servant of the Lord Jesus Christ, and he confesses it, as the Baptist declared that he was the servant of Him who came after Him, but was preferred before Him. All his invectives against Jewish sin are plain, for they were hurled at the same sinful race as the Baptist's invectives were, to lead them to cry out, "What shall we do?" On the other hand, there were some in the dispersion who had heard the glad tidings and listened to the good news, to them he frequently adverts in tender accents, as we may picture the stern Nazarite did when he turned from his rebukes launched at " the generation of vipers," to point his disciples to the " Lamb of God, that takes away the sin of the world."

We conclude therefore that the main purpose of St. James in this Epistle was to preach to the Jews of the *dispersion* the same doctrine of conviction of sin, that the Baptist, and our Lord in the sermon on the mount, had preached to the Jews *in the land of Judæa*, with the same object in view, to lead them through humiliation and godly sorrow and sore compunction to see their lost estate before God, and so to prepare them for the reception of that Gospel which in all its fulness of mercy and free grace, proclaims through Christ pardon, peace, and life, without money and without price, by his blood shedding and all-righteous merits.

THE DATE OF THIS EPISTLE

has been variously assigned, even by those who hold James the Bishop to have been the author. His martyrdom and the fall of Jerusalem fix a certain limit on one side, but where shall the limit be fixed on the other? The ordinary opinion, that it must have been the product of this James late in his life-time, in consequence of the developed condition of the Jewish churches in the dispersion, is quite untenable, as in what, it may be asked, is that development seen? the only development plainly legible in the Epistle is a development of sinful practices, and until it can be shown, which we are thankful to say it has never been, that the defaulters were Christians, this opinion is perfectly baseless. Others, including such men as Neander, Hoffman, etc., on the continent, and the late Dean Alford, place the period of writing before, though not long before, the council at Jerusalem, about A.D. 45.

And Huther advances that after the doctrine of St. Paul, that a man is justified, not by works but by faith, had become generally known, it is inconceivable that St. James could promulgate his doctrine of justification by works in ignorance of that circumstance. The opinion, therefore, concerning the early date is no novelty, although we must say that this supposed collision between St. James and St. Paul must not be allowed for an instant, for it is perfectly plain that, without taking into consideration the great fact of inspiration, if St. James would not have written his chap. ii. after St. Paul had sent his treatises on justification by faith to the churches of Galatia and Rome, surely, *vice versâ*, St. Paul would not have written those and like productions after reading the Epistle of St. James.

But according to our theory all such contradictions and difficulties disappear, and all the phenomena fall into order. St. James the Elder is the author; his death took place at Easter, A.D. 44; this Epistle was written before that period, probably very soon after the death of Stephen, to whose apology before the Sanhedrim this Epistle has strong affinities; all the features of the question harmonize; the Apostle, one of the great three, is honoured with a place amongst the inspired writers, as the other two members of the trio were. He writes to his brethren according to the flesh to carry out the same line of work which the Baptist, and the Lord in the earlier days of his teaching, had done. The Jewish views of justification are those that are opposed. The early date is necessary, both from the mixed condition of believers with unbelievers in the synagogues of the dispersion, and from the date of the writer's death.

GENUINENESS AND CANONICITY OF THE EPISTLE.

The testimonies of the early fathers, real and supposed, have been frequently collected and catalogued; they may be summed up thus:—

Clement of Rome: 'Αβραὰμ ὁ φίλος προσαγορευθείς, *Abraham who was called the friend*, i.e., of God, compare James ii. 23 with Clement's 1 Ep. ad Cor. chap. x. And again, διὰ πίστιν καὶ φιλοξενίαν ἐσώθη 'Ραὰβ ἡ πόρνη, "Because of faith and hospitality Rahab the harlot was saved," compare ii. 25 with *Ib.* chap. xii.

The Shepherd of Hermas: 'Εὰν οὖν ἀντιστῇς αὐτόν (scil. διάβολον)—φεύξεται ἀπὸ σοῦ κατῃσχυμμένος, ii *Mand.* xii. 5. *If therefore you resist him* (i.e., the devil) *he will flee from you ashamed*, compare James iv. 7. There are other passages in the same author which have some similarity to our Epistle.

Irenæus: "Abraham credidit Deo, et reputatum est illi ad justitiam, et amicus Dei vocatus est," *Hær.* iv. 16, 2, *Abraham believed God, and it was imputed to him for righteousness, and he was called the friend of God.* Compare James ii. 23.

Origen quotes the Epistle in several places of his works, and as has been remarked above refers to the Epistle as that which is said to be James', see page ii.

Eusebius classes the Epistle among those writings which were objected against and not universally received, Τῶν δ' ἀντιλεγομένων, γνωρίμων δ' οὖν ὅμως τοῖς πολλοῖς, ἡ λεγομένη 'Ιακώβου φέρεται, κ. τ. λ., *H. E.* iii. 25, *Among the disputed books, although they are well known and approved by many, is reputed that called the Epistle of James*, etc.

Again Eusebius, after relating Hegesippus' account of the martyrdom of James the Bishop of Jerusalem, adds: Τοιαῦτα καὶ τὰ κατὰ τὸν Ἰάκωβον, οὗ ἡ πρώτη τῶν ὀνομαζομένων καθολικῶν ἐπιστολῶν εἶναι λέγεται· ἰστέον δὲ ὡς νοθεύεται μέν. οὐ πολλοὶ γοῦν τῶν παλαιῶν αὐτῆς ἐμνημόνευσαν, *H. E.* ii. 23, *These accounts are given respecting James, who is said to have written the first of the Epistles called Catholic, but it must be known that it is considered spurious. Not many indeed of the ancients mentioned it.*

Once more, Eusebius, quoting from the authority of Clemens Alexandrinus, reports, μηδὲ τὰς ἀντιλεγομένας παρελθών, τὴν Ἰούδα λέγω καὶ τὰς λοιπὰς καθολικὰς ἐπιστολάς, *H. E.*, vi. 14, *Neither omitting those Epistles that are disputed, I mean that of Jude and the rest of the Catholic Epistles.*

Hippolytus cites the former part of chap. ii. 13.

Dionysius of Alexandria quotes part of chap. i. 13. It is worthy of note that Eusebius tells us of his intimacy with the churches in Syria, Arabia, Cappadocia, Pontus, and Bithynia; the last named places, it will be remembered, were those to which St. Peter addressed his first Epistle to the sojourners of the dispersion.

Gregory Thaumaturgus, Bishop of Neo-Cæsarea in *Pontus* (mark the place also), cites the subject matter of chap. i. 17, δῆλον γὰρ ὡς πᾶν ἀγαθὸν τέλειον θεόθεν ἔρχεται.

Chrysostom received this Epistle among the number of the canonical books, as has been stated above, but Leontius of Byzantium, writing at the close of the sixth century, states that Theodore of Mopsuestia, in Cilicia, rejected the Epistle of James, "Ut arbitror ipsam Jacobi Epistolam,—abrogat et antiquat."

Jerome's mention of the Epistle has been already referred to, with his revival of the report that it was published by some one else under the name of James, surnamed the Just, page iii.

It is not included in the Muratorian fragment, which dates at about A.D. 170, but is found in the Laodicene catalogue, A.D. 363. It may be here repeated that the oldest uncial MSS. affix the name of James, either in superscription or subscription.

Of the two versions made in the earliest days of the church, the Peshito-Syriac contained this Epistle, but it would seem that the old Italic Version did not. See, however, page v. The Epistle was eventually received as canonical by the Council of Carthage, A.D. 397, and after this date it was universally admitted as canonical.

The above facts may serve as an outline of the external testimony relative to the question of the genuineness and canonicity of this Epistle. There are strong points and weak points in the evidence; the chief witness is beyond doubt the Peshito-Syriac translation; the references, some intended and some accidental, in the writings of the fathers are weakened by the statements of Eusebius and Jerome. It must be confessed that here, as well as in the case of the authorship, there is some mystery which needs unfolding.

The following suggestions may help to throw some light on the path of our inquiry. The student cannot fail to observe that with the exception of the Epistle to the Hebrews, all the *antilegomena*, or disputed Epistles, are among those called *Catholic*, James, 2 Peter, 2 and

3 John, and Jude. This prompts us to examine into the meaning of this term *Catholic*, as applied to these Epistles. Clement of Alexandria, *Stromat.* iv. 15, gives this name to the missive issued by the Council of Jerusalem, Acts xv. 22-29. In the fourth century it was appropriated to this group of Epistles, as we learn from Eusebius. Two explanations of the title alone deserve notice, that which explains it as encyclical, or intended for no church in particular, but for all churches, and that which connects it with the *dispersion;* as Œcumenius says, these Epistles were written not to one nation, but καθόλου τοῖς πιστοῖς, ἤτοι Ἰουδαίοις ἐν τῇ διασπορᾷ. If the latter be the true interpretation, we have a hint of great importance that the Catholic Epistles were addressed to the Jews of the dispersion, at different dates, and under different circumstances during the apostolic age, and with this the internal evidence of these compositions agrees. It is a coincidence also worth noting that the Epistle to the Hebrews, though not catalogued as one of the Catholic Epistles, perhaps for this very reason, that it was sent to the Jews resident in Palestine, and not to the dispersion, was addressed, as its name imports, to Jews, and that it has passed through a very similar history with reference to its reception by the church as canonical. The 2nd and 3rd John were private communications, whether addressed to persons of Jewish extraction or not we cannot say, neither is our argument much affected by them. The conclusion from the above premises seems natural that these Epistles, sent to members of the dispersion, remained in the possession of churches of strictly Jewish origin; and as every day the separation between the synagogue and the church was growing

wider and wider, those writings came to the knowledge of the general Christian church by accident, and at intermittent times, and even then under feelings of suspicion; hence we may account for the evident scrutiny they were subjected to before they were finally admitted into the canon; hence, taking into consideration this difficulty as accounting *a priori* for the doubts that clung around the composition, coupled with the uncertainty of its authorship, the peculiarity of its contents, mixed so largely with reproof against those who could have no claim to Christianity, we may fairly admit the grounds of hesitation before it was accepted generally.

And on the other hand, from its presence in the Peshito Syriac,* from the undoubted references in Hermas and others, and lastly from the fact that the Council of Carthage, whose members were probably more acquainted with the question than ourselves, ratified its claims, there can be no real ground for doubt that our Epistle has a valid right to its place among the canonical books of Holy Writ. This claim is substantiated tenfold by the view concerning the authorship and purpose of writing advocated in these pages.

We may here add, although beyond the pale of criticism private opinions have no authority, and cannot be admitted like historical facts to evidence, that at the period of the revival of literature and the age of the Reformation, when this question, which had been sleeping in its grave for many centuries, revived, in the Church of Rome Erasmus and Cardinal Cajetan

* This version, it must be remembered, was in a language used by the Jews; this affords additional support to the preceding argument.

entertained doubts on the canonicity of this Epistle, and Luther's opinions are familiar to every student. In his preface to this Epistle in the year 1522 he writes: "But to give my opinion, yet without the prejudice of any one, I count it to be no Apostle's writing;" and in his preface to the New Testament, two years later: "the Epistle of James is a right strawy Epistle;" yet it seems strange and contradictory, after such expressions, that he held, at all events at one time, that the author was the son of Zebedee. This low estimate of the Epistle prevailed for a time among the Lutherans, but subsequently it obtained a better reception among them, and it was acknowledged that St. Paul and St. James agree essentially together. The rationalistic writers, as might be expected, on various grounds throw discredit on the Epistle.

LANGUAGE AND STYLE OF THE EPISTLE.

There are two features that strike the student on perusing the few pages contained in this Epistle. The first is, that the thoughts embodied, the structure of the composition, and the mode of appeal are Hebrew and not Greek; and the second is, that the Greek which is the vehicle of these thoughts, so far as the language is concerned, is unexceptionally good for the period, ranking with the productions of St. Luke in excellency. So much has this been felt that some critics, as Faber, Bolten, and Bertholdt, have been of opinion that it was written originally in Aramaic, and afterwards translated into Greek; this was the case with St. Matthew's Gospel, according to high patristic authority, which was written for Jewish use especially, and also with the Epistle to the Hebrews, which, according to Clement of Alexandria, quoted by Eusebius, *H. E.* vi. 14, was written by St. Paul in Hebrew, and translated into Greek by St. Luke, which is highly probable, both because it was addressed to the Jews of Palestine, who used a Semitic vernacular, and also because the editorial work of St. Luke in translating the treatise would account for some of the internal difficulties found in that Epistle. If our Epistle passed through the same process, the superiority of the Greek would be accounted for as well as the Semitic structure of the composition, but against this hypothesis a grave difficulty presents itself, that this letter was written to the Jews of the *dispersion*, the Hellenists or Grecising Jews, who had in their estrangement from their own country and customs adopted the language of those nations among whom they dwelt. No satisfactory solution has ever been given of this combination of Hebrew thought, identical in character and force with the inspiration of the prophets of the golden age of that language, and the confessed excellence of expression in the Greek tongue; neither is there any ascertained experience in the history of any of the name of James who can lay claim to the authorship of the Epistle that would serve to solve the enigma; the residence of the Bishop of Jerusalem in that city, where so many races met, might be supposed to lend an advocacy to his claims, but his cure of souls was evidently confined to the Jewish believers, who were chiefly of the poorer class, and they were Aramaic in dialect. However, the fact is before us, account for it as we can or will, that the thought and structure of the composition is Hebrew, and that of a high order, and more than this, that our Epistle is penned, not in prose but in poetry, the true and natural utterance of exalted thoughts; Bishop Jebb has beautifully entitled it, "a prophetic poem." It is in short a Hebrew poem in a Greek garb.

It would be quite out of place to introduce here anything like a treatise on Hebrew poetry, even though a knowledge of some of the discoveries made in that interesting field of inquiry is necessary to the intellectual enjoyment of our Epistle. The reader is referred to the well known works on the subject, both foreign and English, the most interesting of which, so far as this Epistle is concerned, is the elegant work of the late Bishop Jebb on "Sacred Literature," based upon the researches of Bishop Louth; to this work the student will observe that the writer is indebted for many hints and examples.

It is well known that Hebrew poetry consists chiefly, if not entirely, of the two classes of poetry known as the lyric and the gnomic, the impulsive and proverbial; both are found represented in our Epistle. The former is finely exhibited in chap. iv. and the early part of chap. v., and the latter in chap. i. 22-27; ii. 26; iii. throughout, etc.

It is familiar to all Bible students that Hebrew poetry consists not in the prosodial laws which govern the poetry of the Aryan races, but in the expression of parallel ideas, grouped in various forms; the simplest of these is the couplet, in which the idea contained is expressed simply or generally in the former of the two lines, and then particularized or augmented, elevated or degraded, in the latter. This is called by Louth synonymous, but by Jebb cognate parallelism; the following may serve as examples:—

"Are ye not making distinctions amongst yourselves,
And become judges of wicked reasonings?"—Chap. ii. 4.

"Thou seest that his faith was co-operating with his works,
And by his works his faith was perfected."—Chap. ii. 22.

But St. James' style is rich in triplets, that is, in arranging his thoughts in three lines connected intimately with each other, the second rising above the first, and the third above the second, or drawing a deduction from the previous two; examples will be found in the following passages:—

"But the humble brother must glory in his exaltation;
But the rich man (grieve) in his humiliation,
Because as the flower of the grass he shall pass away."—
Chap. i. 9, 10.

"Wherefore putting off all filthiness and abundance of malice,
In meekness receive the word that is sown,
Which is able to save your souls."—Chap. i. 21.

"For judgment shall be merciless,
To him that did not mercy;
Mercy glories over judgment."—Chap. ii. 13.

"Therewith we bless the Lord and Father;
And therewith curse we men,
Who after the likeness of God are created."—Chap. iii. 9.

"Be weighed down, and mourn and wail;
Let your laughter to mourning be turned,
And your joy into dejection."—Chap. iv. 9.

"Complain not against one another, brethren,
That ye be not judged:
Lo! the judge before the doors standeth."—Chap. v. 9.

We find also specimens of quatrains, or sentences distributed into four lines, so connected as to make the sense continuous, though sometimes the connection is traceable directly in pairs, and sometimes alternately. Examples of this form of Hebrew poetry are presented in the following passages:—

"If any one thinketh he is rite-religious,
Though not bridling his tongue,
But deceiving his own heart,
This man's rite-religion is vain."—Chap. i. 26.

"Lo, the bits of horses
Into their mouths we put,
That they may be obedient to us,
And their whole body we guide-about."

"Lo, the ships also, so great as they are,
And by violent winds driven,
Are guided-about by a very small rudder,
Wherever the will of the helmsman desireth."—Chap. iii. 3, 4.

1 "Ye lust and ye have not;
3 Ye murder and envy, and cannot obtain,
2 Ye fight and war, ye have not;
4 Because of your not asking."—Chap. iv. 2.

There is another form of Hebrew poetry found in St. James, which Bishop Jebb terms *epanodos*, and defines thus: "Epanodos is literally, *a going* back; speaking first to the second of the subjects proposed: or, if the subjects be more than two, resuming them precisely in inverted order, speaking first to the last, and last to the first. The *rationale* of this artifice in composition I ventured to explain in the following words: Two pair of terms or propositions, containing two important, but not equally important, notions, are to be so distributed as to bring out the sense in the strongest and most impressive manner; now this result will be best attained, by commencing and concluding with the notion to which prominence is to be given, or by placing in the centre the less important notion, or that which from the scope of the argument is to be kept subordinate." Examples of epanodos will be found in the following places of our Epistle :—

"*But let the rich man (grieve) in his humiliation,*
Because as the flower of the grass he shall pass away,
For the sun arose with the Simoom,
And withered the grass,
And the flower of it fell down,
And the grace of its appearance perished,
So the rich man also in his ways shall be blighted."—
Chap. i. 10, 11.

"*But become ye* doers *of the word*
And not only hearers,
Deluding your own selves;
Because if any one is a hearer of the word, and not a doer,
He is like a man considering the face of his nature in a mirror.
For he considered himself, and went away,
And straightway forgot what sort of man he was.
But he that inspected the perfect law
That pertaineth to liberty,
And continued there,
And became not a hearer of forgetfulness,
But a doer of work,
This man blessed in his doing shall be."—Chap. i. 22-25.

"*God haughty men opposeth,*
But to humble men giveth grace,
Submit ye then to God,
But withstand the devil, and he shall flee from you,
Draw nigh to God, and he shall draw nigh you,
Cleanse your hands, O sinners,
And purify your hearts, O double-minded.
Be weighed down, and mourn and wail;
Let your laughter to mourning be turned,
And your joy into dejection.
Be humbled in the sight of the Lord,
And he will exalt you."—Chap. iv. 6, 10.

Before closing these remarks on the poetical structure of this Epistle, we may add that the figure called by grammarians *duadiplosis*, and by logicians *sorites*, is frequent in St. James' composition. It consists in a taking up, or repetition of, in the second clause the predicate in the preceding one, and so on. Bishop Jebb notices only one in our Epistle, chap. i. 15, but gives some fine specimens from other places; we select for an example Luke xii. 58:

" Lest he drag thee to the *judge*,
And the *judge* hand thee over to the *officer*,
And the *officer* cast thee into prison."

See, for other examples, Jno. i. 4, 5; Rom. v. 3, 5; viii. 29, 30; 2 Pet. i. 5-7. Specimens of this figure are found in our Epistle:—

" Knowing that the test of your faith worketh out *endurance*,
But let *endurance* have *perfect* work
That ye may be *perfect* and complete,
In nothing *lacking*,
But if any of you *lacketh* wisdom," etc.—Chap. i. 3, 5.

Again:—

" Let no one when *tempted* say,
' From God I am *tempted*,'
For God is unskilled in evil things,
Neither *tempteth* he any one.
But each one is *tempted* from his own *lust*,
Being drawn away and enticed-by-a-bait,
Then *lust* having conceived bringeth forth *sin*,
And *sin* being accomplished breedeth death."—Chap. i. 13-15.

Enough has been said on the subject of structure to show the reader that the characteristics of this Epistle are essentially Semitic; that it was not only written by a Jew to Jews, but that it was composed also after the exemplar of those ancient prophecies to which their forefathers had listened in the days when the inspired seer uttered his burden, or unfolded his roll "written within and without with lamentations and mourning and woe." The subject matter, like a germ, accreted to itself a body congenial to its nature, and Hebrew thought could not escape the necessity of incarnation in Hebrew rhythm, though it has come down to us clothed in a garb wrought in another language, whose elegance is so striking and suitable, that at first sight the observer would conclude the foreigner to be a native. This Hebrew basis will be more apparent when we enter on the work of interpretation; the quotations, it will be seen, and the references, the logic and the arguments, the doctrines and duties, the circumstances and the customs, in a word, the composition in its essence and its accidents, in its whole and in its parts, is thoroughly Jewish; and the superscription that introduces the Epistle to the critic and the student is proved to be a faithful witness, both by direct and circumstantial evidence, "To the twelve tribes that are in the dispersion."

The Greek text of the Epistle has been revised, the readings adopted, as a general rule, are those supported by the evidence of the most ancient uncial MSS., as will be seen by the notes, except in a very few cases, where the internal evidence is preponderating in favour of readings exhibited by later authorities.

The Hebrew parallelisms have been preserved in arranging both the Greek text and the English translation, and in the latter the position of the words in the original has been observed as far as the different idioms of the two languages would permit. The true emphasis thus gained must plead an apology, if in some places a too great stiffness of expression, or an overweening anxiety for accuracy, should suggest the presence of pedantry.

THE
EPISTLE OF S^T. JAMES.

CHAPTER I.

1 *ΙΑΚΩΒΟΣ Θεοῦ καὶ Κυρίου Ἰησοῦ Χριστοῦ δοῦλος, ταῖς δώδεκα φυλαῖς ταῖς ἐν τῇ διασπορᾷ, χαίρειν.*

1 JAMES, of God and of the Lord Jesus Christ a servant, to the twelve tribes that are in the dispersion, with joyful-greeting.

Ver. 1. *James, i.e.*, Jacob, the Hebrew יַעֲקֹב *supplanter;* the same name as that of the great patriarch. It is to be regretted that the more ancient form of this word has not been retained in translations. The original name became Ἰάκωβος in Greek, and *Jacobus* in Latin, in Italian *Jácomo*, in Spanish *Iago* and *Diego*, in Portuguese *Tiago, Xagme* or *Jayme*, in French *Jacques* and *Jame*, hence our *James*. See the interesting note in the *Bible Dictionary* by Rev. F. Meyrick. For other particulars connected with the author of this Epistle see Introduction.

Of God and of the Lord Jesus Christ a servant. Having stated his name, the writer proceeds to describe his office, he is a *servant*, δοῦλος, *one bound to serve*. This title conveys more than the general notion of one who believes in and obeys God and the Lord Jesus Christ. The call he had received, the mission and special field of labour assigned him are also embodied in the term. It is equivalent to the "servant of the LORD" (עֶבֶד יהוה) of the Old Testament, a designation with which only a few of the members of the Hebrew Church were honoured, who were raised up by God for some specific work, the founding of a covenant, as in the case of Abraham and Moses; the inaugurating of some step in advance or the introduction of some new phase or development of the system, as in the case of Joshua, David, and Zerubbabel. Thus St. James had a special service entrusted to him, which appears in this very Epistle to have been to make an appeal to a particular section of his brethren. See Introduction.

By declaring himself to be a servant of God, St. James makes confession of the Jewish faith, that *he* was a believer in the God of his fathers, and by adding "and of the Lord Jesus Christ" he equally announces his acceptance of Jesus Christ as the Messiah and hope of Israel. It is to be noticed that the name of Jesus Christ occurs only once more in this Epistle, chap. ii. 1, a strong proof, as has been observed in the Introduction, that this Epistle was not addressed by the author to Christians as such, but to his brethren in the flesh generally.

To the twelve tribes that are in the dispersion. It is of the greatest importance for the understanding of this Epistle to retain in mind the persons to whom it was addressed: for the consideration of this question, see Introduction. It will be sufficient for the purpose of this note to remind the reader that St. James is addressing Jews and not Gentiles; Jews as such, and not necessarily Christian Jews; Jews, moreover, not dwelling in Judæa, but Jews of the dispersion, *i.e.*, Jews who were scattered throughout the world in the midst of the Gentiles, the Hellenists or Grecising Jews; the word διασπορά always refers to this portion of the Jewish people, see Jno. vii. 35; 1 Pet. i. 1. The views of those commentators that maintain that the Jews residing in Judæa are included, or that the Christians who were dispersed throughout the world are addressed in a figurative term borrowed from the well-known state of the Jewish people, are quite untenable.

With joyful greeting, χαίρειν, the regular Greek form of epistolary greeting. There is probably a remote radical alliance between this verb and the Hebrew חיה *to live*, with the annexed idea of living prosperously and happily, hence the phrase יחי המלך, *May the king live!* rendered in E.V., "God save the king," 1 Sam. x. 24, etc. χαίρειν as a form of address is found in the epistle sent to the Gentile churches by the council of Jerusalem, Acts xv. 23; this form is not found in the *preface* of any other Epistle in the New Testament, the use of it therefore in this place has been generally considered as furnishing an undesigned coincidence of the common authorship of the above decree and this Epistle. Without seeking to invalidate the force of this testimony as advanced by those who hold the ordinary view respecting the authorship of this Epistle, we may remind the reader that this verb is found in St. Paul's Epistles in the same

2 Πᾶσαν χαρὰν ἡγήσασθε, ἀδελφοί μου,
ὅταν πειρασμοῖς περιπέσητε ποικίλοις,

2 All joy esteem it, my brethren,
When into the midst of various temptations ye fall,

sense, though it rather assumes the form of subscription than of superscription: see 2 Cor. xiii. 11; Phil. iii. 1; iv. 4. We should have expected from the pen of one whose epistle exhibits so much in matter and style that is akin to the writings of the ancient prophets some phrase that savoured more of his nationality and associations, the customary שלום עליכם, εἰρήνη ὑμῖν, *peace be to you:* but when we call to mind that though the author evidently thought in Semitic, and constructed his epistle after a Semitic model, yet he studied to attain excellency in Greek expression, and further, that he was writing to his brethren of the dispersion, to Jews who were mingled with the Greeks and used their language, the propriety of this idiomatic mode of address will be apparent. It may be remarked that St. John, the brother of St. James, uses the word as a form of personal greeting, which is closely akin to the epistolary use of the word in this place: see 2 Jno. 10.

Ver. 2. *All joy.* Esteem every temptation to be a source or cause of rejoicing.

Joy, χαράν. This word seems to have been suggested by the preceding χαίρειν *with joyful-greeting*. When I wish you joy, I would have you regard even your temptations as conducive to joy, which they will prove to be, if you view them as permitted for the establishment of your faith and the refinement of your spiritual character. For a somewhat similar play on this verb see *Eur. Hecuba*, 426, 427.

Temptations. Were it not for the 13th verse we should be induced to think that these temptations were trials and tests of faith merely, such as affliction and persecution, but the prohibition that the tempted man is not to refer the temptation to God, because it arises from his own lusts, plainly proves that in this place we are to interpret the word as including the dark and evil temptations of Satan and our own evil hearts, as well as the trials that come upon us from external sources; the adjective ποικίλοις shows that every kind of temptation is referred to. It is God's prerogative to bring good out of evil, to make even our temptations that burden our hearts, and torture our inner being, to be a means of driving us to Him for succour, and our spiritual sufferings a school of patience, and a pathway to perfection. Temptation is not sin; resisted temptation makes a man stronger; the sin consists not in the assaults of the foe, but in concession to his demands.

3 γινώσκοντες ὅτι τὸ δοκίμιον ὑμῶν τῆς πίστεως
κατεργάζεται ὑπομονήν·

4 ἡ δὲ ὑπομονὴ ἔργον τέλειον ἐχέτω,
ἵνα ἦτε τέλειοι καὶ ὁλόκληροι,
ἐν μηδενὶ λειπόμενοι.

3 Knowing that the test of your faith
Worketh out endurance.

4 But let endurance have perfect work,
That ye may be perfect and complete,
In nothing lacking.

Ye fall-amidst, περιπέσητε. The preposition in composition in this verb imparts the meaning of falling amongst trials, so as to be encompassed by them. The servant of God is thus represented as being hemmed in, as by an iron girdle of trials from which human means can effect no escape; but the things that are impossible with men are possible with God; the same grace that gives the power to endure will also open the way of deliverance: see 1 Cor. x. 13.

Ver. 3. *The test*. The temptations mentioned in the preceding verse serve as a test of your faith, hence their value; gold may be pure and precious, but its excellency is proved by its being cast into the furnace and coming out more brilliant from the ordeal; so faith that is cast into the crucible of temptation, and is neither melted away or wasted by the process, is proved thereby to be a genuine grace, the gift of God. This test works out endurance, an *abiding under* the temptations, a bearing of them, and a sustaining of them without yielding or falling under them, and without impatience to be rid of them.

Ver. 4. *But let endurance have perfect work*. That is, let your endurance of the testing process above named be exercised to the end, let it be no unfinished work. Many run well for a time and then grow weary in the race; many are bold at the onset, but fail before the fight is over; many put their hand to the plough, but look back before they reach the end of the furrow. The trials of the Jewish people in general, and especially of the early converts to Christianity among them, at this period are familiar to all, hence the appropriateness of this exhortation.

That ye may be perfect. There is a Divine and a human perfection; the former is faultless, the latter is relative. Our Lord

5 Εἰ δέ τις ὑμῶν λείπεται σοφίας,
αἰτείτω παρὰ τοῦ διδόντος Θεοῦ
πᾶσιν ἁπλῶς, καὶ μὴ ὀνειδίζοντος,
καὶ δοθήσεται αὐτῷ.

5 But if any of you lacketh wisdom,
Let him ask *it* from God who giveth
To all freely, and reproacheth not,
And it shall be given him.

taught His disciples, Matt. v. 48, " Be ye therefore perfect, even as your Father in heaven is perfect," where the likeness between the original and the copy is apparent, and yet the vast distance between them felt the more by the juxtaposition.

Complete, ὁλόκληροι. This word implies that which has all its full parts and powers in possession; the meaning is well illustrated by the miracle recorded in Acts iii. The lame man healed by Peter and John, in the unrestrained exercise of his newly gained powers walked and leaped, and the apostles pointed at him as a proof of the resurrection of Jesus, who had given him, through their instrumentality, " this *perfect soundness* (ὁλοκληρίαν) in the presence of all." As it was with this man's body so it should be with our souls.

In nothing lacking. A further expansion of the idea contained in the former word, indeed the three characteristics of the man of God form a climax: ye are to be spiritually perfect, having all your graces and virtues in their entirety, and in no one thing are ye to be deficient; the ideal statue is not to present to the view one grace in abundant development, and another of stinted proportions, symmetry not deformity is the model, each part is well balanced with the rest, and all in graceful harmony with the whole; the law of physical is also the law of moral beauty. As the temptations spoken of are various, of divers sorts and kinds, assaulting and testing the various constituents of the whole character, the effect of a successful endurance of them severally would be the perfection of each and all of the members of the inner man, the completion of the godly character, the production of a man after God's own heart.

Ver. 5. *If any of you lacketh wisdom.* The whole of this verse bespeaks Hebrew thought and associations. With them wisdom, הכמה, was the knowledge of the service of God, whereas ignorance of God and irreligion were called נבלה, *folly*. We must not forget, moreover, that "wisdom" in its most comprehensive and expanded sense, as is evidenced by the occasional use of

6 αἰτείτω δὲ ἐν πίστει, μηδὲν διακρινόμενος·
ὁ γὰρ διακρινόμενος ἔοικε κλύδωνι θαλάσσης
ἀνεμιζομένῳ καὶ ῥιπιζομένῳ.

6 But he must ask in faith, nothing doubting;
For he that doubteth is like a wave of the sea
Wind-tossed and dashed about.

the plural form הכמות, was a synonym of the Word of God, to whom the inspired metaphysicians ascribed the creation of the world (see Prov. viii. throughout, and ix. 1; Ps. civ. 24, etc.), and as the prophets and evangelists teach, became incarnate in the person of our Lord Jesus Christ. St. James, therefore, after laying before his brethren the rule of perfection, suggests the thought that some may be lacking in the very essence of all true perfection, the wisdom, the saving knowledge of Him whom to know is everlasting life.

Freely, ἁπλῶς. This is the only place where this adverb is used in the New Testament; we have, however, the cognate noun ἁπλότης in several places in St. Paul's Epistles, Rom. xii. 8; 2 Cor. i. 12 in some MSS., 2 Cor. viii. 2; ix. 11, 13; xi. 3; Eph. vi. 5; Col. iii. 22. The exact import of the adverb in this place has been decided differently by expositors, both ancient and modern; the Syriac Version renders it "copiose," the Latin Vulgate "affluenter," which is followed by Erasmus and Grotius. Bede and Beza "benignè," others "sincerè;" but the true and literal meaning of ἁπλῶς appears to be *simply*, and the best interpretation of the whole clause is, that God is induced simply by the desire of conferring blessings, when He answers the prayers of man; hence, although "freely" (that is, without condition or limit) is somewhat paraphrastic, it is a sound comment on the original, and better suited to explain the intended idea in our language than "simply."

And reproacheth not, μὴ ὀνειδίζοντος. When men give, they often take advantage of the obligation under which they place the recipient, and by some unkind or ill-timed word or insinuation cast in his teeth his position, his wants, or his inferiority. In Ecclesiasticus this verb is several times connected with the act of giving, as in this place, see chap. xviii. 18; xx. 15; xli. 22, where the sense appears to be the same, μετὰ τὸ δοῦναι μὴ ὀνείδιζε. St. James, therefore, teaches us that we may ask of God His best gifts, His largest gifts, and He will confer them on us all freely and fully, unworthy though we be, and will not charge or chide us with our own unworthiness or His liberality.

Ver. 6. Having declared the readiness of God to answer

prayer, St. James proceeds to define the conditions required in the petitioner. He must ask in faith; and this is enforced by him according to a style frequent in our author by the negation of the opposite "nothing doubting." If, as we believe, Jews were addressed in this Epistle, some of whom were believers in Christ, some inquirers, some young and feeble in the faith, and some unacquainted with or even rejecters of the Gospel, how fitting is this exhortation to ask for saving wisdom with a full assurance, or without a doubt that God would guide them to a right conclusion, and give them wisdom in answer to their prayer, as He had done to Solomon, to which episode in Israel's history there is here an unmistakeable reference.

Doubting, διακρινόμενος. Huther has an excellent comment on this word, quoted by Dean Alford, " διακρίνεσθαι *to doubt* is not the same as ἀπιστεῖν *to disbelieve*, but includes in it the essential character of ἀπιστία *unbelief;* while πίστις says *yes*, and ἀπιστία *no*, διακρίνεσθαι is the union of *yes* and *no*, but so that *no* is the weightier; it is an inward giving way, which leans not to πίστις but to ἀπιστία."

For he that doubteth, etc. The play upon the words in this sentence in the E.V., " He that wavereth is like a wave of the sea," is entirely without foundation in the original. It was a grave mistake in the Revisers of 1611 to render the same word by different representatives, it was a graver mistake to confound words that differed, especially when the phraseological form of a sentence was calculated to stamp the expression as a *household word*. " He that hateth suretyship is sure," Prov. xi. 15 ; " The first man is of the earth, earthy," 1 Cor. xv. 47, like the passage before us need only to be pointed out to the student to expose the misleading tendency of such translations.

Like a wave of the sea, wind-tossed and dashed about. The figure of the rolling and rocking of the sea-wave naturally occurs to the mind of the writer, who had spent his childhood and youth on the treacherous waters of the sea of Galilee, and was by no means *Nescius auræ fallacis*. 'Ανεμίζεσθαι is only found in this place, the classical form is ἀνεμοῦσθαι. 'Ριπίζεσθαι is generally connected with ῥιπίς, a *fan*, hence to *fan* into a flame, see Aristophanes' *Ranæ*, 360, " ἀνεγείρει καὶ ῥιπίζει " sc. πολίτας. St. James may here vary the figure from fanning the fire to fanning the waves, but probably he had in mind the more remote derivation of the word from ῥιπή, the *force* or impetus with which anything is thrown, " ῥιπῇ Βορέαο," *Il.* xv. 171, and " ῥιπαὶ κυμάτων ἀνέμων τε," Pindar, P. 4, 346, will sufficiently illustrate our passage. This is the only place in the New Testament where this word is used.

7 μὴ γὰρ οἰέσθω ὁ ἄνθρωπος ἐκεῖνος,
ὅτι λήμψεταί τι παρὰ τοῦ Κυρίου.

8 ἀνὴρ δίψυχος, ἀκατάστατος ἐν πάσαις ταῖς ὁδοῖς αὐτοῦ.

7 For let not that man think,
That he shall receive aught from the Lord.

8 A man double-minded, unstable in all his ways *is he*.

Ver. 7. *Let not that man think that he shall receive aught from the Lord.* Much less the high and precious gift of wisdom : this seems to be the inference suggested.

The Lord, τοῦ Κυρίου. Ὁ Κύριος is a frequent title in our author for God the Father; he uses it as the LXX. had done, as an equivalent for Jehovah. Ὁ Κύριος is a title of Christ in chap. v. 7, 14, 15.

Ver. 8. *Double minded*, δίψυχος. This is the first time this word is used in the Greek language; it was apparently invented by St. James; the meaning of it is the same as the Hebrew phrase לב ולב, Ps. xii. 3, "a heart and a heart," one heart leads in one direction, the other in another. How fitly this description harmonizes with the context will readily appear. The man that lacks wisdom to see the Messiahship of Jesus, which was the great question among the Jews of that day, or when he seeks guidance of God asks not in faith, but doubtingly, he is a man half inclined to believe and half inclined to disbelieve, changeable as a wave that is blown upon first by a wind from one quarter, and then driven back again by an opposite current; a man of two minds, in which, as ever, the worse prevails.

In all his ways. The word "way" is here employed in its metaphorical or figurative sense, as דרך often is in Hebrew: see Gen. vi. 12 ; Is. xl. 27 ; lv. 8 ; Jer. xxxii. 19 ; Prov. xvi. 31, etc. ὁδός is used in the same sense in chap. v. 20 ; Acts xiv. 16; Rom. vi. 6 ; 2 Pet. ii. 15; Jude 11 ; the sense therefore in this place is "in all his plans of thought and action." The next inquiry necessary to be made in this passage is, how are the words to be arranged or connected with the previous subject? The sentence may be arranged as in the E.V., "A double minded man is unstable in all his ways." Regarding the double minded man as generic, as any one of that class, and so making the sentence independent of the previous subject, or connected with it only as an illustrative proverb. Another mode of distributing the

9 Καυχάσθω δὲ ὁ ἀδελφὸς ὁ ταπεινὸς ἐν τῷ ὕψει αὐτοῦ·

9 But let the humble brother glory in his exaltation;

words is to regard them as a further explanation of the character under description, Let not that man think that he shall receive aught from the Lord, inasmuch as he is a double-minded man, unstable in all his ways. The translation, however, that is given in the text is to be preferred to either of these.

Ver. 9. *The humble brother; the rich.* We have here introduced for the first time the two characters that are specially addressed in this Epistle. St. James is a true follower, both in ideas and language, of the psalmists and prophets of the Old Testament. The "poor and needy," עָנִי וְאֶבְיוֹן, Ps. xxxvii. 14, and similar phrases are always descriptive of the truly religious, the meek and lowly in heart, and often predicated of Messiah in His humiliation. The same connection between poverty and religion appears in Zeph. iii. 12, and Zech. xi. 7. Our Lord adopted the same phraseology, see Matt. v. 3, and Luke vi. 20, and associated with that grace of lowliness the assurance of a place in the Gospel kingdom. Whereas the "rich" is an equally well-known epithet of the ungodly, the oppressor, and the enemy of religion, see Ps. xlix. 16; Luke vi. 24. This forms the basis of the parable of Dives and Lazarus, Luke xvi. 19. The rich man was a careless, uncharitable, irreligious man, whereas the poor man was Lazarus, *i.e.*, Eleazar, or one whose *helper is God.* The "poor" and the "rich" therefore are two distinct and opposed classes in this Epistle; the poor and lowly are the converted among them, brethren not only in the flesh but in the Lord, Christian Israelites; and the "rich" are the unconverted, and antagonistic to the Gospel. How commentators can see in the "rich man" a rich *brother* with such passages as *v.* 11; ii. 6, 7; and v. 1-6 in view it is difficult to conceive. The connection with the preceding verses is evident. The lowly believer is one who has made up his mind on the great subject of the Messiahship of Jesus, and he may well rejoice in his exaltation, in the high and holy vocation wherewith he is called, and in the sure and certain hope of the coming kingdom and glory; while the unbeliever who at first was undecided and then adhered to his former unbelief shall be humbled and pass away like a blighted flower. There is a great difficulty in allotting the verb to ὁ πλούσιος, *the rich man.* Some commentators take the "rich" to be a *brother*, parallel to the "lowly brother," and repeat καυχάσθω with the second subject; this, although quite in accordance with the simplest rules of grammar, is perfectly untenable with the position of the "rich" throughout this Epistle. In *vv.* 10, 11, the immediate context of this passage, it is said that the rich man shall "pass away" παρελεύσεται, and be "blighted" μαρανθήσεται; in chap. ii. 6, 7 the "rich" are charged with oppressing the poor and haling them to the law-courts, and being guilty of blasphemy; and in chap. v. 1-3 the "rich" are challenged with the woes that are coming upon them in consequence of their iniquities. In the face of these denunciations against the "rich," who are evidently a class in contradistinction to the "poor" man, who is the representative of another class, it is impossible to regard them as Christian brethren. For the same reason we must reject all milder forms of the same order of interpretation, such as the rich man should rejoice in being brought to repentance through his trials, since this feature is not introduced by the Apostle, but rather a prophecy of judgment. The suggestion of Dean Alford that the indicative καυχᾶται should be supplied falls under this category as an unsuccessful attempt to escape a difficulty. We are rather led to fall back upon a figure found in classical usage, and not unfrequently met with in the New Testament, namely, the borrowing from a word in the preceding clause another word suited to the demands of the following clause: If the lowly brother is to *rejoice* in his exaltation which unites him to the Messiah here, and hereafter will raise him to a place in His kingdom of glory, the rich man is to *grieve* in his degradation from the wealth and luxuries of this world, which were to come to nought at the impending fall of Jerusalem, and in the persecution of the Jews, for then the rich of Israel must fall and fade. This figure, called *zeugma* or *brachylogy*, we find in 1 Cor. iii. 2, γάλα ὑμᾶς ἐπότισα, οὐ βρῶμα, "I have given you milk to *drink*, not food;" here some verb connected with eating must be supplied out of ἐπότισα. Again in chap. vii. 19 a passage occurs more closely allied to ours: ἡ περιτομὴ οὐδέν ἐστι, καὶ ἡ ἀκροβυστία οὐδέν ἐστιν, ἀλλὰ τήρησις ἐντολῶν Θεοῦ; here τὰ πάντα must be supplied out of οὐδέν, its opposite in the preceding clause, "Circumcision is *nothing*, and uncircumcision is *nothing*, but the keeping of the commandments of God *is everything*." Once more in the same Epistle, chap. x. 24, we meet with μηδεὶς τὸ ἑαυτοῦ ζητείτω, ἀλλὰ τὸ τοῦ ἑτέρου; here ἕκαστος must be supplied out of the opposite μηδείς in the former clause, "Let *no one* seek his own good, but *every one* that of the other." Another example may be added from 1 Tim. iv. 3, κωλυόντων γαμεῖν, ἀπέχεσθαι βρωμάτων, where the opposite κελευόντων or some such verb must be borrowed from the preceding verb, "*Forbidding* to marry and *commanding* to abstain from meats." The sense of the passage under consideration will thus be evident, and the teaching of the Apostle be harmonious

10 ὁ δὲ πλούσιος ἐν τῇ ταπεινώσει αὐτοῦ,
ὅτι ὡς ἄνθος χόρτου παρελεύσεται.

11 ἀνέτειλε γὰρ ὁ ἥλιος σὺν τῷ καύσωνι,
καὶ ἐξήρανε τὸν χόρτον,
καὶ τὸ ἄνθος αὐτοῦ ἐξέπεσε,
καὶ ἡ εὐπρέπεια τοῦ προσώπου αὐτοῦ ἀπώλετο·
οὕτω καὶ ὁ πλούσιος ἐν ταῖς πορείαις αὐτοῦ μαρανθήσεται.

10 But the rich man *grieve* in his humiliation,
Because as the flower of the grass he shall pass away.
11 For the sun arose with the Simoom,
And withered the grass,
And the flower of it fell down,
And the grace of its appearance perished.
So the rich man also in his ways shall be blighted.

throughout. The lowly will rejoice in his elevation to Messianic hopes and the coming kingdom, and the rich, the unbeliever, will have cause for sorrow in the loss, as in the example of Dives in the parable, of life and glory, and in expulsion from the inheritance of the saints and from the glory of God.

ὡς ἄνθος χόρτου παρελεύσεται. There is often a similarity traceable between St. James and St. Peter in their style and in the figures employed. They were intimate fellow-apostles, hence the unison of thought; both were of course familiar with the writings of the Hebrew prophets, who furnished a common storehouse; and they were both apostles of the circumcision, hence their field of work was the same. This illustration is common to the two writers, see 1 Pet. i. 24. It is derived from Ps. ciii. 15, 16, and Is. xl. 6-8.

Ver. 11. ἀνέτειλεν γὰρ ὁ ἥλιος, *the sun arose.* This aorist is not merely the aorist of narrative, expressive of an experience, which is supported by frequent examples, but rather equivalent to the prophetic preterite, so constantly met with in the Hebrew prophets. The event predicted is regarded as being so certain of fulfilment that it is spoken of as already accomplished; thus in the original passage, Is. xl. 7, from which this quotation is made we read, יבש חציר נבל ציץ, "withered is the grass, faded the flower." See also Winer's *Greek Grammar of the New Testament,* p. 293.

With the Simoom, σὺν τῷ καύσωνι. Καύσων, from καίω *to burn,* may mean simply *heat,* the heat of the sun; but as the LXX.,

Aquila, Symmachus, and Theodotion have sometimes rendered the Hebrew קדים by this word, it most likely refers to the burning desert-wind, which was suffocating to animals and blighting to vegetation. The sun is here said to arise accompanied by the hot wind, it set in with the sun-rise. קדים is properly the east wind, the quarter from which this destructive blast came. We meet with the word in Matt. xx. 12, where the dissatisfied labourers urge that they have borne τὸ βάρος τῆς ἡμέρας καὶ τὸν καύσωνα; the position of the word here, and the use of the article seem intended to separate it from the preceding subject (see Middleton on the Greek Article). The climax too which was evidently in the minds of the murmurers is thus evident: "who have borne the burden of the day and the Simoom." The same meaning is doubtless intended in the other passage where the word occurs, Luke xii. 55: καὶ ὅταν Νότον πνέοντα, λέγετε ὅτι καύσων ἔσται, "and when (ye see) the south wind blow, ye say there will be a Simoom." This at first sight might seem contradictory to what has been said above, that the Hebrew word signifies the east wind, but in many passages the LXX. translated קדים by Νότος, and for this reason, that in Egypt, where that translation was made, the south wind had the same character that the east wind had in Judæa; hence the word came into general use for a hot wind, the character of the wind more than the quarter from which it blew being intended to be brought into prominence. It would seem not unlikely that Jonah, chap. iv., was the basis of much of this passage; the sacred writers are often in the habit of turning off at a word; some phrase or figure has been employed which is found in an ancient Scripture, this suggests a line of thought, and the original passage and the train of ideas it has awakened will be found to run in parallels. Thus St. James having mentioned the waves of sea tossed by the wind is reminded of Jonah's storm; then the man of two purposes reflects the wavering prophet; then the sun arising with the vehement east wind (see Jonah iv. 8), which withers the gourd (*palma Christi*), is all but reproduced *verbatim* by our author. Many of these subterranean coincidences have been traced, and they seem to bind and unite together the sacred writers as a body corporate, and their writings as one whole and consistent testimony.

εὐπρέπεια, *grace.* The LXX. in Is. xl. 6, and St. Peter in his first Epistle, chap. i. 24, have δόξα for the Hebrew חסד, a word which, like our English "grace," has the double meaning of moral and physical beauty. εὐπρέπεια is only found here in the New Testament.

In his ways, ἐν ταῖς πορείαις, his courses. The idea suggested by this word is that of (apparent) progress, as the grape buds, and blossoms, and promises fruitfulness, but is suddenly blighted

12 Μακάριος ἀνὴρ ὃς ὑπομένει πειρασμόν·
ὅτι δόκιμος γενόμενος
λήμψεται τὸν στέφανον τῆς ζωῆς,
ὃν ἐπηγγείλατο τοῖς ἀγαπῶσιν αὐτόν.

13 Μηδεὶς πειραζόμενος λεγέτω,
"Ὅτι ἀπὸ τοῦ Θεοῦ πειράζομαι·"
ὁ γὰρ Θεὸς ἀπείραστός ἐστι κακῶν,
πειράζει δὲ αὐτὸς οὐδένα.

12 Blessed is the man who is enduring temptation;
Because after becoming approved,
He shall receive the crown of life,
Which He promised to them that love Him.

13 Let no one when tempted, say,
"From God I am tempted;"
For God is unskilled in evil things,
And it is not He that tempteth any one.

and destroyed; so the rich man in his progress, though it seems so prosperous, shall be cut off and perish. The Alexandrine MS. in this place reads πορίαις, a word which is nowhere found in Greek literature; Erasmus and Luther regarded it as equivalent to εὐπορίαις, " in his prosperity or wealth." It is needless to add that the authority of MSS. determines the usual reading to be the correct one.

Ver. 12. This verse re-introduces the tempted man in a higher state of perfection. In the opening of the Epistle the falling into the midst of trials is spoken of as a blessing, if such an experience proved to be a test of his faith, that produced a patient endurance of the trials. In resuming the subject after a digression, St. James starts from the point he had already reached, and represents the tried one as enduring the temptation, and then proceeds to show the blessedness of such an one, for after being tested and approved he shall receive the crown of life: crown is here a symbolical way of expressing *reward*, the reward of eternal life. The genitive is one of apposition, the crown which consists in the *life*, the life which is contrasted with the fading flower, the figure of the rich man who has perished.

Ver. 13. *When tempted*, πειραζόμενος. The reference must be, beyond doubt, made to the πειρασμοί spoken of already: this shows that these temptations must be of an evil character, inasmuch as they did not and could not proceed from God; ἀπό denoting the source and origin. God overrules temptation, makes it subservient to the good of the tempted saint, and if we may so express it, like the wise physician compels even poisons when infused into the cup to minister to the health of the patient; but no temptation is fabricated by God, hence we infer that the temptations spoken of here differ entirely from the case of Abraham's trial, of which we read in Gen. xxii. 1, "God did tempt Abraham;" God put the patriarch to the test, to see if he would obey Him to the last degree. The verb πειράζειν is simply to put to the test or proof, the context must decide whether the test is to be taken in a good or a bad sense. In the New Testament as well as the Old it is employed in the former sense: thus in Heb. xi. 17, where the instance referred to above is cited, we read, Ἀβραὰμ πειραζόμενος. See also 2 Cor. xiii. 5, ἑαυτοὺς πειράζετε εἰ ἐστὲ ἐν τῇ πίστει; and Rev. ii. 2, ἐπείρασας τοὺς λέγοντας ἑαυτοὺς ἀποστόλους: but here it is used in the bad sense, to tempt or lure to evil.

From God. Ἀπό in such a connection denotes the source from which the subject spoken of arises, and we are emphatically warned not to refer the origin of our temptations to God. In the following verse ἀπό is used in the same sense, showing that our temptations arise from our own lust. In both these places the Sinaitic MS. reads ὑπό, which implies the direct agent, but the reading ἀπό is to be preferred; the ordinary punctuation by putting a comma after πειράζεται makes ἀπό to depend upon the participles ἐξελκόμενος and δελεαζόμενος, but the dependence of ἀπό in the 13th verse upon πειράζομαι is sufficient proof that the same connection exists here also.

Unskilled in evil things, ἀπείραστος κακῶν. There is no small difficulty in interpreting these words. In the first place ἀπείραστος is a late form of ἀπείρατος, which signifies either *inexperienced of*, or *untried:* this is the only place in which it is found in the New Testament. The Syriac Version understands it in a passive sense, "God cannot be tempted." But the Æthiopic takes it in an active sense, as intentator, "tempter;" and κακῶν is regarded as masculine, "God is not the tempter of evil men." In such a case as this the context has no small share in settling the question. We have a prohibition not to refer our temptations to God; the next clause which contains this word shows the impossibility of temptation arising from God, inasmuch as He has no skill or experience in evil things, and the following clause states the resulting fact that He tempts no man: this seems to be the connection. The ordinary interpretation that God is untempted of evil is contrary to the use of the word, introduces a truism that is irrelevant, and gives no reason for the prohibi-

14 ἕκαστος δὲ πειράζεται ἀπὸ τῆς ἰδίας ἐπιθυμίας,
ἐξελκόμενος καὶ δελεαζόμενος·
15 εἶτα ἡ ἐπιθυμία συλλαβοῦσα τίκτει ἁμαρτίαν·
ἡ δὲ ἁμαρτία ἀποτελεσθεῖσα ἀποκύει θάνατον.
16 Μὴ πλανᾶσθε, ἀδελφοί μου ἀγαπητοί.

14 But each one is tempted from his own lust,
Being drawn away and enticed by a bait.
15 Then lust having conceived bringeth forth sin,
And sin being accomplished, breedeth death;
16 Do not be-led-astray, my beloved brethren.

tion, although the causal particle γάρ demands that a reason should be assigned for the statement made in the clause which precedes it.

And it is not He that tempteth anyone, πειράζει δὲ αὐτὸς οὐδένα. The point here specially urged is, as stated in the preceding note, that although these temptations abound, and the man of God has to do battle with them, yet they do not proceed from God; He is not the author of them. The translation of the text, though slightly paraphrastic, endeavours to bring out this force of αὐτός.

Ver. 14. This verse describes the true source and origin of temptation, the ἰδία ἐπιθυμία of each man, his own particular lust, his own idiosyncrasy in evil desires.

Ver. 15. The key-passage to the striking metaphors which follow appears to be Prov. vii. 10-27, where the harlot is represented in the act of ensnaring the thoughtless youth. In *vv.* 21, 22 he is pictured as forced and led away, corresponding to ἐξελκόμενος; in *vv.* 16-21 the process of enticement is delineated, corresponding to δελεαζόμενος; and the sin and death that result from his folly are described in *vv.* 22, 27. Here ἐπιθυμία is almost personified; it seizes the man, drags him out of his right course, lures him on to seduction; the consent of the mind and the ἐπιθυμία of the flesh are united; lust becomes pregnant with sin and in due course gives birth to the evil offspring, which coming to maturity breeds death, eternal death: lust and hell are grandparent and grandchild.

Ver. 16. It has been much debated whether the words which compose this verse conclude the previous paragraph or commence the next one, or form a connecting link between them. Believing,

17 Πᾶσα δόσις ἀγαθή,
καὶ πᾶν δώρημα τέλειον
ἄνωθέν ἐστι καταβαῖνον
ἀπὸ τοῦ πατρὸς τῶν φώτων,
παρ' ᾧ οὐκ ἔνι παραλλαγή,
ἢ τροπῆς ἀποσκίασμα.

17 Every good act-of-giving,
And every perfect gift,
Is from above descending,
From the Father of Light,
With whom there existeth no change,
Or of declension a shadow.

as stated above, that the passage in Proverbs forms the foundation of this passage, we find the very lesson here enforced in *v.* 25, " Go not astray in her paths;" these words will therefore most naturally conclude the preceding paragraph with a forcible and nervously expressed application to his readers, Do not be led astray by the lust that works in you, shun and resist the solicitations of the courtezan; " Vitanda est improba Siren."

Ver. 17. Having shown firstly that God tempts no man, but that temptations arise from the evil engendering of lust, which propagates death, our author now proceeds to prove, that on the contrary, all good descends upon us from God; as on the one hand sin breeds (ἀποκύει) in us death, so on the other hand God begat (ἀπεκύησεν) us by the word of truth, *v.* 18; and as we are warned not to go astray in the way that leads to death by holding commerce with lust and procreating sin; so in *v.* 21 we are exhorted to receive the implanted word, the good seed, which gendereth to life, " which is able to save our souls."

Every good act-of-giving, and every perfect gift. δόσις and δώρημα are not easily distinguished in our language, the former expresses the act of the giver, the latter the thing which he gives. Some have supposed that a distinction is here intended between smaller and greater gifts; the point seems rather to be that the very wish to give and the putting forth of power to give have their origin in our Father's heart, and every gift is dispensed by his hands; hence the adjectives also are chosen with marvellous propriety, the very motive in giving is *good,* ἀγαθή, and the gift which God confers is *perfect,* τέλειον.

It is to be noted that this sentence forms an Hexameter verse:—
Πᾶσα δόσις ἀγαθὴ καὶ πᾶν δώρημα τέλειον.

The *cæsura* after the first foot being lengthened by *arsis*. This metrical distribution of the words was purely accidental there can be little doubt. Similar examples of Hexameters are found, besides the quotation in Tit. i. 12 from Epimenides, and the part of Hexameter in Acts xvii. 18 from Aratus, in Heb. xii. 13:—

Καὶ τροχιὰς ὀρθὰς ποιήσατε τοῖς ποσὶν ὑμῶν,

and in Rev. xix. 12:—

Καὶ ἐπὶ τὴν κεφαλὴν αὐτοῦ διαδήματα πολλά.

To these may be added the Trimeter Iambic in 1 Cor. xv. 33, which is a quotation from the *Thais* of Menander:—

Φθείρουσιν ἤθη χρησθ' ὁμιλίαι κακαί,

where, however, the MSS. preserve the form χρηστά without elision. Some approximations to rhythmical composition, more or less forced, have been pointed out in other passages.*

The Father of Light, τοῦ πατρὸς τῶν φώτων. The explanations of this title of the Supreme Being are many and various: the following are the chief:—

1. φώτων refers to the Urim and Thummim in the breastplate of the high priest, by which God gave information of His will to His people. *Urim*, אורים, signifies *lights*. It might be thought that τέλειον *perfect* in the last clause put the author in mind of *Thummim, perfections*, and hence this reference to the Urim and Thummim.

2. That all moral excellencies are denoted by this word.

3. That good and holy men who are spiritual luminaries are intended.

4. That all spiritual light comes from God.

5. That natural light is referred to, the sun, moon, and stars, as we read of them under this comprehensive name in Ps. cxxxv. 7, φῶτα μεγάλα: see also Jer. iv. 23; LXX.

6. That the first creation of light, Gen. i. 3, was the thought in the writer's mind, " God said, Let there be light; and there was light."

Several of these interpretations are closely allied and interpenetrate or overlap one another, it would be undesirable therefore to narrow the title to any one special class of these figures.

Another explanation is possible: that τῶν φώτων is equivalent to τῆς δόξης, chap. ii. 1, and as that phrase explains further who the Lord Jesus Christ is, namely, the *Shechinah*, so here *lights* would serve to show the attributes of the Father, God, who is light, essentially, originally, perfectly. Thus viewed it would be parallel to 1 Jno. i. 5, ὁ Θεὸς φῶς ἐστιν. Or, again, inasmuch

---

* On the subject of verses occurring in the Greek Testament see Winer's *Greek Grammar*, pp. 662, 663.

18 βουληθεὶς ἀπεκύησεν ἡμᾶς λόγῳ ἀληθείας,
εἰς τὸ εἶναι ἡμᾶς ἀπαρχήν τινα τῶν αὐτοῦ κτισμάτων.

18 He willed *so*, and begat us by the word of truth,
That we should be a kind of firstfruits of His creatures.

as St. Paul, Eph. i. 17, entitles God "the Father of the glory," ὁ πατὴρ τῆς δόξης, which is further explanatory of ὁ Θεὸς τοῦ Κυρίου ἡμῶν Ἰησοῦ Χριστοῦ, "The God of our Lord Jesus Christ." It is possible that φώτων is the plural of excellence or majesty, and God is described as the Father of Him who came to reveal Him, who himself declared, "I am the light (τὸ φῶς) of the world," Jno. viii. 12. In this case there would be a striking connection between the good giving and the perfect gift of the former clause and this, as God giving His only Son was the best of giving and the best of gifts. It is difficult to make choice among so many possible solutions; the words that follow are also capable of several meanings, so that they do not necessarily lead us to any one conclusion.

No change, or of declension a shadow. The notion of astronomical terms in these words has been abandoned by the majority of interpreters, but without sufficient reason. A comprehensive figure capable of embracing many allusions is likely to awake in a poetical mind, such as St. James evidently possessed, many side-thoughts, and the fundamental idea first conceived would be likely to attract to itself various after thoughts, suggested by the terms employed. All light which we enjoy on earth is subject to change, the alternating vicissitudes of day and night, summer and winter, witness of mutability; this is a natural and inherent law in the heavenly bodies, but not so with God, who is light and the source of all light, both physical and spiritual; with Him no such imperfection is inherent. Ἔνι is abbreviated for ἔνεστι. The Sinaitic MS. reads simply ἐστιν in this place, but ἔνι has both external and internal evidence in its favour.

Ver. 18. The connection between this and the former verses is progressive. Every good gift comes from God, who is light and the fountain of light; He is subject to no change; His purpose knows no alteration; He is not a man that He should repent; our very creation is the result of His fixed and unalterable will; He willed and then worked, or rather His will was His work; His " Let be " and " there was " are scarcely separable.

βουληθείς, *willing it:* at the time of creation. This verb is constantly employed by Homer of the will of the gods, because with them will is effect. See Liddell and Scott's *Lexicon.*

ἀπεκύησεν. Sin breeds (ἀποκύει) death, *v.* 15. God begat us by the word of truth to life.

λόγῳ ἀληθείας, *by the word of truth.* The genitive of apposition, the word which is truth. This is one of those passages in which it is difficult to determine whether the personal or the written word is intended. The same difficulty exists in the two passages which are most closely allied to this one. In Jno. xvii. 17 we read, 'Ἁγίασον αὐτοὺς ἐν τῇ ἀληθείᾳ σου, Ὁ λόγος ὁ σὸς ἀλήθειά ἐστι, where, inasmuch as in chap. xiv. 6, our Lord had declared ἐγώ εἰμι ... ἡ ἀλήθεια, and λόγος is so emphatically the title of the Lord in this Gospel, it is more probable that He used this form of speech as a synonym for Himself: "Sanctify them through thy truth (that is, through me), thy word (that is myself, the manifestation of thee) is truth." So also in 1 Pet. i. 22, Ἀναγεγεννημένοι διὰ λόγου ζῶντος Θεοῦ καὶ μένοντος. It is uncertain whether the begetment here spoken of is of God through the personal Word or by the instrumentality of the written or preached word. John i. 12 seems to favour the view of the personal Word, and to my mind settles the question: "Ὅσοι δὲ ἔλαβον αὐτόν, ἔδωκεν αὐτοῖς ἐξουσίαν τέκνα Θεοῦ γενέσθαι, τοῖς πιστεύουσιν εἰς τὸ ὄνομα αὐτοῦ· οἳ οὐκ ἐξ αἱμάτων, οὐδὲ ἐκ θελήματος σαρκός, οὐδὲ ἐκ θελήματος ἀνδρός, ἀλλ' ἐκ Θεοῦ ἐγεννήθησαν, where the begetment of the saints from God is certainly defined as being brought about by the power and authority of the λόγος or Word, which forms the subject of the grand preface of this Gospel.

The next question of importance in this clause is, Who are the ἡμᾶς, who constituted the ἀπαρχήν τινα? Inasmuch as St. James was addressing Jews, it is impossible to shut out the reference to their early selection from among the nations to be the chosen people of God, and the depositaries of His word and promises. The very mention of the paternity of God seems to have suggested a remembrance of Ex. iv. 22 to the mind of the Apostle, "Israel is my firstborn;" this seems to be the key to the passage before us. The reference to the call of Israel does not exclude, but rather include, the Christian or spiritual begetment, in the case of the believing portion of the Jews to whom he was writing, as Christianity was the appointed ratification and fulfilment of all the blessings and promises contained in, and shadowed forth by, the earlier dispensation.

Ἀπαρχήν τινα, *a kind of firstfruits.* The firstfruits of men, cattle, and productions of the land were to be consecrated to God by Israel, and in like manner God took the nation of Israel itself as the firstfruits of the nations of the earth. It is worthy of note that St. Paul in treating of the purposes of God concerning Israel employs the same figure and the same word, though in a somewhat different connection, see Rom. xi. 16.

Κτισμάτων, *creatures.* From the very connection human

19 Ἴστε, ἀδελφοί μου ἀγαπητοί,
ἔστω δὲ πᾶς ἄνθρωπος ταχὺς εἰς τὸ ἀκοῦσαι,
βραδὺς εἰς τὸ λαλῆσαι, βραδὺς εἰς ὀργήν.

19 Ye know *this*, my beloved brethren,
But let every man be swift to hear,
Slow to speak, slow to wrath.

creatures must be signified, not the animal kingdom. πᾶσα ἡ κτίσις has clearly the same reference to all mankind that are outside the Jewish pale in Mark xvi. 15; Rom. viii. 22; Col. i. 23.

Ver. 19. *Ἴστε, ye know (this).* The Received Text reads here ὥστε after κ and L, MSS. of the ninth century, and the Syriac Version, whereas the Alexandrine, Vatican, and the Codex Ephraemi read ἴστε; the Sinaitic has ἴστω, which is afterwards corrected into ἴστε; the Latin Vulgate also reads *scitis:* there can be little doubt therefore that ἴστε is the true reading, for as Dean Alford has well argued, it would have been impossible for the easy reading ὥστε to be altered into the difficult ἴστε, whereas the easier word might readily assume the place of the harder one. There will then arise another question, whether ἴστε is indicative or imperative? If the former it will refer to what precedes, and form a connecting link between the two paragraphs. The Vulgate took this view. On the other hand the imperative would relate to what follows; this is favoured by the primary reading of the Sinaitic MS., ἴστω, " My beloved brethren, let every man know this, and let him be," etc.: there is much to be advanced on both sides. We have, however, two other instances of ἴστε in the New Testament, Eph. v. 5, where the ancient MSS. read ἴστε instead of the Received ἐστέ, and Heb. xii. 17; in both these places the verb is indicative, hence it is a fair and probable conclusion that it is so here also. The argument of this passage will then be, Ye know this, that we are a firstfruits of creation, but let your knowledge of this privilege and blessing be manifest in your character, according to the precepts that follow. It will be observed that in the second clause δέ is inserted, which is not found in the Received Text, but is found in this place in the Vatican and Sinaitic MSS., and an equivalent καί in the Alexandrine; the Vulgate also has *autem*, and the Syriac a similar connection.

Swift to hear, etc. Proverbial sayings of this kind were common amongst the Jews, both in Scripture and apocryphal writings: see Prov. x. 19; xvii. 27, 28; Eccl. v. 2; Sirach v. 11. " Swift to hear" is borrowed from the duty of the pupil, who

20 ὀργὴ γὰρ ἀνδρὸς δικαιοσύνην Θεοῦ οὐκ ἐργάζεται.
20 For the wrath of a man worketh not the righteousness of God.

should be ready to drink in all that is delivered to him. "Slow to speak" from the attitude of the teacher, who should be deliberate in weighing well what he teaches. "Slow to wrath" warns us against the excitement which is so often the companion of debate, when we hear statements with which we cannot agree. I cannot help thinking that the real point, in this exhortation is, that the nation of the Jews was at this time divided on the subject of the Messiah, whether Jesus was the Christ or not. This, then, is the wise counsel of St. James based upon, and borrowed from, the language of the schools of the Rabbis. You Jews, he says, to his brethren in the flesh, are the firstfruits of God's creation; you are aware of that. Remember, therefore, that it is your duty to weigh and consider well the important question now before you. Be swift to hear the evidence and arguments which are adduced by the Christian teacher; slow to speak in contradiction, and slow to wrath, slow to run into an excited opposition to the doctrine and the preacher, faults most common amongst the Jews at this period, as is everywhere evident in the history of the New Testament. For the reason, see next verse.

Ver. 20. *For the wrath of a man worketh not the righteousness of God.* Wrath, ὀργή, is the *feeling* of wrath, the conception of anger, the inner excitement of the mind; θυμός, akin to the Latin *fumus*, the *exhibition* of wrath; the former is the subterranean wave, the latter the volcano in eruption.

Of a man, ἀνδρός. The reference is to πᾶς in the former verse, not therefore man in general, though such a statement would be equally true, but a man, the man in particular who might be tempted to think otherwise. The choice of the word ἀνήρ is probably intended to mark the self-assertion and presumption of the individual who should fall into the mistake against which St. James warns his readers. *Man* is certainly not used here with reference to his sex or age, *i.e.*, in contradistinction to *woman* or *child*, as Bengel, Lange, etc., hold.

Does not work, οὐκ ἐργάζεται. This is the reading of the most ancient MSS. instead of the Received κατεργάζεται, the difference between the two is that the former represents the habit and continued practice, the latter the precise accomplishment; the one is more of a general, the other of a particular application.

The righteousness of God. There can be only one interpretation

21 Διὸ ἀποθέμενοι πᾶσαν ῥυπαρίαν καὶ περισσείαν κακίας,
ἐν πραΰτητι δέξασθε τὸν ἔμφυτον λόγον,
τὸν δυνάμενον σῶσαι τὰς ψυχὰς ὑμῶν.

21 Wherefore putting off all filthiness and abundance of malice,
In meekness receive the word that is sown,
Which is able to save your souls.

tenable here, the *righteousness* here spoken of cannot be God's attribute of righteousness, neither can it be the forensic righteousness with which Christ justifies the believer, but can only mean *that which is righteous in the sight of God:* Take heed how ye hear the evidence of the Messiahship of Jesus of Nazareth, be slow and deliberate in your judgment, let not any inner feeling of anger or excitement hurry you on to rash words in opposition, to contradict and blaspheme, for remember it is a true proverb that, a man's wrath worketh not that which is approved as right in the sight of God.

Ver. 21. Διό, *wherefore.* This verse again exemplifies the character of those to whom this Epistle was addressed, the reference is plainly to the parable of the sower, Matt. xiii. In that parable the process only of sowing the seed of the word is described, and the fruitfulness or failure that followed; the means by which the glebe was prepared so as to render it different from the wayside, the rocky ground and thorny patches being pre-supposed. Here, on the contrary, this special preparatory work of the Holy Ghost is insisted on, the harrow must be applied, the land cleared of the rubbish, ῥυπαρίαν, and of the overgrowth, περισσείαν, the refuse and weeds which vitiate the soil. This purifying process having been accomplished, the ground will be ready to receive the seed of the word which is sown, ἔμφυτον; this word must not be rendered "engrafted," as that is not the figure here employed. So do ye, St. James would say, as wise husbandmen, cleanse your souls from the filthiness and abundance of malice (κακίας belongs to both the preceding substantives) which naturally clings to the old man (see for a parallel passage chap. iv. 8), and receive into your souls with meekness the word which the Great Sower plants, the word that is living and quickening, able to make wise unto salvation. The conclusion we should arrive at from this allusion to the first parable of our Lord is that those to whom St. James was writing

22 Γίνεσθε δὲ ποιηταὶ λόγου,
καὶ μὴ μόνον ἀκροαταί,
παραλογιζόμενοι ἑαυτούς.

22 But become ye doers of the word,
And not only hearers,
Deluding your own selves.

were in the same stage of spiritual experience as those whom the Lord addressed, having no clear or settled views concerning the character of Messiah or His kingdom, and having not yet determined the question whether Jesus were the Christ or not; and hence St. James echoes the words of his Master, that they should receive the word into an honest and good heart, for sincerity of purpose and holiness of heart are the lenses through which the Spirit of God sends the pure ray of truth into the inner chamber of the soul of man. See Introduction, *To whom was this Epistle written?*

Some interpreters, among whom Bishop Wordsworth may be numbered, press the radical meaning of ἔμφυτον in this place, *innate*, τὸ ἐν φύσει, and explain it of the incarnate Word, which was planted in our nature, Emmanuel, God with us; or in the other rarer sense of the word, *engrafted*, as the branch is engrafted on the stock so Christ was engrafted in our nature. It has been observed in the former note that it is impossible to separate the idea of the personal Word from the written word in many passages, the former so frequently involves the latter, in such passages sometimes the one will be more emphasised than the other; both are included here, but the word, as brought to bear upon them by exhortation and teaching, seems uppermost in the writer's mind.

Ver. 22. *But become ye doers of the word.* As in the parable of the sower we read that those who received the seed into an honest and good heart brought forth manifold, hence we have here also a parallel exhortation to fruitfulness, couched in the words " Become *doers* of the word."

And not only hearers. The seed that fell on the wayside and other sterile places met with no deep and true reception, so a man may be a hearer of the word, but the truth may not penetrate down to his heart: this merely superficial hearing of the Gospel will be of no avail, but rather prove a detriment, for the man that places any reliance on such an external accident will delude himself. The plea that Christ has taught in our streets, and that we have eaten and drunk in His presence, will not secure a sentence of approval in the last day.

23 ὅτι εἴ τις ἀκροατὴς λόγου ἐστί
καὶ οὐ ποιητής,
οὗτος ἔοικεν ἀνδρὶ κατανοοῦντι τὸ πρόσωπον
τῆς γενέσεως αὐτοῦ ἐν ἐσόπτρῳ·

24 κατενόησε γὰρ ἑαυτὸν καὶ ἀπελήλυθε,
καὶ εὐθέως ἐπελάθετο ὁποῖος ἦν.

23 Because if any one is a hearer of the word,
And is not a doer,
He is like a man considering the face
Of his nature in a mirror.

24 For he considered himself, and went away,
And straightway forgot what sort of man he was.

Ver. 23. Hereupon follows an illustration of the futility of giving a passing hearing only to the Gospel, for the hearer but non-doer, the unconverted and unfruitful man, resembles one who looks at his face in a mirror; nothing is so evanescent as the impression made on our memory by our own features; of course the comparison is not to be pressed too closely, the general fact that we are less acquainted with, and less retentive of, our own appearance than that of others is all that is necessary for the purpose of illustration.

The face of his nature, τὸ πρόσωπον τῆς γενέσεως αὐτοῦ. That is, the face with which he was born, Vulgate, *nativitatis suæ*, and hence the face which naturally distinguished him from other men; the word seems to point to the idiosyncrasy of each man's physiognomy, which ought to make it more easy of remembrance; αὐτοῦ strengthens the emphasis of this reference.

ἐν ἐσόπτρῳ, *in a mirror*, not a *glass*. Looking-glasses are of modern date, probably not older than the thirteenth century. The mirrors of the ancients were for the most part made of a mixture of copper and tin, a compound metal which was susceptible of the highest polish.

Ver. 24. κατενόησεν, ἀπελήλυθεν, ἐπελάθετο. Mark the tenses: he considered himself; the act done and over, he went away, and continued away; he forgot, once for all. "We find neither the aorists nor the perfect put for the present, but the case supposed for illustration in v. 23 assumed as matter of fact, and the Apostle falling into the strain of narration." Winer's *Gk. Gram. of New Test.*, p. 293.

25 ὁ δὲ παρακύψας εἰς νόμον τέλειον
τὸν τῆς ἐλευθερίας,
καὶ παραμείνας,
οὐκ ἀκροατὴς ἐπιλησμονῆς γενόμενος,
ἀλλὰ ποιητὴς ἔργου,
οὗτος μακάριος ἐν τῇ ποιήσει αὐτοῦ ἔσται.

25 But he that inspected the perfect law
That *pertaineth* to liberty,
And continued *there*,
And became not a hearer of forgetfulness,
But a doer of work,
This man blessed in his doing shall be.

Ver. 25. In this verse the figure contained in the preceding verse is resolved; the mirror is explained to be the perfect law, that is to say, the new law of liberty or freedom from the yoke of the Mosaic law; and the man that looks into the mirror is described as bending down for the purpose of instituting a more accurate observation. Moreover, he does not go away and forget, but remains on the spot engaged in the examination. Such an one is no longer a hearer characterized by forgetfulness, but a doer of the work enjoined; such an one the writer pronounces to be blessed in such practice.

τέλειον, *perfect.* The perfect law is further explained as τὸν τῆς ἐλευθερίας, that is to say, the law which belongs to liberty. This law is not the Gospel in opposition to the law, as though the Gospel were perfect and the law imperfect, but rather the law which becomes perfect by the Gospel; the law was a preparation for the Gospel, the guide that led us to the school of Christ. (See Gal. iii. 24.) This was the basis also of the Sermon on the Mount. Paraphrastically, therefore, this phrase would read: The law whose perfections are established and rendered manifest by its development into the liberty which Christ has brought to light in the Gospel. Law and Gospel are not antagonistic, but both co-operate in their times and spheres for the instruction and salvation of man. An excellent comment on this passage is, "whose service is perfect freedom." *Church of England Prayer Book.*

ἀκροατὴς ἐπιπλησμονῆς ... ποιητὴς ἔργου. The former of these is acknowledged to be a Hebrew genitive, a hearer marked

26 Εἴ τις δοκεῖ θρῆσκος εἶναι,
μὴ χαλιναγωγῶν γλῶσσαν αὐτοῦ,
ἀλλὰ ἀπατῶν καρδίαν αὐτοῦ,
τούτου μάταιος ἡ θρησκεία.

26 If any one thinketh he is rite-religious,
Though not bridling his tongue,
But deceiving his own heart,
This man's rite-religion is vain.

or characterized by forgetfulness, as κριταὶ διαλογισμῶν πονηρῶν, "judges of evil thoughts," that is, characterized by evil thoughts, chap. ii. 3. The latter, however, is regarded as simply a dependent genitive, *a doer of work*, but it is better to view it as parallel in construction to the former, a doer characterized by work.

ποιήσει. The act of doing, the practice; the performance of the duties enjoined by the perfect law of liberty.

Ver. 26. δοκεῖ, *thinks* to himself, not *appears* to others.

θρῆσκος *a rite-religious man*, and θρησκεία *rite-religion*. An apology is almost demanded for the introduction of this compound word. We have, however, no term in our language to express the original, which refers to the outward circumstance of religious profession, the ceremonial garb in which our faith is vested. These words have been beautifully commented upon by Archbishop Trench, *Synonyms of the New Testament*. The reference is to the externals of religious worship, the *cultus exterior*, the ceremonial, the ritual of worship. The noun and its cognate verb are found in Wisdom xi. 16; xiv. 16, 18, 27, in connection with idolatry. Philo has a passage very similar to our text: θρησκείαν ἀντὶ ὁσιότητος ἡγούμενος. St. James throws into contrast the old law with its gorgeous and imposing exhibitions, with the humble simplicity of the Gospel, and the self-denying duties it enjoins. If religion needs a ritual, an outside by which its highest and holiest service may be made manifest to the world, let all that is external be evidenced in the visiting of orphans and widows in the hour of their woe and want, and in a holy separation from the defilements of a wicked world.

μὴ χαλιναγωγῶν γλῶσσαν αὐτοῦ, *not bridling his tongue*. This is anticipatory of the substance of the third chapter of this Epistle, where the government of the tongue under the same figure is more fully illustrated and enforced.

27 θρησκεία καθαρὰ καὶ ἀμίαντος
παρὰ τῷ Θεῷ καὶ πατρὶ αὕτη ἐστίν,
ἐπισκέπτεσθαι ὀρφανοὺς καὶ χήρας ἐν τῇ θλίψει αὐτῶν,
ἄσπιλον ἑαυτὸν τηρεῖν ἀπὸ τοῦ κόσμου.

27 Rite-religion pure and undefiled
With God the Father is this,
To visit orphans and widows in their tribulation,
Spotless himself to keep from the world.

Ver. 27. τῷ Θεῷ καὶ πατρί, literally, *Him who is God and Father.* The article referring to, and so uniting the reference in both nouns to the same person, best rendered in idiomatic English *God the Father.* Father is evidently inserted to bring out the relation in which God stands to the fatherless and widows, see Ps. lxviii. 5.

As this represents the duty of the religious man to his neighbour, so the next clause lays down his duty to himself, *to keep himself spotless from the world.* The figure here again is doubtless derived from the Jewish law; the touch of the ceremonially defiled, of a grave, a carcase, a bone, or an unclean animal, imparted pollution to a man, and he had to submit to a cleansing process before he could join in the temple services or associate with his brethren. The world is graphically pictured as a graveyard, a leper-house, a den of unclean beasts, through which the believer must pick his way so carefully and circumspectly that he may escape contact with the all-surrounding corruptions, and come forth with his purity unsullied and unstained.

CHAPTER II.

1 Ἀδελφοί μου, μὴ ἐν προσωπολημψίαις
ἔχετε τὴν πίστιν τοῦ Κυρίου ἡμῶν Ἰησοῦ Χριστοῦ,
τῆς δόξης.

1 My brethren, do not with respect for appearances,
Hold the faith of our Lord Jesus Christ, the Shechinah.

Ver. 1. The transition to the following subject is suggested by the remarks that have gone before concerning the outward forms of religion. Θρησκεία reminded the writer of the synagogue and its ritual; and the picture just drawn of the true worshipper visiting orphan children and widowed women suggested the striking contrast to this, which was so often witnessed in the congregations that assembled in the synagogues, the respect and reverence servilely paid to the wealthy and well clothed, and the disregard and all but disdain exhibited to the poor and meanly clad.

μὴ ... ἔχετε, *do not hold*, etc. There are many difficulties in this verse. It is clear from the next verse that the Jewish synagogue, and not the upper chamber or Christian church, was the scene of the impropriety which St. James so severely reprimands. It would appear that the Jewish Christians attended the temple service till the last, when they left the city before the final blow destroyed the "beautiful house," and doubtless they also frequented the synagogues, both in Judæa and also throughout the *dispersion*. The sharp separation which took place between the church and the synagogue had not yet arranged their respective adherents into a recognised antagonism, hence we find in this chapter Christian and non-Christian Jews addressed; in what sense then are we to understand, μὴ ἔχετε, *do not hold?* Some have suggested that the sentence should be read interrogatively, "do ye hold? etc. Surely not." Others have regarded ἔχετε as equivalent to κατέχετε, *do not hold down*, or *suppress:* the meaning rather is, *do not hold, i.e.*, ye cannot hold, etc. Considering the mixed character of the congregation addressed, it is better to suppose that he had in his mind's eye both sections, the Jewish and the Christian; for the latter he would entertain a fear lest they should be carried away by the influence of their superiors in worldly wealth, see vv. 5-7 ; and for the former he would have a word of reproof. If you are enquiring into the claims of Jesus of Nazareth, do not think you can embrace and hold that faith and still continue to exercise so unjust and unkind a practice as preference for the rich above the poor in God's house, where all are equal. The words that follow show that they were specially addressed who were the appointed officials of the synagogue, whose duty it was to provide accommodation for the members of the congregation: these must have been Jews and not Christians. Hence it will appear that the ἀδελφοί μου are brethren, as being of the stock of Israel; the brotherhood of Christianity lies in the background, to be appropriated by those who held the faith of Jesus as the Christ; but the scene, the synagogue, and the thoroughly Jewish character of the fault, the desiring the chief seats in the synagogues (see Matt. xxiii. 6), all prove that we are on Jewish ground.

ἐν προσωποληµψίαις, *in respect for appearances*. The well known Hebrew phrase פנים נשא, which originally signified *to raise the face*, and hence *to show kindness*. In the Old Testament the phrase is employed in a good sense. In later times it appears to have changed its application, and to signify the partiality and servile respect shown to a man's external circumstances. The plural form of the word is usually explained of the different modes in which this servility was paid and the frequency of such occurrences. It is true, that in the Greek word, from the necessity of the case, the plural part of the word belongs to the *respectings*, but in the Hebrew phrase it would belong to the *appearances;* as the Hebrew phrase would be that which would at once be suggested to the Jewish readers, it would become the rule whereby they would expound the Greek word. This appears to be one out of many instances in which the original expression must determine the exact sense of its translation into another tongue ; the plural therefore does not imply the variety or the frequency of the sin, but is the natural and necessary form of the word, as there must be a plurality of appearances among men before we can select some as objects of our respect, and this adulation is not paid to one alone but to many.

τὴν πίστιν τοῦ Κυρίου ἡμῶν Ἰησοῦ Χριστοῦ τῆς δόξης, *the faith of our Lord Jesus Christ, the Shechinah. The faith of our Lord*, etc. This is the objective genitive, the faith concerning our Lord, in other words, the Gospel of His revelation.

This is the only place in the body of the Epistle where our Lord Jesus Christ is spoken of by name, and only one other example is found, and that is in the superscription, see chap. i. 1. The composition of this whole sentence is important. *Our Lord* stands first in the most emphatic position ; it contains a confession on

2 ἐὰν γὰρ εἰσέλθῃ εἰς συναγωγὴν ὑμῶν
ἀνὴρ χρυσοδακτύλιος ἐν ἐσθῆτι λαμπρᾷ,
εἰσέλθῃ δὲ καὶ πτωχὸς ἐν ῥυπαρᾷ ἐσθῆτι,

2 For if there come into your synagogue
A man with a gold ring on his finger, in handsome garb,
And there come in a poor man also in shabby garb,

the part of the writer, an exhortation to those whom he was addressing to acknowledge Him also, and there is a declaration it would seem in the words Χριστοῦ *the Messiah*, and τῆς δόξης *the glory*, that in Him was found a fulfilment of the hopes of Israel; Jesus is at once the Messiah and the glory.

τῆς δόξης. Various opinions have been held by a long list of commentators concerning the construction of the sentence and the meaning of this word. The Authorised Version makes the genitive τῆς δόξης depend upon Κυρίου, repeated from above, "*the Lord* of glory."

δόξης has been interpreted in the sense of *opinion*, opinion about the Lord, etc.

It has been connected with Χριστοῦ, *the Christ of glory*, or *the glorious Messiah*.

Again, it has been made dependent on τὴν πίστιν, and made the governing word of τοῦ Κυρίου, *the faith of the glory of our Lord Jesus Christ*, or, *the faith of the glory*, i.e., *the glorious faith*.

There can be little doubt that Bengel (*vide Gnomon Novi Test.*) has proposed the most tenable view, because it may be illustrated so abundantly from both the Old and New Testament Scriptures, and is in accordance with Jewish tradition and expectations. This construction makes τῆς δόξης to be in apposition to 'Ἰησοῦ Χριστοῦ, *the Lord Jesus Christ, the glory*. The antithesis between the *appearances*, πρόσωπα, of men, and the *visible glory*, δόξα, of the Messiah must not pass unnoticed. For a further discussion of this passage see *Excursus*, in the Appendix.

Ver. 2. συναγωγήν. This word, as above remarked, proves that the Jewish place of worship, and not that of the Christians proper, is the scene of this impropriety. The use of ἐπισυναγωγήν in Heb. x. 25 being addressed to Jews also, as this Epistle was, proves nothing to the contrary. The Christian assemblies proper were called ἐκκλησία, or the place of meeting was designated by ὑπερῷον, or simply ἐπὶ τὸ αὐτό. The Jewish Christians at Jerusalem still frequented the temple, and those among the *dispersion* the synagogues, hence there is no cause for surprise in finding Christians mixed with unconverted Jews at

3 καὶ ἐπιβλέψητε ἐπὶ τὸν φοροῦντα τὴν ἐσθῆτα τὴν λαμπράν,
καὶ εἴπητε, " Σὺ κάθου ὧδε καλῶς,"
καὶ τῷ πτωχῷ εἴπητε, " Σὺ στῆθι ἐκεῖ,
ἢ κάθου ὑπὸ τὸ ὑποπόδιόν μου·"

3 And ye look-with-respect-at him that wears the handsome garb,
And say, " Be thou seated here in honour; "
And to the poor man say, " Do thou stand there,
Or, be seated under my footstool,"

this period in a common place of worship. The people sat in the synagogue according to their social rank or trade, and St. James fastens on this exhibition of pride on the part of the higher classes as a ground of convincing them of sin and of violation of the spirit of the law, which enjoined " Thou shalt love thy neighbour as thyself." A further argument that the Jewish synagogue is spoken of is, that we learn from the context that strangers came in who were provided with seats that happened to be vacant. This would occur constantly in the synagogue, but in the upper chamber of the Christians it would be most unlikely that persons of wealth and eminence, as here described, should thus freely enter the congregation of the despised Nazarenes. A graphic delineation follows of the casual worshippers, for casual they must have been, as the regular comers would have their seats allotted them. The one is wealthy and proud, the other poor and lowly; the force of this contrast will appear the more when we remember that the Christian portion of the Jewish community was chiefly gathered out of the lower ranks in the social scale. The rich man is described as having a gold ring or rings on his fingers, for it was a common custom to wear a number of these ornaments; he is clad also in handsome (λαμπρᾷ) attire, literally *shining*, most likely with reference to the gloss of the texture of his raiment; and the poor man is represented as clothed in shabby (ῥυπαρᾷ) attire, most probably with reference to the soil contracted in labour.

Ver. 3. Mark again the pictorial character of the sequel: Ye look, and that with respect, at (ἐπιβλέψητε) the man of wealth and style, and say, *Be thou seated here in a place of honour*, ὧδε καλῶς. This refers to the upper end of the building, where the ark or chest which contained the law was placed. It was here that *the first seats in the synagogue* (πρωτοκαθεδρίαι) stood, which the Pharisees and Scribes desired to occupy, see Matt. xxiii. 6.

4 οὐ διεκρίθητε ἐν ἑαυτοῖς,
καὶ ἐγένεσθε κριταὶ διαλογισμῶν πονηρῶν;
5 Ἀκούσατε, ἀδελφοί μου ἀγαπητοί,
οὐχ ὁ Θεὸς ἐξελέξατο τοὺς πτωχοὺς τῷ κόσμῳ,
πλουσίους ἐν πίστει, καὶ κληρονόμους τῆς βασιλείας,
ἧς ἐπηγγείλατο τοῖς ἀγαπῶσιν αὐτόν;

4 Are ye not making-distinctions amongst yourselves,
And become judges of wicked reasonings?

5 Hearken ye, my beloved brethren,
Did not God elect the poor in the world,
To be rich in faith, and heirs of the kingdom,
Which He promised to them that love Him.

Whereas there is no look of respect directed to the poor man, but he is simply bidden to stand during service, at a distance, or if he sit down, it is to be under the footstool of the officer who presides over the arrangements of the synagogue. Mark the antithesis between ὧδε and ἐκεῖ, the *here* of honour and the *there* of dishonour. The plan of the Christian church, it is said, was formed on the original of the Jewish synagogue, and it is much to be feared that the early Christians who met together on the footing of equality in the name of one common Lord in the upper chamber, when they adopted the architecture of the synagogue, fell also into these abuses, which called forth from St. James this well merited rebuke.

Ver. 4. διακρίθητε, *do ye not make distinctions*, etc. The tense is aorist; whenever you have acted as described above, did you not then make distinctions between yourselves, etc. Of all the various meanings of which this verb is capable, none is so well suited to the context as this, when you showed respect to the rich and disdain to the poor, did ye not make a distinction which you ought not. There is evidently also a connection between this verb and κριταί, *judges*, in the parallel clause, in *adjudging a distinction* between fellow worshippers ye became *judges* of evil reasonings. διαλογισμῶν πονηρῶν is like ἀκροατὴς ἐπιλησμονῆς, chap. i. 25, the genitive which explains the character of the governing word, *judges characterized by evil reasonings*. It is not unlikely that the parable of the unjust judge, ὁ κριτὴς τῆς ἀδικίας, Luke xviii. 6, the judge who was characterized by injustice, who neglected the appeal of the poor widow, passed through the mind of St. James as he was penning these words.

Ver. 5. ἐξελέξατο κ.τ.λ., *elect, or choose out, the poor in the world*, etc. This seems to have characterized God's dealings in

6 ὑμεῖς δὲ ἠτιμάσατε τὸν πτωχόν.
οὐχ οἱ πλούσιοι καταδυναστεύουσιν ὑμῶν,
καὶ αὐτοὶ ἕλκουσιν ὑμᾶς εἰς κριτήρια;

7 οὐκ αὐτοὶ βλασφημοῦσι τὸ καλὸν ὄνομα
τὸ ἐπικληθὲν ἐφ' ὑμᾶς;

6 But ye dishonoured the poor man.
Do not the rich domineer over you?
And is it not they that drag you to the law-courts?
7 Is it not they that blaspheme the honourable name,
Which was invoked upon you?

all ages. The Hebrews were fewer and feebler than all people, yet He chose them in the prison-house of Egypt, and made them heirs of the kingdoms of Canaan. This reference probably underlies this passage, and suggests a tacit rebuke to the conduct he has been reprehending. This is rendered the more likely from the reading of the Alexandrine and Sinaitic MSS., ἐπαγγελίας *promise*, instead of βασιλείας *kingdom*. The same mode of proceeding was evidenced in our Lord's choice of the Apostles when inaugurating the new covenant. The moral of both dispensations is, "God chose the weak things of the earth to confound the mighty."

The τῷ κόσμῳ must be correlative with ἐν πίστει, *poor in the (things of the) world, rich in faith*.

Ver. 6. *But ye dishonoured the poor man*, i.e., the poor man we saw treated with so much contempt in the synagogue. How different were God's dealings with you from your dealings with your fellow creatures!

A question of some difficulty and importance arises here: Who are the "rich" who domineer over the people that St. James is addressing, and who blaspheme the honourable name that had been invoked on them? They could not be *Christian* rich men; this is utterly impossible, not only from this place, but also from the way in which the "rich" are reprimanded in the first and fifth chapters. Were they Gentiles or Jews then? For the former, it may be advanced that our Lord, when speaking of the tyranny of the Roman power (Matt. xx. 25) uses this word, οἴδατε ὅτι οἱ ἄρχοντες τῶν ἐθνῶν κατακυριεύουσιν αὐτῶν; if they were Gentiles then the honourable name might refer to the profession of the Jewish religion, as the Jews were defined as the nation on whom "God's name was called," see Deut. xxviii. 10; 2 Chron.

4

8 Εἰ μέντοι νόμον τελεῖτε βασιλικόν,
κατὰ τὴν γραφήν,
'Ἀγαπήσεις τὸν πλησίον σου ὡς σεαυτόν,'
καλῶς ποιεῖτε·

8 If surely ye perform the law of *our* king
According to the Scripture,
"Thou shalt love thy neighbour as thyself,"
Ye do well.

ᶠii. 14, and they were held in contempt by the heathen. But the "rich" here named must clearly be the same class as the man with the gold ring and the fine apparel in the synagogue, and the same with the "rich" who are described as a blighted flower, chap. i. 11, and bidden to weep and howl for the miseries that were impending, chap. v. 1. These marks would scarcely be appropriate to the Roman rulers; they would·not attend the synagogue service, and the day of Jerusalem's destruction would rather be the period for their prosperity. It would seem then that the "rich" were wealthy Jews (see notes on chap. i. 10), who out of hatred to Christianity tyrannized over their brethren, and dragged them into the justice courts. The honourable name would then refer to the profession of Christianity, and the invocation of the name upon them to the ordinance of baptism into the name of the Lord.

Ver. 8. *If surely*, εἰ μέντοι. It is much disputed what the connection is in this word. Some suppose an objection is raised to the teaching of·the preceding paragraph, as though St. James had instructed them to despise the rich, or that his words might be viewed as capable of such a construction, and that in this verse he corrects this misapprehension of his words. Another opinion is, that St. James is not replying to an objection already raised against his teaching, but is guarding his expressions from a wrong interpretation.

Again, it has been proposed to explain the passage thus: The Jewish Christians boasted of the law, and to this feature the μέντοι *indeed*, refers, "If indeed ye fulfil," etc.

I should rather regard this and the following verses as a summing up merely of the preceding arguments. There is no objection to be met from an adversary, no fence to be set up to guard or correct a previous statement, but a recapitulation of the lesson enforced: You reverence the rich, you make distinctions amongst yourselves in their favour and to the disparagement of the poor, and that unrighteously, forgetting that God made choice

9 εἰ δὲ προσωποληπτεῖτε, ἁμαρτίαν ἐργάζεσθε,
ἐλεγχόμενοι ὑπὸ τοῦ νόμου ὡς παραβάται.

10 ὅστις γὰρ ὅλον τὸν νόμον τηρήσῃ,
πταίσῃ δὲ ἐν ἑνί,
γέγονε πάντων ἔνοχος.

9 But if ye respect-appearances, ye work sin,
Being convicted by the law as transgressors.

10 For whosoever the whole law shall have kept,
But stumbled in one *particular*,
He has become guilty of all.

of the poor to be His people and inheritance, and that the rich are your persecutors and blasphemers of your religion. If indeed, or surely, instead of such practices ye fulfil the law of *our King*, " Thou shalt love thy neighbour as thyself," ye do well; but if ye respect external appearances, ye are working sin, being convicted by that very law of which I am speaking as being transgressors.

Νόμον βασιλικόν. This phrase must either mean the chief of all laws, *i.e.*, that God's commands are paramount to all other laws, or, which is far better, the law which belongs to and proceeds from the King, the King of Israel. Then the question arises whether God the Father is intended by the king, or Christ as the King of the Jews and Christians also ? I think the former, not only because the words are addressed to the members of the synagogue, but also from the 11th verse, where the commandments contained in the law of Moses are specified.

In the reference to our *King* there is a tacit reminder that God was the common king over both rich and poor, and that both are His subjects, hence all that are subjects are in that respect equal, and all are neighbours to each other.

Ver. 9. *But if ye respect appearances, ye work sin*, ἐργάζεσθε. This word combines the ideas of practice and perpetration, see Matt. vii. 23.

ἐλεγχόμενοι, *convicted, proved to be guilty*.

ὡς. The ὡς of reality, *as being*, and actually being, transgressors.

Ver. 10. *The whole law*, ὅλον τὸν νόμον. All the commandments contained in the law.

But stumble in one particular, ἐν ἑνί (understand μέρει).

Guilty of all, πάντων ἔνοχος. The meaning is not, as the following verse shows, that a man who breaks one commandment

4*

11 ὁ γὰρ εἰπών, " Μὴ μοιχεύσῃς,"
εἶπε καί, " Μὴ φονεύσῃς·"
εἰ δὲ οὐ μοιχεύεις, φονεύεις δέ,
γέγονας παραβάτης νόμου.

12 Οὕτω λαλεῖτε καὶ οὕτω ποιεῖτε,
ὡς διὰ νόμου ἐλευθερίας μέλλοντες κρίνεσθαι·

11 For He that said, "Commit no adultery,"
Said also, "Murder not."
But if thou committest not adultery, but dost murder,
Thou hast become a transgressor of the law.

12 So speak ye, and so do,
As by the law of liberty going to be judged,

actually breaks all, the transgressor of the sixth commandment is not necessarily the transgressor of the seventh, but the law is viewed as a perfect circle, and if any point in its circumference is ruptured the perfection of the figure is gone; God's mind is one, though recorded to us under ten heads or divisions; in violating one of these particular sections the sinner transgresses against the whole system, the one revealed mind of God. This exposition increases the heinousness of sin, and proves that what man regards as little sins are not little in the sight of God, and by inference shows plainly that by the deeds of the law no flesh can be justified. It is said that the Rabbis have a similar sentiment to this, and from this source our author doubtless borrowed the argument as well known amongst those to whom he was writing. Rabbi Jochanan says of the thirty-nine precepts of Moses, "But if a man does all, but leave out one, he is guilty of all and of each."

Ver. 12. Having thus explained the strict letter of the law, and how it involves the sinner in condemnation, he derives a practical lesson: Speak and act *so*, that is, as you ought, seeing ye are about to be judged by the law of liberty, διὰ νόμου ἐλευθερίας. The law of liberty, what is this? It is usually explained as meaning the Gospel, the law of liberty in contrast to the law of works, but surely this would introduce a new element into the argument. The whole discourse is upon the law of Moses, and the transgression of its commandments by these members of the synagogue. Surely νόμος here must be the same as νόμος in each of the preceding four verses. What then can be the force of the explanatory genitive ἐλευθερίας, *of liberty?*

13 ἡ γὰρ κρίσις ἀνέλεος τῷ μὴ ποιήσαντι ἔλεος·
κατακαυχᾶται ἔλεος κρίσεως.

13 For the judgment *shall be* merciless
To him that did not mercy;
Mercy glories over judgment.

This seems to refer to the purpose of God's law, which enjoined love to our neighbour without respect of persons. This was liberty, religious brotherhood amongst all classes; but by their respect of persons they had introduced a bye-law of bondage, which subjected class to class; and this distinction depended not on *religious* pre-eminence, but on the *earthly* accident of wealth, the meanest ground' on which to erect a system of servitude.

There is great point in this warning: Ye who have thus perverted a law which was designed to give freedom amongst brethren into a code of tyranny and oppression, are on the threshhold of being judged by the very law which ye have so distorted. When we compare this and the following verse with the early part of the fifth chapter, we cannot fail to see that the day of vengeance on Jerusalem, which fell so heavily on the Jews, was the judgment immediately before our writer's eyes.

Ver. 13. *For the judgment*, ἡ κρίσις, refers back to the κρίνεσθαι of the previous verse: The judgment of which I speak shall be without mercy, untempered, unassuaged, unaccompanied by the considerations of mercy to him that did not practice mercy. The aorist tense ποιήσαντι transfers the mind to the period when the inquisition shall be made and the judgment executed.

Mercy glories against judgment. What is the connection between this clause and the former subject? The Received Text unites them by a καί, and the Alexandrine MS. and one of the correctors of the Sinaitic by a δέ after κατακαυχᾶται. The usual mode of explaining these words is that judgment in the case of the merciless shall be merciless, yet in the case of the merciful mercy glories against judgment, so as to ward off its stroke, and deliver the merciful man, so that mercy does not fear judgment, but rather glories against it and over it. The whole lesson teaching us, in Bengel's words, that judgment shall be to every one as every one shall have been. But this exposition seems to bring in another subject, quite foreign to the writer's argument; he is not treating of mercy or the merciful man, but of the unjust man and of judgment. Surely, if the mode of deciding the verdict of the merciful man had been intended, some mention of that character would have found a place. It seems better to

14 Τί τὸ ὄφελος, ἀδελφοί μου,
ἐὰν πίστιν λέγῃ τις ἔχειν,
ἔργα δὲ μὴ ἔχῃ;
μὴ δύναται ἡ πίστις σῶσαι αὐτόν;

14 What is the use, my brethren,
If any one saith he hath faith,
But hath not works?
Can his faith save him?

regard this clause as a sort of climax to the preceding statement: You are about to be judged by the law which enjoins liberty, and the judgment which will be passed by God according to that law will be unaccompanied by *mercy* against the man that did not show mercy, even though it is characteristic of God's *mercy* to glory against judgment. His mercy often spares when we deserve the blow, but it shall not be so then. You have judged and rejected others, you shall be judged and rejected yourselves. As you have sown, so shall you reap.

Ver. 14. With this verse begins the passage which has ever proved the *Crux Interpretum*.

Commentators not heeding the fact that this Epistle was addressed to the twelve tribes of the dispersion of the Jews as such; and starting with the foregone conclusion that notwithstanding this superscription all who were addressed were Christians in some degree or another, and shutting their eyes to the awful state of immorality in which the rich and powerful among them had fallen, or evading these evident tokens of non-Christianity, settled it in their minds that the faith here spoken of is the Christian faith, the faith of the Gospel, the faith in Jesus Christ as the one atonement for sin, the faith in his justifying righteousness; and consequently have been driven into a wondrous variety of interpretations, each commentator exercising his own theological or logical ingenuity to harmonize the teaching of this paragraph with the doctrinal and dogmatic statements laid down by St. Paul.

Some theologians, giving up the task of reconciliation of the twain as hopeless, elected St. Paul to be in the right, and have all but reviled the author of this Epistle, accusing him of ignorance, or valuing his treatise as "one of straw." This was one way, at least, of escaping the difficulty; others, with more reverence, taught that St. Paul spoke of true and living faith, whereas St. James treated of a dead and lifeless faith; others, again, that St. Paul had in his mind the justification of man before God, but St. James the justification of men in the sight of men; others, that there are two kinds of, or two stages, in justification, the first is obtained by faith without works, the second is the perfecting or completing of that justification by works. Again, as some elevated St. Paul to the seat of authority, and held that St. James must be reconciled to him, so others, *per contra*, inverted this order by explaining St. Paul by the definitions of St. James. Lastly, it is largely held that St. Paul excepted against works done under the Mosaic law as meritorious, but did not except from justification works of Christian obedience.

The schoolmen taught that the faith of St. James was *fides informis*, and that of St. Paul *fides formata*.

This is not the place to investigate the various tenets that have been held on the important doctrine of justification by the various churches and communities of Christendom, for although St. James' teaching in this place has had a large share in the moulding or modifying articles of faith on this subject, yet it is more than doubtful whether his statements here have any more than a very remote reference to the point at issue; the principle that he applied to the members of the synagogue may be applied to the members of the church, but the faith of the one and of the other are very distinct. It will be enough to remind the reader that the whole context which has led us up to this point is occupied on exclusively Jewish ground, the synagogue is the scene, not the upper chamber of the Christian congregation. The law not the Gospel is the subject under discussion. There is no mention of sacrifice, atonement, or any other standpoints of Christian dogma. The confession of faith or creed with which this discussion on faith and works is connected, is the Jewish creed that "God is one," the well known *Sh'ma Israel*, Deut. vi. 4. The parallel is not to be found in the writings of St. Paul to Christian churches, but in the preaching of John the Baptist to the Jews who came forth to hear him on the banks of Jordan, and in the exposition of the law unfolded by our Lord on the mount, and in the solemn charge of St. Paul, when he deals with Judaism stilted on its Abrahamic descent, "Thou that makest thy boast in the law, through breaking the law dishonourest thou God." Rom. ii. 23. "For not the hearers of the law are just before God, but the doers of the law shall be justified." Rom. ii. 13.

It is observable at this point that St. James institutes a kind of climax in his teaching. In chap. i. 27 he seems to refer to the gorgeous ritual of the temple, and shows that the external worship is useless in itself unless it has spiritual accompaniments; the outside of religion should be not show, but care for the afflicted, and purity from the defilements of the world. In chap. ii. 1, 7, he proceeds to teach them that the service in the synagogue was also of no avail, if disfigured by partiality to the rich and

15 ἐὰν δὲ ἀδελφὸς ἢ ἀδελφὴ γυμνοὶ ὑπάρχωσι
καὶ λειπόμενοι τῆς ἐφημέρου τροφῆς,
16 εἴπῃ δέ τις αὐτοῖς ἐξ ὑμῶν,
"Ὑπάγετε ἐν εἰρήνῃ,
θερμαίνεσθε καὶ χορτάζεσθε,"
μὴ δῶτε δὲ αὐτοῖς τὰ ἐπιτήδεια τοῦ σώματος,
τί τὸ ὄφελος;

15 But if a brother or sister naked be,
And lacking their daily sustenance,
16 And some one of you say to them,
" Go away in peace
Warm·yourselves and satisfy yourselves,"
But ye do not give them the necessaries for their body,
What is the use?

contempt for the poor. And in the passage we are now entering upon, he further instructs them that even the orthodox faith might be taught and received among them, but yet be dead and inoperative. His object is to convince them that in all that concerned their religion they had no matter of boasting in themselves, no merit before God, but contrariwise needed pardon for the iniquities even of their holy things.

τί τὸ ὄφελος, *What is the use?* What is the profit or the good? What benefit can arise to the professor?

ἐάν λέγῃ τὶς ἔχειν, *if a man say*, that is, makes a profession of having faith. The form of expression is evidently chosen with a purpose to intimate that the man had not what he professed to have.

What is the *faith* here referred to? In this, the opening of the subject, *faith* is introduced indefinitely, or its definition at least is deferred till a later stage in the treatise. At the present point all that is said is, that a man professes to have faith, or *a* faith, but he has not works; he says he has an inward and invisible disposition of mind, but he has no external and visible evidences, which serve as proofs of the truth of his profession.

Can his faith, ἡ πίστις, the faith he says he has, save him, him αὐτόν, the supposed character? It is a mere figment of his fancy, and not a living principle of power and reality.

Ver. 15. This verse introduces an illustration of the subject up to the point at which the writer has arrived: If a person is in want of ordinary necessaries, and one of you were to say kind words and express good wishes for his welfare, making a profession of benevolence, but not carrying the profession into practice,

17 οὕτω καὶ ἡ πίστις, ἐὰν μὴ ἔχῃ ἔργα,
   νεκρά ἐστι καθ' ἑαυτήν.
18 ἀλλ' ἐρεῖ τις,
   " Σὺ πίστιν ἔχεις κἀγὼ ἔργα ἔχω·
   δεῖξόν μοι τὴν πίστιν σου χωρὶς τῶν ἔργων,
   κἀγὼ δείξω σοι ἐκ τῶν ἔργων μου τὴν πίστιν."
19 σὺ πιστεύεις ὅτι εἷς ἐστιν ὁ Θεός·
   καλῶς ποιεῖς·
   καὶ τὰ δαιμόνια πιστεύουσι,
   καὶ φρίσσουσι.

17 So also your faith, if it have not works
   Is dead by itself.
18 But some one will say,
   " Thou faith hast, and I works have,
   Show me thy faith apart from its works,
   And I will show thee out of my works, the faith."
19 Thou believest that God is one.
   Thou doest well,
   Even the devils believe *this*,
   And shudder.

what would be the good of such frothy utterances? So *the* faith, the faith which the man who is the subject of this hypothesis says he has, is dead by itself, furnishing no evidence, or proof of its existence. It is like a man boasting of large possessions but living in poverty and never producing a farthing to public view; or as one who talks of his knowledge of music and painting, and yet never touches the canvass or the chord.

Ver. 18. Here a further objection is raised to the man in error by the introduction of another disputant on the scene, who, admitting the possibility for argument's sake, of the separation between faith and works, thus deals with the question: Thou, for thy part, hast faith, and I, for my part, have works; shew me, display and evidence to me thy faith separate from its works, the works that belong to it. But such a process involves a patent impossibility; for even if a moral condition could *exist* without making any manifestation, it could not be exhibited without a manifestation. And I, he continues, will show you the faith out of, as evidenced and manifested by, my works; the articles are articles of reference.

Ver. 19. σὺ πιστεύεις ὅτι εἷς ἐστὶν ὁ Θεός. This is the pivot

20 θέλεις δὲ γνῶναι, ὦ ἄνθρωπε κενέ,
ὅτι ἡ πίστις χωρὶς τῶν ἔργων νεκρά ἐστιν;

20 But art thou willing to know, O empty man,
That thy faith apart from its works is dead?

on which the whole interpretation of the passage turns. Faith has hitherto been spoken of indefinitely; we have been left in the dark as yet as to the object to which the faith spoken of is directed; here, then, we have the definition. It is not Gospel faith, it is not faith in our Lord Jesus Christ, in His blood and righteousness; we have no mention made of any of the distinctive doctrines of Christianity, but the faith is defined and limited to be that "God is one," the *Sh'ma Israel*, the one great article of the Jewish creed to this very day; the platform is not Christian but essentially Jewish. Surely it is but missing the point of the writer's argument to say this creed was common to both Jews and Christians. It was so, and as such is well suited to the purpose, according to our theory of this Epistle, that it was addressed to Jews as Jews, and not to Christians as Christians. The mixture of the latter with the former was an accident, and hence they are often addressed and consoled, but the bulk of the letter is directed against Jewish error. A definition of faith to a Christian congregation would not have failed to have contained some special reference to our Lord Jesus Christ. Moreover, we must remember that this is only one part of a consistent whole. We have seen that this Epistle was addressed to the twelve tribes, that the scene lay in the synagogue, the commandments quoted are from the Jewish law, and now the very definition of faith is emphatically the creed of Israel.

Thou doest well. There is no doubt about the correctness of this creed, but if you stop at this point, you will fall far short of salvation; a barren belief in the unity of God, although it is a Jewish boast against the Gentile world, is possessed by those that are irremediably lost, for even the devils hold this article of faith, and what is more, "shudder." This creed brings them neither respite nor redemption, but rather adds to their terrors. How like the old Hebrew prophets is this style of bitter irony; how forcible and fearful the picture painted by these words: "Even the devils believe this, and shudder," literally, *their hair stands on end with terror.*

Ver. 20. *But art thou willing to know.* θέλεις. This word suggests the unwillingness of the man in error to see the true force of the argument: Are you really willing and ready to know, or is not your will perverse, and hence your judgment wrong?

21 Ἀβραὰμ ὁ πατὴρ ἡμῶν
οὐκ ἐξ ἔργων ἐδικαιώθη,
ἀνενέγκας Ἰσαὰκ τὸν υἱὸν αὐτοῦ ἐπὶ τὸ θυσιαστήριον;

21 Abraham, our father,
Was not he by works justified
In offering-up Isaac his son on the altar?

Empty, κενέ. Not only *foolish*, or *void of sound sense*, but also with a certain amount of satire, *empty of works*, *void of fruit*.

ἡ πίστις. Not faith in the abstract, but the article refers to the case of the man before us, this faith of which you speak, your faith; apart from *its* works (mark again the force of the article of reference τῶν) is dead.

Dead, νεκρά. There is some difference of opinion about the reading in this place, the MS. B, and the first corrector of C read ἀργή, *unproductive, useless, idle*, but the ordinary reading is found in ℵ, A, C, K, L; the Latin Vulgate also supports this, there can be no doubt that this reading is therefore the best supported.

Ver. 21-23. *Abraham our father*. Mark here again the evidence that this Epistle was addressed to Jews; compare Rom. iv. 1, where St. Paul was addressing the Jewish portion of his readers.

Justified by works. In order to see the force of this passage, and the seeming opposition between it and the teaching of St. Paul, it may be well to place them side by side:—

St. Paul, Rom. iv. 1-3.

"What shall we say then that Abraham our father, as pertaining to the flesh, hath found? For if Abraham were justified by works, he hath whereof to glory; but not before God. For what saith the Scripture? Abraham believed God, and it was counted unto him for righteousness."

St. James ii. 21, 22.

"Was not Abraham our father justified by works, when he offered Isaac his son upon the altar? Thou seest how his faith was co-operating with his works, and by his works his faith was perfected."

It is noticeable that the same example is brought before us by the two writers, the very term *Abraham our father* is common to them both; the testimony of Scripture that Abraham believed God, and it was counted to him for righteousness, is advanced by both alike; the only difference seems to be that the standpoint of St. Paul is the promise of the *birth* of Isaac, and that of St. James

22 βλέπεις ὅτι ἡ πίστις συνήργει τοῖς ἔργοις αὐτοῦ,
καὶ ἐκ τῶν ἔργων ἡ πίστις ἐτελειώθη;

23 καὶ ἐπληρώθη ἡ γραφὴ ἡ λέγουσα,
"'Επίστευσε δὲ 'Αβραὰμ τῷ Θεῷ,
καὶ ἐλογίσθη αὐτῷ εἰς δικαιοσύνην,
καὶ φίλος Θεοῦ ἐκλήθη."

22 Thou seest that his faith was co-operating with his works,
And by his works his faith was perfected,

23 And the Scripture was fulfilled, which saith,
"And Abraham believed God,
And it was reckoned to him as righteousness,
And the Friend of God he was called."

the *offering* of Isaac; the argument and the illustration are so nearly alike that we are puzzled at the apparent discrepancy of the conclusion. But is there any real difference between them? Both agree that Abraham's belief was counted for righteousness. St. James adds that his faith co-operated with his works, and by his works his faith was perfected, or brought to its proper end and completion. St. Paul asserts that the patriarch was justified by the unseen principle of faith; St. James, by that principle as evidenced and brought to full development in its fruits. The former teaches that Abraham's works, as such, did not justify him, but his faith; the latter, that his faith co-operated with his works, and that the works were simply the perfection of his faith. In both the vital force is the same, but in one it is treated in the abstract, in the other in concrete. It must nevertheless be borne in mind that the faith spoken of is the Jewish faith concerning the unity of God, and not the Christian faith relating to atonement and salvation by the Gospel of grace.

Ver. 23. εἰς δικαιοσύνην, *for righteousness*. The rendering of לצדקה, the ל or εἰς, *for*, is expletive almost in our language. It would be best left untranslated or represented by *as*.

Friend of God, φίλος Θεοῦ. See 2 Chron. xx. 7, and Is. xli. 8, where the participle active is used, and therefore the sense would be a *lover of God:* see φίλος τοῦ νυμφίου, φίλος τοῦ κόσμου, etc. This title of Abraham is common amongst the Arabs to this day.

24 Ὁρᾶτε ὅτι ἐξ ἔργων δικαιοῦται ἄνθρωπος,
καὶ οὐκ ἐκ πίστεως μόνον;
24 Behold ye, that by works a man is justified,
And not by faith only!

Ver. 24. This verse forms a conclusion of the argument so far as it is illustrated by the case of Abraham, but Abraham was called and owned of God, and therefore to strengthen the position, St. James adduces the example of a heathen woman, Rahab, a harlot, πόρνη. This word is not to be understood in a figurative sense as an idolatress, one guilty of spiritual fornication, that is, a heathen, nor as a keeper of an inn or resting place for travellers, but literally. It is remarkable that St. Paul, in writing to the Hebrews (for we believe that Apostle to have been the author of that Epistle), teaches that Rahab was saved by faith; here again is the same apparent contradiction as above in the case of Abraham, but as there St. Paul looked at the motive, the inner impression on the secret springs of thought and will, and St. James at the outward evidence of these invisible powers, so the two writers pursue the same course respectively in treating of Rahab.

It must not be forgotten in reading this whole paragraph that the key note is sounded in the nineteenth verse. The faith here treated of is a bare belief that " God is one;" this is a definition of Jewish faith. It is not enough to save a man. But although the same argument might be applied to the Christian, yet we contend that the writer is not speaking of Christian faith, but Jewish faith. Even the illustrations he uses prove that his concern was not with the distinctive doctrines of the Gospel. Abraham had received a promise that in " his seed all nations should be blessed," and when called upon to offer his son on the altar, he believed that God would still keep His word, even though it were necessary for Him to raise Isaac from the dead. (See Heb. xi. 19.) Abraham's faith was a reliance on God that He would not forfeit His word. The same may be said of Rahab: she had heard how God had destroyed Egypt and delivered Israel, and she believed that God would also destroy Canaan, and so she saved the spies. Thus neither in the definition of the faith here spoken of, nor in the illustrations of that faith, have we any mention made of the doctrines of the Gospel of the grace of God. No word is found about the blood and righteousness of Christ. Even in Heb. xi. all that St. Paul advances is that these saints of old showed a spirit of trustfulness in God, and reliance on the evidence which He furnished them; and hence a lesson is derived to ourselves who have full light and a perfect revelation. It is true that by implication and inference the necessity of Christian

25 ὁμοίως δὲ καὶ 'Ραὰβ ἡ πόρνη
οὐκ ἐξ ἔργων ἐδικαιώθη, .
ὑποδεξαμένη τοὺς ἀγγέλους,
καὶ ἑτέρᾳ ὁδῷ ἐκβαλοῦσα;

26 ὥσπερ γὰρ τὸ σῶμα χωρὶς πνεύματος νεκρόν ἐστιν,
οὕτω καὶ ἡ πίστις χωρὶς τῶν ἔργων νεκρά ἐστι.

25 But likewise Rahab also the harlot,
Was not she by works justified,
In receiving-secretly the spies,
And by a different way dismissing them?

26 For as the body apart from breath is dead,
So faith also apart from its works is dead.

faith producing Christian works, which no one would deny, is enforced, only that is not the point here, the object of the writer being to convince his Jewish readers of their shortcomings, and as the Baptist, when he bade the people bring forth fruit meet for repentance, and as our Lord, when He preached the sermon on the mount, raised the standard of the law to prove the sinfulness of man, so St. James shows the Jews, to whom he wrote, that neither their ceremonial, nor their knowledge of the law, nor their faith in one God, could save their souls. He was thus driving them from self-trust, to the embracing of the life-giving doctrines of the Gospel.

Ver. 25. *The messengers*, τοὺς ἀγγέλους. In the parallel passage in the Epistle to the Hebrews (xi. 31) κατασκόπους, *spies*, Heb. מרגלים, Josh. ii. 1.

ὑποδεξαμένη. The preposition in composition suggests the secrecy with which she received the spies, and that in ἐκβάλουσα the speed with which she dismissed them.

ἑτέρᾳ ὁδῷ, *by a different way.* They came in by the gate, they were dispatched through a window in the wall.

Ver. 26. This verse seems to present no small difficulty, as we should have expected that *faith* would have been represented by *breath*, and *works* by the *body*. This has been noticed by all commentators. The comparison here is clearly not between the body and faith, and breath and works in every point of view, but only in this, that when we see a body, we know that it is alive by its breathing; so when we see a man professing to have faith, we discern its living reality by the visible exhibition of good works. Breath here is viewed as the manifestation of life, not as the cause.

CHAPTER III.

1 Μὴ πολλοὶ διδάσκαλοι γίνεσθε, ἀδελφοί μου,
εἰδότες ὅτι μεῖζον κρίμα λημψόμεθα·
2 πολλὰ γὰρ πταίομεν ἅπαντες.
εἴ τις ἐν λόγῳ οὐ πταίει,
οὗτος τέλειος ἀνήρ,
δυνατὸς χαλιναγωγῆσαι καὶ ὅλον τὸ σῶμα.

1 Do not many of you become teachers, my brethren,
Knowing that greater condemnation shall we receive.
2 For in many things stumble we all,
If any one in word stumbleth not,
He is a perfect man,
Able to bridle his whole body also.

Ver. 1. *Do not many of you become teachers.* Here, again, we have tokens of the Jewish character of the persons addressed; the office of rabbi or teacher was one of great honour among them, and consequently one much sought after.

We see this in the Gospel narrative, where our Lord reproves them as loving to be called *Rabbi, Rabbi*, Matt. xxiii. 7. The same features of self-sufficiency and arrogance are prominent in the Judaizing teachers who disturbed the early church, as is clear from many passages both in the Acts and Epistles.

Teachers not *masters*, in the modern sense of the word. *Become*, not *be:* Do not introduce into the church this fault that is prevalent in the synagogue. The object of St. James in this portion of his Epistle seems to be to convince the teachers of sin in the performance of their official duties, as he had hitherto the members of the synagogue in their daily walk in life.

The sin of the teacher is more glaring, creates a greater scandal, and is visited with severer punishment. How strikingly is this implied in our Lord's words to Nicodemus, "Art thou a master (ὁ διδάσκαλος) of Israel and knowest not these things?" Jno. iii. 10.

Ver. 2. *In many things.* πολλά is frequently used adverbially

3 Ἴδε τῶν ἵππων τοὺς χαλινοὺς
εἰς τὰ στόματα βάλλομεν
εἰς τὸ πείθεσθαι αὐτοὺς ἡμῖν,
καὶ ὅλον τὸ σῶμα αὐτῶν μετάγομεν.

3 Lo! the bits of horses,
Into their mouths we put,
That they should be obedient to us,
And their whole body we guide-about.

for *often*, but there seems to be a distinction drawn here between the general faults of which all are guilty and the particular sin of an unbridled tongue, this is supported by the Syriac and Vulgate.

We stumble, πταίομεν, akin to πίπτω, to *fall*, to *stumble* in the path of duty.

All, ἅπαντες. A comprehensive word; ἅμα πάντες, *all together*. "There is not a just man upon earth that doeth good and sinneth not." Eccles. vii. 20. But of all sins the most difficult to avoid and restrain are sins of the tongue, hence St. James tells us that the man who stumbles not in word is a perfect man. *Perfect*, τέλειος; absolute perfection is not intended by this word, but relative, the nearest approach to faultlessness is the man who governs his tongue; the truth of this is evident: speech is the channel through which our thoughts find expression, the angry feeling begets the angry utterance, and hence becomes known; the foul thought is published by the foul word; the tongue is the index of the whole man; "out of the abundance of the heart the mouth speaketh;" to keep the tongue in subjection is to hold in control all the evil tossings and risings of the flood of iniquity within us; the man who can bridle his tongue, as a practised rider checks the restiveness of a fiery steed, can curb (χαλιναγωγῆσαι) and direct the whole of his body; the tongue is the master-position, this secured, the mutiny of our members is under our power.

Ver. 3. ἴδε, *lo!* Instead of ἴδε the MSS. A, B, K, L, read εἰ δέ, *but if*, and ℵ, εἰ δὲ γάρ. The Vulgate also has *si autem*. On the other hand C reads ἴδε, and the Syriac, *but lo!* The authority, therefore, for εἰ δέ is preponderating; moreover, it is the harder reading, and therefore more likely to have been altered to an easier one. Yet in a question of this kind the style of the writer must have considerable weight in determining the question. St. James, after the example of the old Hebrew prophets, continually prefaces his illustrations and exhortations by this interjectional form: see vv. 4, 5 of this chapter, and chap. v. 4, 7, 9, 11. It is

4 Ἰδοὺ καὶ τὰ πλοῖα τηλικαῦτα ὄντα,
καὶ ὑπὸ ἀνέμων σκληρῶν ἐλαυνόμενα,
μετάγεται ὑπὸ ἐλαχίστου πηδαλίου,
ὅπου ἂν ἡ ὁρμὴ τοῦ εὐθύνοντος βούληται.
5 οὕτω καὶ ἡ γλῶσσα μικρὸν μέλος ἐστί,
καὶ μεγαλαυχεῖ.
Ἰδοὺ ἡλίκον πῦρ ἡλίκην ὕλην ἀνάπτει·

4 Lo! the ships also, so great as they are,
And by violent winds driven,
Are guided-about by a very little rudder,
Wherever the will of the helmsman desireth.
5 So the tongue also a little member is,
And boasteth greatly.
Lo! how little a fire,
How great a forest kindleth!

a strong argument for this reading that the two illustrations that follow immediately on this are introduced by ἰδού. It is not at all unlikely that the confusion in the reading arose from an *itacism*, a clerical error which is so frequent in ancient MSS. This mistake in vowels and diphthongs which have nearly the same sound, arose either from the copyist writing from the dictation of a reader, or from a careless manner of pronouncing such words, leading to an incorrect way of spelling them. In the most ancient MSS. the chief *itacisms* were between ι and ει, αι and ε; this would account for the doubt which hangs over this place: see Scrivener's *Introduction to the Criticism of the New Test.*, p. 10.

The three illustrations so poetically introduced give a sort of popular explanation of the somewhat startling statement, that he who governs his tongue is a perfect man; the small bit in the mouth of the horse governs and guides his whole body; the little rudder manages the whole ship, even when wind and wave conspire to drive the bark into rebellion; the spark that accident lets fall envelopes the wide forest in flames. Such is the power of the little tongue amongst the many members and the whole body of man; if we control and curb it, all the tumult of passion will be held in subjection, but if the bit be broken, the rudder unhinged, the spark dropt, the whole man will be the victim of his own unbridled fury, and the fire will spread and embrace in its destructive arms the whole circle of the society in which he moves.

Ver. 4. ὁρμή is the will manifested in action and effort.
Ver. 5. *How small*, ἡλίκον. The Received Text here reads

6 καὶ ἡ γλῶσσα πῦρ,
ὁ κόσμος τῆς ἀδικίας.
ἡ γλῶσσα καθίσταται ἐν τοῖς μέλεσιν ἡμῶν,
ἡ σπιλοῦσα ὅλον τὸ σῶμα,
καὶ φλογίζουσα τὸν τροχὸν τῆς γενέσεως,
καὶ φλογιζομένη ὑπὸ τῆς γεέννης·

6 And the tongue *is* a fire,
The world of iniquity *the forest!*
The tongue is constituted among our members,
The defiler of the whole body,
And inflamer of the orb of creation,
And inflamed by Gehenna.

ὀλίγον, *little.* The authority for this reading is A, the revise of C; K, and L. Whereas ἡλίκον is found in A revised, B, ℵ, and the first hand of C; the Vulgate *quantus* also supports this. ἡλίκος refers to size, either *how great* or *how small,* according to the requirements of the context.

Forest, ὕλην. The word *matter,* found in the English Version, is borrowed from the Latin *materies,* which sometimes signifies *fuel;* the literal rendering is far more graphic, as reminding the reader of those sudden disasters that sometimes arise in hot countries from the accidental spark falling on the dry herbage, and extending to whole forests.

Ver. 6. *And the tongue is the fire, the world of iniquity (the forest).* Both Wordsworth and Alford, together with most commentators, render the article in ὁ κόσμος by *that, that* world of iniquity, in apposition to ἡ γλῶσσα, *the tongue,* in the former clause. But as the article in ἡ γλῶσσα, *the tongue,* marks it as the subject in its own clause, so it is more natural to regard the article in ὁ κόσμος as performing the same office in its clause. It has however been already hinted at, chap. i. 9, that in Hebrew parallelisms it often happens that one line of thought is stated fully in one member, but in the following member or members of the group the subject only is expressed, the predicate being involved, and to be supplied from the preceding parallel clause. Thus ἡ γλῶσσα has for its predicate πῦρ expressed, but derived from the sentence immediately preceding, so ὁ κόσμος has for its predicate ὕλη, derived from the preceding sentence, though not expressed; thus the *tongue* corresponds with the *spark,* and the *world* with the *forest.* This is the view adopted in the Syriac Version, a high authority, as being in a tongue cognate with Hebrew; the translator has only slightly varied the metaphor by changing it into a simile. Bishop Jebb in his *Sacred Literature*, pp. 285-287, resists this construction as an innovation, and rejects it on the ground of the demands of the parallelism, but although the parallelism is not preserved precisely in the same form, it is not destroyed; and it is a strong argument for this mode of arranging the parallels, that the article in ὁ κόσμος is properly accounted for. As to the argument that it is strange that if this were the reading, copyists could, without an exception, have departed from it, is beside the mark; it is not contended that the Greek text ever read ὕλη, but that the nature of Hebrew parallelism demands or permits such a transference of a predicate from a preceding clause.

Before the second ἡ γλῶσσα the Received Text inserts οὕτως; this is omitted in all the ancient MSS., the style is more nervous and forcible without it.

καθίσταται, *is constituted*. This rendering is rather too strong. We have scarcely any word in our language that gives the exact force; *has its place* would, probably be the nearest.

St. James proceeds to show the tremendous capabilities of the tongue for evil. It bespatters with foul spots (σπιλοῦσα) our whole body, and inflames the *orb*, or, *universe of creation*.

τ. τροχὸν τ. γενέσεως. This expression has received a vast number of interpretations. A few may be named: *the course of our life; the term of our life; the succeeding generations of mankind;* thus the Syriac: another mode of expressing *the whole body* just mentioned; *the world at large, orbis terrarum;* or, by change of accent, τρόχος, *the race of man*. Classical usage and figures are of little importance in helping us to decide a question like this. An Old Testament passage must be sought for, as the whole basis of thought and expression in the New Testament generally, and very specially in this Epistle, is Hebrew. Such a passage is found in Ps. lxxvii. 19, in E.V. 18, "the voice of thy thunder was in the *heaven*," E.V. בגלגל, literally, *in the wheel*. This passage is, moreover, rendered by the LXX. (which is of great importance here) φωνὴ τ. βροντῆς σου ἐν τ. τροχῷ. This *wheel* or *orb* it will be perceived is in contrast to the *world* and the *earth*, and hence seems clearly to denote the heavenly sphere or universe. I am aware that many scholars of note disapprove of this interpretation. Some suggesting a *rolling sound;* this has the support of Aben-Ezra, Maurer, Böttcher, etc.; others, as Hengstenberg, *a whirl*, denoting the rapidity with which the thunder-peals follow on each other; and others, as J. D. Michaelis and Ewald, *a whirlwind*. But none of these explanations have better ground than the first mentioned; the comparison of the concave of heaven to a *wheel* or *orb*, with its revolutions of day and night, seems the most natural: this view was adopted by Kimchi. If this passage in the psalm is the original ground of the phrase in St. James, and

7 πᾶσα γὰρ φύσις θηρίων τε καὶ πετεινῶν,
ἑρπετῶν τε καὶ ἐναλίων,
δαμάζεται καὶ δεδάμασται τῇ φύσει τῇ ἀνθρωπίνῃ·
8 τὴν δὲ γλῶσσαν οὐδεὶς δύναται ἀνθρώπων δαμάσαι·
ἀκατάστατον κακόν μεστὴ ἰοῦ θανατηφόρου.

7 For every nature both of wild-beasts and birds,
Both of reptiles, and sea-monsters,
Is being tamed and has been tamed by human nature.

8 But the tongue no one of men can tame,
It is a disorderly evil, full of deadly poison.

of this little doubt can be entertained, the figure presented to us is that of the tongue, a central power, that defiles the whole body of its possessor; but its danger does not end here, it sets on fire the whole creation: as the little spark falling on the blades of grass spreads the fire to the forest, and none can tell where the conflagration will end, so the tongue, by emitting sparks of wickedness, may involve the whole universe in disaster. This explanation receives strength also from the statement that follows, that the fire with which the tongue is kindled is derived from Gehenna; the *highest* and the *lowest* points in creation are thus contrasted, the evil at the centre of the circle is diffused to the most distant points in the circumference: " Set a watch, O Lord, before my mouth, keep the door of my lips."

Gehenna, גיהנם, the valley of Hinnom. It was here that the Jews sacrificed their children to Moloch, and after it had been polluted for this reason by Josiah, 2 Ki. xxiii. 10, it became the place of refuse for Jerusalem. In consequence of the corruption that was always festering there, and the fire that was ever kept burning to consume the filth, this valley was regarded as a type of the place of endless torment, and its name was transferred to that dread abode. After the judgment of death, whether by sword or stoning, had been passed on a criminal, the casting of his carcase into the valley of Hinnom was regarded as the greatest *post-mortem* dishonour: see Matt. v. 22, 23.

Ver. 7. φύσις, *nature.* Not *species,* but the nature proper to every creature, is now daily in course of being tamed, and has long been so, by the superior nature that is proper to man; yet though man has this power over the wild creatures, he has not control over his own tongue.

Ver. 8. ἀκατάστατον, *unstable, restless.* The Received Text reads ἀκάσχετον, *uncontrollable.* The former is the reading of the more ancient Uncial MSS., and the latter of the more recent ones.

ST. JAMES, III. 53

9 ἐν αὐτῇ εὐλογοῦμεν τὸν Κύριον καὶ πατέρα,
καὶ ἐν αὐτῇ καταρώμεθα τοὺς ἀνθρώπους
τοὺς καθ' ὁμοίωσιν Θεοῦ γεγονότας·

10 ἐκ τοῦ αὐτοῦ στόματος ἐξέρχεται εὐλογία καὶ κατάρα,
οὐ χρή, ἀδελφοί μου, ταῦτα οὕτω γίνεσθαι.

11 μήτι ἡ πηγὴ ἐκ τῆς αὐτῆς ὀπῆς
βρύει τὸ γλυκὺ καὶ τὸ πικρόν;

9 Therewith we bless the Lord and Father,
And therewith curse we men,
Who after the likeness of God are created.

10 From the same mouth proceeds blessing and curse!
My brethren, these things ought not thus to happen.

11 Doth a spring from the same aperture
Emit the sweet and the bitter?

Full of deadly poison. This seems to be a reference to Ps. cxxxix. 3, "the poison of asps is under their lips." Probably both passages have their common origin in the history of the first temptation and the serpent tempter.

Ver. 9. *The Lord*, Κύριον instead of Θεόν, is the reading of the most ancient MSS.

In the likeness of God. Mark here again the reference to the early part of Genesis i. 26, 27.

Ver. 10. χρή. It may be worth noticing that this is the only place in which this verb occurs in the New Testament.

The perversion of the use of the tongue is sharply rebuked by exhibiting the unnaturalness of such a misappropriation of its powers; this is done by the parables of the Fountain and the Fig-tree. These two comparisons teach each its own lesson; the former, the inconsistency and impossibility of the tongue uttering both good and bad, as though it were actuated by two distinct agencies; "What communion hath light with darkness," 2 Cor. vi. 14, contains a similar thought. Such a blending together of opposites cannot exist. The latter, since the tongue is evil (for the case of the wicked man's tongue only is under consideration): Do not suppose that the blessings you pronounce upon God's name, in the exercise of your forms of religious worship, are acceptable to Him, for He will only receive a pure offering from a pure source; "Do men gather grapes of thorns or figs of

12 μὴ δύναται, ἀδελφοί μου, συκῆ ἐλαίας ποιῆσαι,
ἢ ἄμπελος σῦκα;
οὔτε ἁλυκὸν γλυκὺ ποιῆσαι ὕδωρ.

13 Τίς σοφὸς καὶ ἐπιστήμων ἐν ὑμῖν;
δειξάτω ἐκ τῆς καλῆς ἀναστροφῆς
τὰ ἔργα αὐτοῦ ἐν πραΰτητι σοφίας.

12 Can, my brethren, a fig-tree produce olives,
Or a vine, figs?
Neither (can it) salt-sweet water.

13 Who is there wise and understanding among you?
Let him show out of his good mode-of-life
His works in meekness of wisdom.

thistles?" Matt. vii. 16; and "a good man out of the good treasure of his heart bringeth forth good things; and an evil man out of the evil treasure bringeth forth evil things," Matt. xii. 35, contain a parallel lesson to this figure.

Ver. 12. The Received Text has here οὕτως οὐδεμία πηγή, and after ἁλυκόν, καί. These words are not found in the most ancient MSS.; but though probably not forming part of the original it is a correct gloss, as by the parallelism we expect such a subject to correspond with what goes before; hence I should not conclude, as most commentators, that ἁλυκόν formed the subject with δύναται understood for the verb, "(Can) salt (water) bring forth sweet water?" but the primary subject of the sentence is sustained throughout; the absence of the article with ἁλυκόν also points in the same direction (see also note on 6th verse); the omission of the καί adds great force to the figure "salt-sweet," an *oxymoron*. The terseness of the expression refers chiefly to the double produce supposed in *v.* 11, though it will be at once felt that the other thought is not excluded but involved.

Ver. 13. *Who is there wise and understanding.* The former σοφός refers to the general ability, the latter ἐπιστήμων to the particular application of that ability. The interrogative form, "Who is?" suggests the thought, If there is any one among you of this character, then let him manifest his wisdom in meekness.

14 εἰ δὲ ζῆλον πικρὸν ἔχετε
καὶ ἐρίθειαν ἐν τῇ καρδίᾳ ὑμῶν,
μὴ κατακαυχᾶσθε καὶ ψεύδεσθε κατὰ τῆς ἀληθείας.
15 Οὐκ ἔστιν αὕτη ἡ σοφία ἄνωθεν κατερχομένη,
ἀλλ' ἐπίγειος, ψυχική, δαιμονιώδης.
16 ὅπου γὰρ ζῆλος καὶ ἐρίθεια,
ἐκεῖ ἀκαταστασία καὶ πᾶν φαῦλον πρᾶγμα.
17 ἡ δὲ ἄνωθεν σοφία πρῶτον μὲν ἁγνή ἐστιν,
ἔπειτα εἰρηνική, ἐπιεικής, εὐπειθής,
μεστὴ ἐλέους καὶ καρπῶν ἀγαθῶν,
ἀδιάκριτος ἀνυπόκριτος.

14 But if bitter jealousy ye have,
And selfishness in your heart,
Do not boast or lie against the truth.
15 This is not the wisdom from above descending,
But *is* earthly, animal, devilish.
16 For where *there is* jealousy and selfishness,
There *there is* disorder and every naughty deed.
17 But the wisdom from above, firstly indeed is pure,
Secondly *is* peaceful, kind, readily-obeying,
Full of mercy and good fruits,
Making-no-distinctions, void-of-hypocrisy.

Ver. 14. ἐριθείαν, *selfishness*. This word is derived from ἔριθος, *a hired labourer*, and hence means *self-seeking, greed, selfishness*. In Rom. ii. 8 it is found, as here, in connection with opposition to the truth.

Ver. 15. ψυχική, *animal*. A most difficult word to render in our language, as we have no proper equivalent. It really signifies *pertaining to the soul, soulish*. The use here seems to picture to us the soul or *anima* of man left in its fallen state, with its affections and appetites fixed on the lower world, degraded to the level of the beasts: hence this wisdom is spoken of as earthly, as opposed to heavenly, animal, as opposed to spiritual, and devilish, as opposed to divine. For a full discussion of the ψυχή, see Delitzsch's *Biblical Psychology*.

Ver. 16. Mark the reference in ἀκαταστασία, *disorder*, to the 8th verse, where the tongue is called ἀκατάστατον κακόν, *a disorderly evil*.

Ver. 17. ἐπιεικής, *kind*, from εἰκός, *reasonable*. A beautiful

18 καρπὸς δὲ δικαιοσύνης ἐν εἰρήνῃ σπείρεται
τοῖς ποιοῦσιν εἰρήνην.

**18 And the fruit of righteousness in peace is sown
By the producers of peace.**

word, which perhaps would be best paraphrased in our language by, *though having right, not insisting on that right:* see Aristotle's *Ethics*, v. 14; and for a pleasant account of the word, Trench's *Synonyms of the New Testament.*

εὐπειθής, *readily obeying.* The disposition that submits where it ought, when it ought, and to whom it ought, is represented in this word, rather than a susceptibility of persuasion. The Vulgate renders by *suadibilis*, which is rather the mark of a weak than of an humble mind.

ἀδιάκριτος. Not as E.V., *without partiality*, which is not sufficiently pointed; nor *without doubting*, as Alford; but referring to the distinctions that these Jews were in the habit of making between the rich and the poor, see chap. ii. 4. The wisdom from above teaches us not to respect persons, but to be equitable and kind to all alike.

ἀνυπόκριτος, *without hypocrisy.* These qualities above named must not be a semblance but a fact, the heavenly wisdom is truthful and wears no mask.

Ver. 18. There is some difficulty in tracing the exact line of thought in this verse. To clear the ground, it may be concluded that τ. ποιοῦσιν is the dative of the agent. Then, perhaps, it has not been sufficiently considered that the phrase ποιεῖν εἰρήνην is borrowed from the produce of nature, the *peace* being regarded as the fruit yielded; it is the עשׂה פרי of Hebrew, see *v.* 12. Next, that καρπὸς δικαιοσύνης is the genitive of apposition, *i.e.*, fruit which is righteousness. The idea then evolved is, The fruit, namely *righteousness*, is sown in peace by the producers of peace, that is, those who produce peace, as trees do their fruit, sow the fruit of righteousness in peace; they commit the harvest of good seed to good ground again, *peace in peace*, so that each harvest becomes the seed-crop of another, an ever accumulating store, a reflexive blessing to themselves, and a benefit even extending to others.

CHAPTER IV.

1 Πόθεν πόλεμοι καὶ πόθεν μάχαι ἐν ὑμῖν;
οὐκ ἐντεῦθεν, ἐκ τῶν ἡδονῶν ὑμῶν
τῶν στρατευομένων ἐν τοῖς μέλεσιν ὑμῶν;
2 ἐπιθυμεῖτε, καὶ οὐκ ἔχετε·
φονεύετε καὶ ζηλοῦτε, καὶ οὐ δύνασθε ἐπιτυχεῖν·
μάχεσθε καὶ πολεμεῖτε οὐκ ἔχετε,
διὰ τὸ μὴ αἰτεῖσθαι ὑμᾶς·

1 Whence *are* wars, and whence strifes among you?
Are they not from hence, from your pleasures,
That wage-warfare in your members?
2 Ye lust, and ye have not;
Ye murder and envy and cannot obtain,
Ye fight and war, ye have not,
Because of your not asking.

Ver. 1. St. James in this paragraph turns upon the ungodly Jews, the unconverted, the selfish and rebellious, and rebukes them with all the energy and severity of the ancient Hebrew prophets, whose language and poetic style he most strikingly adopts. How any one in reading such a passage as this can suppose that the writer was addressing members of the Christian church at such an early period of its existence, even if the date is fixed at the latest possible point, it is difficult to imagine. The state of the Corinthian church, which is sometimes adduced as a parallel, is not at all similar: see Introduction, *To whom was this Epistle addressed.* The state of the Jewish people in the period between the crucifixion of our Lord and the destruction of Jerusalem, as detailed by Josephus, is the best comment on this portion of the Epistle.

πόθεν is repeated before μάχαι in ℵ, A, B, C.

Ver. 2. φονεύετε, *ye murder.* In consequence of commentators failing to perceive that this Epistle is addressed to the twelve tribes, that is to Jews, and determining that it was an Epistle addressed to

3 αἰτεῖτε, καὶ οὐ λαμβάνετε,
διότι κακῶς αἰτεῖσθε,
ἵνα ἐν ταῖς ἡδοναῖς ὑμῶν δαπανήσητε.

4 μοιχαλίδες, οὐκ οἴδατε ὅτι ἡ φιλία τοῦ κόσμου
ἔχθρα τοῦ Θεοῦ ἐστιν;
ὃς ἂν οὖν βουληθῇ φίλος εἶναι τοῦ κόσμου,
ἐχθρὸς τοῦ Θεοῦ καθίσταται.

3 Ye ask, and ye have not,
Because ye ask wickedly,
To squander in your pleasures.

4 Adulteresses!
Know ye not that the love for the world
Is hatred against-God?
Whoso therefore prefers to be a lover of the world
A hater of God is constituted.

Christians as such, great difficulty has always been felt in accounting for this fearful charge, that those to whom St. James was writing were not unfrequently guilty of murder, hence all sorts of evasions of the plain and literal meaning of the word have been invented, such as *murder in thought, coveting even to death*, etc.; and lastly, some have even proposed to read φθονεῖτε, *ye envy*, although there is not a manuscript, uncial or cursive, that authorises such a reading; but if we admit that St. James was writing to the Jews, as such, composed of unbelievers, as well as believers, in the Messiahship of Jesus, all is clear; this part of his Epistle will refer entirely to the former section, and the sins which he charges them with, it is well known, were of daily occurrence.

Ye fight and war, i.e., with one another, or against the ruling authorities; most likely St. James had in his mind's eye the struggles of the faction of the Zealots; yet you do not obtain what you desire; you omit the duty of prayer, of asking for what you want from the only source from whence it can come. But perhaps you plead that you do ask, yet you do not receive, because you ask wickedly, with an evil purpose, that you may squander it in the enjoyment of your carnal pleasures.

Ver. 4. In the Received Text this verse begins with Μοιχοὶ καί, *adulterers and*, etc., but the ancient MSS., א, A, B, omit these words; the Syriac and Vulgate Versions have only *adulteri*.

ST. JAMES. IV. 59

5 ἢ δοκεῖτε ὅτι κενῶς ἡ γραφὴ λέγει,
" Πρὸς φθόνον ἐπιποθεῖ
τὸ πνεῦμα ὃ κατῴκισεν ἐν ἡμῖν; "

5 Think ye, that the Scripture vainly saith,
" The spirit that He made-to-dwell in us
With jealousy desireth *us*?"

The insertion of the words, which appear first in a revision of א, in κ and L, and in the Philoxenian Version, is an attempt to explain a nervous poetical figure in a prosaic form. No comparison is more frequent in Scripture, or more familiar to ourselves through that source, than that marriage "signifies unto us the mystical union that is between Christ and his church." See for some examples Ps. xliv.; Is. liv. 5; Jer. ii. 2; iii. 14; Rom. vii. 4; 2 Cor. xi. 2; Eph. v. 22-33. And the turning aside of the people of God to idolatry, false doctrine, or evil practice is portrayed by the rupture and profanation of the marriage vow. See Hosea throughout; Jer. iii. 1-11; Ezek. xvi. throughout. Our Lord takes up the old Hebrew strain, and rings its awful echoes in the ears of the unbelieving sign-seekers, "an evil and adulterous (μοιχαλίς) generation." Matt. xii. 37; Mark viii. 38; compare also 2 Pet. ii. 14 and Rev. ii. 4.

τοῦ κόσμου and τ. Θεοῦ are genitives of the object.

βουληθῇ, *has a wish*, and consequently makes a choice between God and the world.

καθίσταται, see chap. iii. 6, *settles down to be, becomes, takes his stand as*.

Ver. 5. Many difficulties exist in this verse; the first task will be to settle the reading; the Received Text is κατῴκησεν, *dwelt*, and so the Vulgate *habitat*, but κατῴκισεν, *He made to dwell*, is the reading of א, A, B, which is doubtless the best reading. The next question that meets us is, Is λέγει used intransitively, "Are ye of opinion that the Scripture *speaks* in vain? and so does the following sentence form a separate question? or does ἡ γραφὴ λέγει introduce the following sentence in the form of a quotation? The ordinary use of λέγει and the phrase ἡ γραφὴ λέγει determine the question in favour of the transitive use, and therefore the following sentence will be the object of the verb.

Next, who is the τὸ πνεῦμα? This is at once answered if the reading κατῴκισεν is accepted, *the Spirit of God*.

What then is the meaning of πρὸς φθόνον? This will readily appear when we consider the figure introduced at the

6 μείζονα δὲ δίδωσι χάριν·
διὸ λέγει,
"'Ο Θεὸς ὑπερηφάνοις ἀντιτάσσεται,
ταπεινοῖς δὲ δίδωσι χάριν."

7 Ὑποτάγητε οὖν τῷ Θεῷ.
ἀντίστητε δὲ τῷ διαβόλῳ καὶ φεύξεται ἀφ' ὑμῶν·

6 But greater grace *the Scripture* giveth,
Because it saith:
"God haughty men opposeth,
But to humble men giveth grace."

7 Submit ye then to God,
But withstand the devil, and he shall flee from you;

commencement of this paragraph. St. James has apostrophized the Jews whom he was addressing as "adulteresses," and just as in the passages cited in the foregoing note, we find the Lord inviting the erring wife back again to allegiance and love, so St. James reminds them that though they had gone astray from God, yet the Spirit which God had made to dwell among his people desired them with jealousy; God, the jealous God, who "will not give His glory to another," saw the idolatry of His people, and longed to lead them back again.

Our last enquiry is, Are we to regard the sentence as a direct or a general quotation? Here, again, opinions are as numerous as the commentators themselves; probably that view is to be preferred that makes the sentence a compound of several well known passages, which describe the jealousy of God over His people, and His right to their obedience and love from the fact that *He dwelt* among them.

Ver. 6. δίδωσιν, *giveth*. The subject of this verb may be *God*, as the Author of Scripture, or the Spirit, which He gave His people, who is the Inspirer of Scripture, or, which is grammatically most probable, ἡ γραφή in the former verse is carried on; the sense is practically the same. The quotation that follows, which is found also in 1 Pet. v. 5, is probably taken from Prov. iii. 34; the same thought is found frequently in Scripture: see for examples Job xxii. 29; Ps. cxxxviii. 6; Matt. xxiii. 12, etc.

8 ἐγγίσατε τῷ Θεῷ, καὶ ἐγγιεῖ ὑμῖν.
καθαρίσατε χεῖρας, ἁμαρτωλοί,
καὶ ἁγνίσατε καρδίας, δίψυχοι.

9 ταλαιπωρήσατε καὶ πενθήσατε καὶ κλαύσατε·
ὁ γέλως ὑμῶν εἰς πένθος μεταστραφήτω,
καὶ ἡ χαρὰ εἰς κατήφειαν.

8 Draw nigh to God, and He shall draw nigh you,
Cleanse *your* hands, O sinners,
And purify your hearts, O double-minded.

9 Be weighed-down, and mourn and wail;
Let your laughter to mourning be turned,
And your joy into dejection.

Ver. 8. *Cleanse your hands.* This refers to "ye will," and "purify your hearts" to "ye lust" of verse 2.

δίψυχοι, *double-minded.* The reference is here again to the main figure of this paragraph. These spiritual adulterers professed to love God and serve Him, and yet were slaves to the vilest and worst sins; they were trying to effect the impossibility, the serving of God and mammon: compare Ps. xii. 2, and the Hebrew phrase בלב ולב, "with a heart and a heart." This whole passage while denouncing sin in the strongest terms, yet inculcates, and urges to, repentance. God's reproofs are always conservative; the purpose of our Father in His chastisements is corrective. These haughty sinners must be humbled, these murderers must wash away their guilty stains, and then they should find grace, and pardon, and exaltation. They had tried to attain a crown without a cross by sinful ambition, and had failed; now let them repent in dust and ashes, and God would give them a crown through the cross.

Ver. 9. ταλαιπωρήσατε, *be weighed down.* The radix of this word is τλῆμι, τλάω, hence the idea suggested is the burden of sin and a consciousness of that burden: the thought is Hebrew. Sin was regarded by the Israelite as a load, a grievous load too heavy to bear, and forgiveness was conceived of as the lifting up of the load, hence the phrase נשא עון, Is. xxxiii. 24, and compare Ps. xxxii. 1; hence I apprehend our Lord's evangelical office was so fitly described as the Lamb of God who takes away ὁ αἴρων τὴν ἁμαρτίαν, the lifter up and remover of the *intolerable* burden. The same thought underlies his well known and precious invitation, "Come unto me, all that labour and are heavy laden,"

10 ταπεινώθητε ἐνώπιον Κυρίου,
καὶ ὑψώσει ὑμᾶς.

11 Μὴ καταλαλεῖτε ἀλλήλων, ἀδελφοί·
ὁ καταλαλῶν ἀδελφοῦ ἢ κρίνων τὸν ἀδελφὸν αὐτοῦ,
καταλαλεῖ νόμου, καὶ κρίνει νόμον·
εἰ δὲ νόμον κρίνεις,
οὐκ εἶ ποιητὴς νόμου, ἀλλὰ κριτής.

10 Be humbled in the sight of the Lord,
And He will exalt you.

11 Speak not against each other, brethren,
He that speaketh against a brother, or judgeth his brother,
Speaketh against the law and judgeth the law;
But if the law thou judgest,
Thou art not a doer of the law, but a judge.

πεφορτισμένοι, Matt. xi. 28. Mark the climax in this verse, the oppression of guilt, the sorrow for guilt, and the exhibition of their sorrow.

κατήφειαν, *the casting down of the eyes*, the mark of penitence: see the description of the tax-gatherer in the temple, Luke xviii. 13.

Ver. 11. Some difficulty has been found in St. James here calling those whom he addressed as "brethren," whereas just above he had designated them as "adulteresses," as sinners, and double-minded. The difficulty, however, vanishes when we remember that he was not addressing them as Christian brethren, but Jewish brethren; the relationship was national, no more. There is also another point of view from which this mode of address may be regarded: the title "brethren" does not so much relate to them with reference to himself, but to them with reference to themselves and the connection in which they stood to each other. The word "brethren" would emphatically remind them how deeply they violated the ties of brotherhood by their unbrotherly judgment and slander of each other. It is as if he said, Speak not against one another, inasmuch as ye are brethren. This is clear from the following part of this verse. So far from this being a milder mode of expression than the epithets used re, the reproof is enhanced and the guilt made more manifest ord which reminds them of a natural duty, and that duty ed and abandoned. 'See, for a similar force of the word,

12 εἷς ἐστιν ὁ νομοθέτης καὶ κριτής,
ὁ δυνάμενος σῶσαι καὶ ἀπολέσαι·
σὺ δὲ τίς εἶ ὁ κρίνων τὸν πλησίον;

13 Ἄγε νῦν οἱ λέγοντες,
" Σήμερον ἢ αὔριον πορευσόμεθα εἰς τήνδε τὴν πόλιν,
καὶ ποιήσομεν ἐκεῖ ἐνιαυτὸν ἕνα,
καὶ ἐμπορευσόμεθα, καὶ κερδήσομεν."

12 One is the law-giver and judge,
Who is able to save and to destroy;
But who art thou that judgest *thy* neighbour?

13 Come now, ye that say,
To-day or to-morrow we will go into this city here,
And spend there a year, and trade and gain.

Luke xv. 32. The meaning of this verse seems to be this, You are all brethren under the same law, if any one of you presume to pass judgment on another, that man usurps the place of the law, and thus instead of obeying the law which governs all alike, is condemned of setting himself up against its jurisdiction.

Ver. 12. There is *one and only one* who combines in Himself the offices both of lawgiver and judge (καὶ κριτής is added in ℵ, A, B, and Vulgate), of laying down what is law, and seeing to the measure of obedience that is rendered to its demands by every one of His subjects.

Who is able to save and to destroy. See Matt. x. 28. This evidently points to the future awards of life and death: compare 2 Cor. v. 10.

Who art thou that judgest thy neighbour? The Received Text reads here, ὃς κρίνεις τὸν ἕτερον, *who art judging the other one*, but ℵ, A, B have ὁ κρίνων τὸν πλησίον; the former would imply the act simply, the latter the habit and (self-constituted) office of the judge.

Ver. 13. Another class of spiritual adulterers now presents itself to the writer's mind: Come *now* (νῦν), it is the time that I should administer a rebuke to you also who form your plans as though you had a lease of your life, and utterly disregard the overruling providence of God.

To-day or to-morrow. The reading ἤ seems preferable to καί; ℵ and B adopt the former, followed by the Vulgate and Syriac; A the latter. The former describes the careless security of the

14 οἵτινες οὐκ ἐπίστασθε τὸ τῆς αὔριον·
ποία ἡ ζωὴ ὑμῶν;
(ἀτμὶς γάρ ἐστε) ἡ πρὸς ὀλίγον φαινομένη,
ἔπειτα καὶ ἀφανιζομένη·

14 And yet ye know not the *hap* of the morrow;
For what is your life?
(For ye are a vapour) that for a little while appeareth,
Then disappeareth also.

speaker, To-day we will do this, or if we should find it will suit us best, to-morrow. The latter, the presumed certainty of life; The going to this city will take two days, to-day and to-morrow we will execute the journey.

This city, τήνδε τὴν πόλιν; *this city here.* Generally explained to be the city under the speaker's consideration; but if we remember that St. James was at Jerusalem, and that he was writing from that place to the twelve tribes scattered abroad, he would naturally be putting himself in their position, purposing to come up to this city where he dwelt, for the prosecution of their business; the doom which he knew to be impending over the city would add to the uncertainty of their plans and the folly of their boastings.

Spend a year. Almost equivalent to our common phrase, "make a year of it." This suggests the thought that the supposed speakers promised themselves many years of life, health, and prosperity: compare Is. lvi. 12, and the parable in St. Luke xii. 16-21.

ἕνα is omitted in ℵ, and B, and Vulgate.

Great varieties are found in the form of the verbs in this verse, the difference consisting in the choice between o and ω, that is, between the future indicative and the aorist subjunctive. In the former case we have the self reliant determination of the speakers brought out most forcibly. This reading in all the verbs is best. Out of the four verbs ℵ has 1, 3, 4 in the future indicative and 2 in the aorist subjunctive; A has 1, 2 in the aorist subjunctive and 3, 4 in the future indicative; B has all four in the future indicative. The Vulgate also has the future throughout.

Ver. 14. οἵτινες, *and yet ye.* Containing a delicate irony: Ye who settle on your plans thus are ignorant of what will happen on the morrow.

τὸ τῆς αὔριον, *the of the morrow.* The ellipsis may be filled up with such words as *circumstances, misfortunes, evils, incidents,* or the like.

15 ἀντὶ τοῦ λέγειν ὑμᾶς,
"'Ἐὰν ὁ Κύριος θελήσῃ, καὶ ζήσομεν,
καὶ ποιήσομεν τοῦτο ἢ ἐκεῖνο."

16 νῦν δὲ καυχᾶσθε ἐν ταῖς ἀλαζονείαις ὑμῶν·
πᾶσα καύχησις τοιαύτη πονηρά ἐστιν.

17 εἰδότι οὖν καλὸν ποιεῖν,
καὶ μὴ ποιοῦντι,
ἁμαρτία αὐτῷ ἐστιν.

15 Instead of your saying,
 "If the Lord will, we shall both live,
 And do this or that."
16 But now ye boast in your vauntings;
 Every such boasting is wicked.
17 To *the man* therefore that knows to do good,
 And *yet* doeth it not,
 Sin to him there is.

(ἀτμὶς γάρ ἐστε.) There is a great variety in the readings of this place: א omits the words altogether; A reads ἔσται, which some think the same, by a frequent clerical error, as ἐστε, but the future was more likely intended to convey a prediction of their being suddenly cut off in the impending disaster of Jerusalem, compare chap. v. 1-3; B has ἐστε, *ye are a vapour*, not their life only but themselves, compare chap. i. 10; 1 Pet. i. 24. The Vulgate supports the common reading, the Syriac that of B.

ἡ φαινομένη, ἀφανιζ. Mark the use of the article with participle, showing the nature of such a vapour. The reading of καί instead of δέ in the last clause is attested by א, A, B, and the Vulgate.

Ver. 15. The reading of the future indicative in the verbs ζήσομεν, ποιήσομεν, instead of the aorist subjective, is found in א, A, B; the Vulgate supposes the ἐάν to have been repeated, "Si Dominus voluerit; et; si vixerimus, faciemus hoc."

Ver. 17. The force of this closing moral seems to be this: You know, if you will but ponder on the subject, the uncertainty of life, and your entire dependence on the providence of God, and yet ye vaunt as though all things were in your own power, and at your own disposal. You know what is right and yet do wrong, and so are convicted of sin.

CHAPTER V.

1 Ἄγε νῦν οἱ πλούσιοι,
κλαύσατε ὀλολύζοντες
ἐπὶ ταῖς ταλαιπωρίαις ὑμῶν ταῖς ἐπερχομέναις.

2 ὁ πλοῦτος ὑμῶν σέσηπε,
καὶ τὰ ἱμάτια ὑμῶν σητόβρωτα γέγονεν·

1 Come now, ye rich men,
Weep ye and howl
At your woe-burdens that are coming on.

2 Your riches are rotted,
And your garments become moth-eaten.

Ver. 1. ἄγε νῦν. The νῦν is emphatic, as in chap. iv. 13, "*Now* it is time you should weep," etc. Probably the text in St. James' mind was Is. xiii. 6, where the prophet denounces the judgments that should be executed in the day of the Lord; the parallelism between these utterances of the Old and New Testament prophets is unmistakable, compare verse 8.

πλούσιοι, *rich*. See note on chap. i. 9.

ταλαιπωρίαις, *woe-burdens*. See chap. iv. 9. There he bade them be weighed down, ταλαιπωρήσατε, with penitential sorrow, to mourn and *wail*, κλαύσατε. It would seem that with prophetic eye he foresaw they would not listen to the warning voice, and so with piercing irony he reverts to the charge he had given them, and takes up the very words he had uttered before: Ye would not bend under the burden of penitence, but a burden of woe shall weigh you down and crush you. Ye would not wail for sin, but ye shall for suffering. Ye would not mourn and sigh for your iniquities, but ye shall howl in your despair and destruction.

ταῖς ἐπερ., *that are coming on* (*you*). The rapidly approaching ruin of Jerusalem, and the sufferings of the Jewish people throughout the world, as foretold by our Lord, were here before the writer's mind.

Ver. 2. ὁ πλοῦτος. This passage is evidently built upon our Lord's words, Matt. vi. 19, 20: They would lay up treasure on the earth

3 ὁ χρυσὸς ὑμῶν καὶ ὁ ἄργυρος κατίωται,
καὶ ὁ ἰὸς αὐτῶν εἰς μαρτύριον ὑμῖν ἔσται,
καὶ φάγεται τὰς σάρκας ὑμῶν ὡς πῦρ·
ἐθησαυρίσατε ἐν ἐσχάταις ἡμέραις.

4 ἰδοὺ ὁ μισθὸς τῶν ἐργατῶν
τῶν ἀμησάντων τὰς χώρας ὑμῶν,
ὁ ἀφυστερημένος ἀφ᾽ ὑμῶν, κράζει·
καὶ αἱ βοαὶ τῶν θερισάντων
εἰς τὰ ὦτα Κυρίου Σαβαὼθ εἰσεληλύθασιν,

3 Your gold and silver are rusted,
And their rust for witness against you shall be,
And shall eat your flesh like fire,
Ye stored-up in the last days.

4 Lo! the wages of the workmen
That mowed your fields,
Which is held back *from them* by you, clamoureth;
And the cries of the reapers
Into the ears of Jehovah Sabaoth have entered.

instead of in heaven, and lo, the treasure itself is fading and perishing under the blight of a curse. Mark the perfects σέσηπεν and γέγονεν, the prophetic preterite so frequent in the Old Testament predictions. God's purposes, though future in their execution, are so certain that they are spoken of in the past tense.

Ver. 3. ὁ χρυσός. It is advanced that gold is not subject to the action of rust, hence various ways of explaining this passage have been invented, such as a moral sense of the word "rusted:" in God's sight your gold is corroded; or a material explanation, such as, the vessels referred to were of base metal, gilt with gold only. But prophetic declamation not unfrequently delights in such rebukes as involve the unexpected or impossible; the very impossibility according to man's mind heightens the picture, and shows how dim the gold has become, how reprobate the silver, and how unlooked for, and consequently severe, the punishment.

φάγεται. The Hellenistic form of the future φαγήσεται. See Luke xiv. 15; xvii. 8; Jno. ii. 17; Rev. xvii. 16.

ἐν, *in the last days.* Not *against*, or *for*, but that particular period, when earthly wealth can be of no profit.

Ver. 4. ἀφ᾽ ὑμῶν. A difficulty has been found in the use of this preposition. Some grammarians, refusing to allow that ἀπό can be employed in any sense as an equivalent for ὑπό, connect the preposition with the following word κράζει, *crieth out from you,*

5 ἐτρυφήσατε ἐπὶ τῆς γῆς, καὶ ἐσπαταλήσατε·
ἐθρέψατε τὰς καρδίας ὑμῶν ἐν ἡμέρῃ σφαγῆς.

5 Ye lived-deliciously in the land, and wantoned;
Ye fed-up your hearts in a day of slaughter.

that is, from the treasury where you have secured the ill-gotten gain; *crieth out for judgment.* Others regard the preposition as denoting that the *act proceeded* from these men, and that the act is fairly represented by ἀπό. See Luke ix. 22. This is perhaps the best explanation. See Winer's *Gk. Gram.*, p. 389, Note. The Sinaitic MS. reads here ἀφυστερημένος in place of the Received ἀπεστ.

Κυρίου Σαβαώθ, *the Lord*, *i.e.*, *Jehovah Sabaoth.* The Hebrew word Sabaoth is retained here as in Rom. ix. 29; in the latter it is in a direct quotation; in St. James probably in a reference to Mal. iii. 15.

There is great difficulty in explaining this word, though it is familiar to us in the Old Testament under the translation "Hosts." (1) It may be that all created worlds, the armies of the skies, are intended; this is clearly the case where the word occurs for the first time, Gen. ii. 1. (2) It may refer to the armies of Israel which are called צבאות יהוה, "the hosts of the Lord," Ex. xii. 41. (3) It may comprehend both; in the sense that whatever things are created, whatever powers there be, whether in heaven or earth, material or immaterial, angelic or human, Jehovah is God of them all. In all these cases the phrase יהוה צבאות is explained to be equivalent to יהוה אלהי צבאות, "*Jehovah God* of hosts." (4) It is, however, far more likely that this word is a title of Jehovah, placed in apposition, explanatory of the *executive* omnipotency of the Divine Being. As *Elohim* represents the *source* and *seat* of omnipotence, so *Sabaoth* represents all the *manifestations* of the majesty and mightiness of God. It is to be noticed that this title of God, *Jehovah Sabaoth, Lord of Hosts*, is not found in the books of Moses, Joshua, Judges, or Ruth. It appears first in the books of Samuel; it does not occur in Ezekiel; it is abundantly frequent in the Jehovistic psalms and the minor prophets.

St. James evidently employs the phrase in this place to remind them of the power of God whom they were provoking, and of the executive character of that power. The passage to which he refers, indeed almost quotes, is Mal. iii. 15, as observed by Bishop Wordsworth, where the *Lord of Hosts* is spoken of as coming to judgment against those that *oppress the hireling in his wages;* the passage is rendered by the LXX., τοὺς ἀποστεροῦντας μισθὸν μισθωτοῦ.

Ver. 5. St. James' words here are of a highly tragical character, and therefore the sentences are brief, abrupt, concise, and broken; the graphic metaphor reminds us in style of the outpourings of Hosea. The difficulty here, as in other examples of the same kind of composition, is to catch the logical relation of the thoughts expressed, and trace out the consecutiveness of the clauses. He had charged them with laying up riches *in the last days*. There his purpose was to point out their folly with reference to the *time* in which they were engaged in their ungodly gain. Now he proceeds to show *where* they were doing this, in the *land*, the land of Israel, which was on the very point of being given over to the avenger. In the former chapter the visiting of the city by the rich for the purposes of gain has been adverted to, now he supposes them upon the spot, and the day of vengeance at hand. Jerusalem was the central spot on which the thunderbolt was about to fall that would paralyze all Israel, Hebrews and Hellenists. As a matter of history it is well known that vast numbers of the dispersion were involved in the catastrophe of the holy city. This passage, however, though addressed to, and by direct implication comprising the dispersion, yet evidently conveys a prophetic warning and denunciation against the whole family of Israel, on whom the judgment was about to descend.

ἐτρυφήσατε. This word describes the luxury and carnal delights in which they revelled; ἐσπαταλήσατε, the squandering and dissolute expenditure by which this selfish indulgence was gratified.

The interpretation of the following words is attended with some difficulty. Some interpreters take σφαγῆς in the sense of *sacrifice*, and explain the meaning to be that these devoted ones feasted and rejoiced as though it were a day of religious observance and festivity. Others, explaining σφαγῆς as *slaughter*, think that such a day is described as that of Nabal's feast, 1 Sam. xxv.; see *v.* 11; or such as that depicted in the parable of the marriage feast, "My oxen and my fatlings are killed," Matt. xxii. 4. This seems to be the view of the Syriac Version.

These interpretations are to a great extent based on the Received Text, which inserts ὡς before ἐν, but this particle of comparison is not found in ℵ, A, and B, or the Vulgate. The nervous and unconnected sentences must not lead us to suppose that there is no link between the thoughts expressed. It would seem that St. James employs here a biting satire: In these last days, in this devoted land ye feed up your hearts, but it is a day of slaughter; "the days of vengeance," when ye shall fall by the edge of the sword: compare Jer. xii. 3; xxv. 34. The rendering of the Vulgate seems to favour this interpretation, "in die occisionis." The next sentence reminds us of the mad cry of the crucifiers of Christ, "His blood be on us and on our children."

6 κατεδικάσατε, ἐφονεύσατε τὸν Δίκαιον·
οὐκ ἀντιτάσσεται ὑμῖν.

6 Ye condemned, ye murdered the Just One,
He is not opposing you.

Why is this doom awaiting you, why? Ye condemned, ye murdered the Just One; therefore all this is coming on you.

He is not opposing you. You are left to yourselves, to fill up the measure of your iniquities, but when the cup is full, then the judgment will fall upon you.

Ver. 6. τὸν Δίκαιον, *the Just One.* There can be no doubt that the Messiah is referred to under this well known title. David, in Ps. xxxiv. 19, had prophesied about the trials and deliverance of the *Righteous One,* צדיק, where the reference to our Lord is made clear by the following verse, " He keepeth all his bones, not one of them is broken," which was so signally fulfilled at the crucifixion, see Jno. xix. 36. Isaiah, chap. liii. 11, entitles Messiah the "*Righteous* Servant" of the Lord. In Jer. xxiii. 6 He is called " Jehovah our *Righteousness,*" and the same title is repeated in chap. xxxiii. 16; the " she shall be called " should be in our language *it,* referring to "the branch of righteousness," regarded as a composite feminine subject; for, though צמח *branch* is masculine, צדקה *righteousness* is feminine, and hence the whole phrase is viewed so, and thus the two passages will be really at one in their reference to the coming King. In the New Testament the epithet δίκαιος, *righteous* or *just,* seems to have been a familiar synonym of the Messiah. The centurion at the foot of the cross evidently employed it in this meaning, for according to St. Luke xxiii. 47 he cried, Ὄντως ὁ ἄνθρωπος οὗτος δίκαιος ἦν, truly this man was *Just,* used as a proper name, or almost so; whereas, according to St. Matthew's account, his confession was, " this man was the Son of God." In the Acts we frequently meet with this title: see chap. iii. 10; vii. 52. This is an important text, as the Jews are there charged with being the murderers, φονεῖς, of the *Just One;* the very sin that is charged on them here, and the same words are employed : see again Acts xxii. 14; 1 Pet. iii. 18; 1 Jno. ii. 1. In the two last named texts the word is used as a proper name without the article as here. Probably St. James made choice of this title to bring this attribute of our Lord into sharp contradistinction to their injustice in wronging the labourer of his hire, at the same time reminding them that though the Lord did not interfere with this generation which was given over to destruction, yet He was, and would prove eventually, the " Righteous Judge." See Hosea iv. 17; Matt. xxiii. 32-38.

7 Μακροθυμήσατε οὖν, ἀδελφοί,
ἕως τῆς παρουσίας τοῦ Κυρίου.
ἰδοὺ ὁ γεωργὸς ἐκδέχεται τὸν τίμιον καρπὸν τῆς γῆς,
μακροθυμῶν ἐπ' αὐτῷ,
ἕως λάβῃ (ὑετὸν) πρώϊμον καὶ ὄψιμον·

8 μακροθυμήσατε καὶ ὑμεῖς,
στηρίξατε τὰς καρδίας ὑμῶν,
ὅτι ἡ παρουσία τοῦ Κυρίου ἤγγικε.

7 Be-long-patient therefore, brethren,
Until the presence of the Lord.
Lo! the farmer waits for the precious fruit of the land,
Being long patient over it,
Until it receive (rain) the early and latter.

8 Be ye also long-patient.
Fortify your hearts,
Because the presence of the Lord is nigh.

Ver. 7. St. James here turns from the unbelieving section of his readers to those that believed and had accepted Jesus as their Messiah, and were expecting His prophecies to be fulfilled.

Long patience, the grace of self-restraint based upon faith and hope, and the assurance that God will avenge His own elect. This curb upon the outburstings of a rebellious impetuosity, and check to the frettings of anxiety, is constantly insisted on in Holy Writ.

οὖν, *therefore.* Seeing that the cries of the oppressed have entered into the ears of the Lord, seeing that the condemnation of your enemies lingereth not, have you, brethren, my brethren, both in the flesh and in the Lord, long patience up to the time which is the expectation and object of longing of the believers in the Gospel, the personal advent and presence of the Lord, the Lord Jesus. Ὁ Κύριος is the frequent title of our Lord in the New Testament. In this Epistle it is so used in chap. i. 1; ii. 1.

παρουσίας. Not merely *coming*, but actual personal presence. The reign of righteousness and truth in the age to come will not consist in a spiritual influence shed abroad by an unseen power as now, but in the visible glory of the King of kings, dispensing His laws and scattering His blessings over a regenerate and rejoicing world. St. James, like the rest of the inspired writers, speaks of the winding up of God's dealings with mankind and the establishment of the kingdom to come as near at hand. This is perfectly consistent. Our Lord told His disciples that none knew that day, neither man nor angel, nor was it a part of the commission He had received to impart the exact dates of times and seasons: see Mark xiii. 32. After His resurrection He replied to His inquisitive disciples that it was not theirs to know the times or the seasons which the Father had put in His own power: see Acts i. 7. And throughout St. Paul's Epistles we trace the evidences of the same retention of the great secret, for the apostle always speaks of the day as imminent, and of the quick at the return of Jesus Christ as "*we* which are alive."

How far in the midst of this unrevealed mystery the inspired writers in their own minds associated or dissociated the final judgment with or from, the destruction of Jerusalem, it may be difficult to say. The type and antitype might form one common completion, or one be held to be, as it is in fact, a prelude to the other, or a promissory fulfilment of an event, which will only be fully exhausted when time shall give place to eternity.

ὁ γεωργός. As our Lord, the Great Teacher, constantly borrowed illustrations of the work of grace from the teachings of Nature, so St. James abounds in pictures painted from the same original; the withering grass, the surging sea, the gushing fountain, the olive and fig trees, the land, the rain, furnish material for the exposition of doctrine or duty. Here the husbandman appears upon the scene, he has sown his seed, it is precious and valuable, he waits and watches through its various stages of growth, his patient expectation of hope rests on the harvest day; the graphic pen delineates him as though he were standing over his corn-fields, and exercising an intent and patient gaze upon the rising crop until it should receive those great necessaries to fertility, the early and the latter rain. καρπός is the best subject for λάβῃ.

(*Rain*) *the early and the latter*. There is a peculiar variety of readings in this passage. The Received Text, which has ὑετόν before πρώιμον, is supported by Α, Κ, L, and the Syriac; Β, and the Vulgate omit the word, and א has καρπόν, *fruit*, instead of ὑετόν, *rain*. The early rain, the יורה of the Old Testament, fell in the autumn, and by softening and fertilizing the soil rendered it fit for the reception of the seed. The latter rain, מלקוש, fell in the spring, perfecting the full development of the corn. The interval which seems to have occurred between the two rain-seasons, and to be predicted as to occur again in the future, is not now marked by any regular cessation of downfall, but the whole period from October to March is characterized by stormy weather in greater or less degree.

9 Μὴ στενάζετε κατ' ἀλλήλων, ἀδελφοί,
ἵνα μὴ κριθῆτε·
ἰδοὺ ὁ κριτὴς πρὸ τῶν θυρῶν ἔστηκεν.
10 Ὑπόδειγμα λάβετε ἀδελφοί μου τῆς κακοπαθείας,
καὶ τῆς μακροθυμίας,
τοὺς προφήτας οἳ ἐλάλησαν τῷ ὀνόματι Κυρίου.
11 ἰδοὺ μακαρίζομεν τοὺς ὑπομείναντας.
τὴν ὑπομονὴν Ἰὼβ ἠκούσατε,
καὶ τὸ τέλος Κυρίου εἴδετε,
ὅτι πολύσπλαγχνός ἐστιν ὁ Κύριος καὶ οἰκτίρμων.

9 Complain not against one another, brethren,
That ye be not judged;
Lo! the judge before the doors standeth.
10 *As* example take, my brethren, of sore-suffering and long-patience,
The prophets, who spoke in the name of the Lord.
11 Lo! we deem them blessed that endured.
The endurance of Job ye heard of,
And the end of the Lord ye saw
That very-tender-hearted is the Lord and merciful.

Ver. 9. We are here reminded of the sermon on the mount, Matt. vii. 1, to which this Epistle bears a striking resemblance in many places. This passage appears also to give a further expansion to chap. iv. 1; there the speaking evil of one another is condemned, here the grumbling and complaining against one another.

κριθῆτε is the reading of ℵ, A, B.

Ver. 10. St. James now turns to another argument, to enforce the duty of patient endurance, namely, the ills and woes to which their forefathers, the prophets, had been subjected. We cannot but call to mind the words of our blessed Lord as recorded in Matt. xxiii. 29-39, words so applicable to the oppressors of this period. St. Stephen's speech before the Sanhedrim, Acts. vii. 52, forms a connecting link between the utterances of our Lord and these words of St. James: You are, says he, the rightful and legitimate successors of these servants of the Most High, inheritors of their graces, their calling, their sufferings, and their hopes. "Stemmata quid faciunt," Juvenal might say, *Sat.* viii. 1, but the remembrance of such a pedigree would nerve to the suffering of sorrows, and give assurance of the crown in reversion.

Ver. 11. ὑπομείναντας, *that endured.* This is the reading

of א, A, B; of the Syriac and the Vulgate, *qui sustinuerunt*, and is preferable to the reading of the Received Text, ὑπομένοντας, *that endure*. The connection between this clause and the following one is rendered more clear: "We deem them blessed that endured;" and out of this company of confessors we single Job as a type of the class who suffered and yet were saved. We canonize these worthies of old time; let then their example be a strength to us in the hour of our trial and temptation. We are forcibly reminded again of the sermon on the mount, Matt. v. 11, 12, where the persecution of the prophets is instanced, as in this place, to encourage and console those that are persecuted for Christ's sake.

Two questions of some interest may receive some amount of light from this reference to the patriarch Job in this place. It has been constantly held by orthodox interpreters that the mention of Job in our Epistle, and in the 14th chapter of Ezekiel, establishes the fact of his real historical existence, and refutes the theory of his mythical character and fabulous existence, as taught first by Samuel Bar Nachman and Hai Gaon, and perhaps Maimonides, amongst the Jews, and followed by many Christian commentators: but, secondly, the antiquity of Job and the date of his history (a subject which has been even more vigorously disputed) may be remotely referred to and probably elucidated. St. James, in treating of a class, and in exhibiting an example of that class, would most likely select the *first* instance that held a prominent place in the pages of the Bible. Surely, if Job had lived in the days of the captivity, as Umbreit and others teach, he would not have been so fitted for our author's purpose, as many others besides them had passed through the same waters of affliction and had reached the same shore of safety. The same remark is applicable to the theory of Ewald and Renan, that Job flourished in the time of Manasseh. Perhaps the most popular opinion at the present day is that espoused by the learned pen of Professor Delitzsch, that this book is the product of the Solomonic period. Without entering on the arguments adduced from the *wisdom-character* of the book, we may say that David would have furnished St. James with an equally good example to illustrate his teaching; we are thus pushed back to the earliest days of Hebrew history, and whether we adopt the belief that the book of the great sufferer was edited by Moses, as the Talmud teaches, as Origen and Jerome held, and as in modern times has been elaborated by Professor Lee, or whether we entertain the opinion that this chronicle was the actual writing of Job himself, as Schultens believes, or was the compilation of Elihu from the facts his eyes witnessed, we may at all events find some ground for assigning the remotest date to the lifetime of the patriarch from the circumstance that St. James made choice of him to represent the fatherhood of the suffering, as St. Paul did Abraham to represent the fatherhood of the faithful.

εἴδετε, *ye saw*. The Alexandrine MS. reads here ἴδετε, the imperative mood, which is favoured by Alford, Lange, and others, but the received reading has the support of א, B, the Syriac, and the Vulgate; the sense is more natural and connected, and the imperative at the end of the sentence would be, to say the least, out of its proper place.

The end of the Lord, τὸ τέλος Κυρίου. The almost universally adopted explanation of these words is, the end which the Lord gave Job, that is, prosperity, after all his troubles, making Κυρίου the genitive of the cause. The older interpretation is, however, much to be preferred, which makes *the end*, τὸ τέλος, to refer to the completed work and sufferings of the Lord Himself, for (1) τοῦ Κυρίου has only just dropped from the writer's pen, *v.* 7, as a title of the Lord Jesus, and therefore it is but consistent the same title should have here the same attribution. (2) In *v.* 11 the context speaks of those who endured in the plural, whereas if the whole illustration refers to Job only, we have but one example of the enduring. (3) The end endured by the Lord would properly be set in opposition to the charge contained in the 6th verse of the Jews having condemned and murdered the Just One. (4) Christ's mercy was especially manifested in His sufferings endured for us: see 1 Pet. ii. 19-25 for an expansion of the teaching of this passage; hence the following clause will harmonize with this interpretation. (5) Lastly, if viewed chronologically all will fall into order : Job was the first great sufferer, himself a type, in his humiliation, sufferings, and triumph ; Christ was the last great sufferer, the antitype stooping from heaven, bearing the cross, and exalted to glory. Between the type and the antitype is included the whole race of those who have endured and prevailed. The word τέλος, *end*, must not be limited to our familiar use of the word as denoting finality, termination, etc., but in connection with St. James' use of the kindred adjective and verb as implying *completion, fulfilment, viz.*, of Christ's work and office and ministry on earth ; all these were marked with suffering and patient abiding under afflictions. Hence we cannot doubt that St. James here, like St. Peter in the parallel passage referred to above, sets before us the Divine exemplar as the great model for our imitation.

πολύσπλαγχνος. This word is not found anywhere else. εὔσπλαγχνος is used by St. Paul, Eph. iv. 32, and by St. Peter, 1 Pet. iii. 8. πολύσπλ. is evidently a literal rendering of the Hebrew רַב־חֶסֶד, *great in mercy*, and affords a beautiful illustration of the elasticity of the Greek language to compound in one word a great wealth of thought.

12 Πρὸ πάντων δέ, ἀδελφοί μου, μὴ ὀμνύετε
μήτε τὸν οὐρανὸν, μήτε τὴν γῆν, μήτε ἄλλον τινὰ
ὅρκον·
ἤτω δὲ ὑμῶν τὸ ναὶ, ναὶ, καὶ τὸ οὒ, οὔ·
ἵνα μὴ ὑπὸ κρίσιν πέσητε.

13 Κακοπαθεῖ τις ἐν ὑμῖν; προσευχέσθω·
εὐθυμεῖ τις; ψαλλέτω.

12 But above all things, my brethren, swear not,
Either by the heaven or the earth, or any other oath,
But let your yea be yea, and your nay, nay,
That under judgment ye fall not.

13 In sore-suffering-is any one among you? let him pray.
Rejoicing is any one? let him sing-praise.

Ver. 12. St. James here proceeds to give a few final exhortations which he felt were necessary for those whom he was addressing. In the first injunction, "swear not," we are carried back once more to the sermon on the mount, Matt. v. 34, 35, where the same command is given almost *verbatim*. It would seem that this dehortation was suggested by the natural tendency of man to break out under provocation and ill-treatment; the following verse evidently refers back to the 10th verse, so that it is impossible to suppose, as some commentators do, that there is no connection between this verse and the preceding context.

This swearing comprises not only imprecatory language, but also that strange medley of oaths which the Jews, it would appear from the more diffuse passage in St. Matthew, were in the habit of using, a habit still in painful prevalence among that nation. It has been observed by a host of commentators on these two passages that swearing in the name of God is not mentioned, nor are judicial oaths forbidden, see Art. XXXIX. of the Church of England. It is the rash invocation of some created object, and therefore involves idolatry. Every oath must be based upon an appeal to the Great Infallible, and consequently creature-oaths are a violation of the first and great commandment.

ὑπὸ κρίσιν. This is the reading of ℵ, A, B, Syriac, and Vulgate, which is far preferable to the reading of the Received Text, εἰς ὑπόκρισιν.

Ver. 13. κακοπαθεῖ. This returns to the subject of *sore-suffering* he has been already treating of above. Our afflictions and persecutions should not produce in us the bitter fruits of

14 ἀσθενεῖ τις ἐν ὑμῖν;
προσκαλεσάσθω τοὺς πρεσβυτέρους τῆς ἐκκλησίας,
καὶ προσευξάσθωσαν ἐπ' αὐτόν,
ἀλείψαντες αὐτὸν ἐλαίῳ ἐν τῷ ὀνόματι τοῦ Κυρίου.

14 In sickness-is any one among you?
Let him call to *him* the elders of the church,
And let them pray over him,
Anointing him with oil in the name of the Lord.

dejection and despair, much less of passion and swearing, but lead us to the cross in prayer for ourselves, that we may have grace to bear the burden, and that God in His own good time, when His purposes of chastisement are perfected, would lighten and remove the pressure; and for our enemies, that God would have mercy upon them, and " turn their hearts."

Is any one rejoicing? let him sing praise. ψάλλειν primarily signifies to pull or twang with the fingers, hence to play on a stringed instrument, as a harp, etc.; afterwards it was used of singing an accompaniment to a harp; the cognate noun ψαλμός has passed through the same stages, and finally given us *psalm*. St. James here gives directions to true and consistent Christians in all ages. Our joy is not to be manifested in worldly revelling and carnal licentiousness, but in praising God for his goodness, and so making each season of joy a prelude of our heavenly occupation, where endless joy will call forth endless praise.

Ver. 14. This verse has a special interest belonging to it, which would never have existed had not the Church of Rome founded mainly upon this basis the sacrament of extreme unction. The best way of investigating the question will be to examine fairly and faithfully what is the literal and plain teaching of the words before us, and then state what is the doctrine and practice of the Roman Catholic Church on this subject.

The central point is the sick man. St. James teaches that it is his duty to call to him the elders of the church; these, doubtless, were the recognized ministers of the Gospel. See especially the use of this word in the closely allied Epistle of St. Peter, 1 Pet. v. 1-5. It may be an open question whether the plural is here to be enforced, and that, so to speak, a rubric is laid down directing the presence of more than one elder, that the joint prayer might be lifted up for a blessing.

τῆς ἐκκλησίας, of course, means that particular portion of the one church of which the patient was a member. In that early day there was no schism in the body.

15 καὶ ἡ εὐχὴ τῆς πίστεως σώσει τὸν κάμνοντα,
καὶ ἐγερεῖ αὐτὸν ὁ Κύριος·
κἂν ἁμαρτίας ᾖ πεποιηκώς,
ἀφεθήσεται αὐτῷ.

15 And their prayer of faith shall save the sufferer,
And the Lord shall raise him up;
And if he be having committed sins,
Forgiveness shall be granted him.

When come to the sick man, their duty was to pray *over* the sufferer, this is clearly the force of ἐπί here; leaning over him they were to raise the prayer of intercession on his behalf. With this outpouring of prayer is united an action, "anointing him with olive-oil in the name of the Lord." To what purpose was this? There are two passages in the New Testament which lend their aid to throw light on this question. St. Mark, vi. 13, relates the mission of the twelve, and they are stated to have "anointed with oil many that were sick and healed them." The other passage is Luke x. 34, where we find the good Samaritan pouring on the wounds of the unfortunate traveller oil and wine. Nothing can be more evident than that the wine was employed medicinally, to wash out the corruption and prevent mortification, and the oil was applied to mollify the wound, to keep out the air, and promote healing. In both passages oil is a remedial agent; this is also mentioned by Isaiah, i. 6, and ancient physicians and writers, it is needless to say, prescribe or mention the application of oil as a healing medicine, not only for wounds but for other ailments. There can be no doubt that the prescription before us has the same purpose. Thus viewed, St. James enjoins the elders to use the prayer of faith, and at the same time to employ the means, the ordinary means, of medical science and treatment. The whole process was to be performed in the name of the Lord, their trust was to be placed, not in the instrumentality employed, but in the Lord. No means can be salutary unless He vouchsafes the blessing.

Ver. 15. *The prayer of faith,* ἡ εὐχὴ τῆς πίστεως, brings before us an additional feature. At this period of Christianity miraculous powers were dispensed to the church; "gifts of healing" are enumerated amongst these by St. Paul, 1 Cor. xii. 9. The prayer of faith is the prayer that springs from the inner and inspired assurance that the miracle will be wrought. We are next told that this prayer of faith shall *save* the sick, σώσει; this salvation in its first aspect refers certainly to the body of the sufferer: see for such use of the cognate verb, Matt. ix. 22; Mark vi. 56, etc.

It is worthy of our notice that the success of the administration is not attributed to the oil, but to the prayer of faith as the instrument, and to the Lord as the real agent, "the Lord shall raise him up." The text continues, "and if he be having committed sins," ᾖ πεποιηκώς; the form of the expression seems to imply that the visitation of sickness was consequent upon sin, and therefore in the healing of the body there was involved also a healing of the soul. As when our Lord said to the palsied, "Thy sins are forgiven thee;" and afterwards argued with the Pharisees, " Which is the easier, to say, Thy sins are forgiven thee, or to say, Rise up and walk? but that ye may know that the Son of man hath power upon earth to forgive sins, he said unto the sick of the palsy, I say unto thee, Arise, and take up thy couch, and go into thine house," Luke v. 20-24, thus showing by the outward evidence of restoration to health the inner and invisible miracle of pardon and salvation. So here the prayer of faith shall be accepted for his bodily disease, and also for his soul's malady, "the Lord shall raise him up... remission shall be his."

Notwithstanding this evident meaning of the passage, these words have been laid as the foundation of the practice of extreme unction in the Church of Rome, which ordinance is numbered amongst her seven sacraments. It is most probable that while the gifts of healing were continued to the church of Christ the outward application of oil was employed as an outward sign and means whereby health might be restored, but such medicinal use was had recourse to for the express purpose of *recovering* the patient; the σώσει in our passage is sufficient to prove this. It is the prayer of faith that shall restore the sufferer. The teaching of the Church of Rome is quite opposed to this; the ordinance is held to be of an entirely spiritual character as a benefit to the soul; indeed, so far from being viewed as a healing agency, it is never administered till all hopes of amendment have vanished, and the sick man is in the very article of death, and no food is permitted to be received after the rite; the oil used is consecrated by a bishop, and the form of administration is the application of the oil to the five senses of the sufferer, with the words, "Per hanc sacram unctionem, et suam piissimam misericordiam indulgeat tibi Deus quicquid peccasti, per visum, auditum, olfactum, gustum, et tactum," the word proper to each sense being uttered as the organ of each sense is anointed.

There is very slight foundation for this practice. No writer of antiquity mentions it. We search in vain till we come to the fifth century before we find any notice of this ordinance; the first mention of it is in a letter of Pope Innocent I. to Decentius, Bishop of Eugubium; the question that had been proposed for solution was whether the sick might be anointed with the oil of *chrism*, and whether the bishop might perform that office. To which he replied that the words of St. James in this place apply to the faithful who are sick, and that they may be anointed with the chrism, and that this may be used not only by priests, but by all Christians, both for themselves and their friends, and that the bishop who made the chrism might as a matter of course use it.

It is observable that the oil here referred to was not the ordinary oil-olive now in use in the Church of Rome, but the oil of chrism, which from early times, it is well known, was in use in connection with baptism, confirmation, and ordination; and that if this chrism had been from the first employed in extreme unction no bishop would have had occasion to write to another bishop such a letter of inquiry, and that no bishop would have made such a reply, as all sacramental rites legitimately established must have been well known among the higher clergy, to say the least. The conceded use of the chrism for private use by the laity is a corollary proof of the association of its use with medicinal treatment. No further reference to this subject is found for a long interval. The ritual lore of the succeeding centuries contains no evidence in favour of this rite. The deaths of saints, when related, are not stated to have been comforted with this *viaticum*, but by that of the Eucharist.

It has been alleged that the Sacramentary of Gregory, A.D. 590, contained an office for this ordinance, but this assertion is without foundation in fact. Daniel in his *Codex Liturgicus*, says distinctly that the old MSS. of the Gregorian Sacramentary do not contain the services for unction. The first MS. that has anything of this sort is ascribed to the ninth or tenth century, and seems to have belonged to a monastery in Rheims. Another, that belonged to a monastery at Corbei, was said to contain nothing that did not belong to Gregory, and was published by the Benedictines as the genuine work of that author, but Daniel says, "multa continet quæ Gregorium auctorem nequaquam agnoscunt," Vol I., 9, 309.

The custom, to whatever extent it prevailed, which seems to have been very circumscribed, appears to have retained its original character of *materia medica*, it was not till the twelfth century that it was called or treated as *extrema unctio*. Seven centuries passed away between Innocent I. and his namesake the third at that period before mention is made of the rite in a sacramental character. The failure of the process to restore bodily health doubtless prompted the teaching that it healed the soul; the oil was applied at this mediæval period to the portions of the body that were afflicted by the disease; after this had obtained for a while, the schoolmen dogmatized on the subject, and the Council of Florence, A.D. 1439, established the rite, and the Council of Trent, A.D. 1551, passed four canons to ratify its

16 Ἐξομολογεῖσθε οὖν ἀλλήλοις τὰς ἁμαρτίας,
καὶ εὔχεσθε ὑπὲρ ἀλλήλων, ὅπως ἰαθῆτε.
πολὺ ἰσχύει δέησις δικαίου ἐνεργουμένη.

16 Confess therefore to one another your sins,
And pray for one another to be healed,·
Of much avail is the entreaty of a righteous man
when it is energized.

sacramental character. The Greek Church retains the custom of anointing, but does not regard it as a sacrament, but as medicinal treatment for the body. The first Prayer Book of Edward VI. retained the form and permitted the use of unction, if the patient desired its administration, with prayer for pardon of sin and recovery to bodily health. All the subsequent Prayer Books of the English Church omit the practice altogether.

Ver. 16. This verse again has been rendered celebrated by the superstition built upon it by the Church of Rome. The most ancient MSS. insert οὖν, *therefore;* this evidently connects this injunction with the preceding sentence, to which it is parallel. The sick man is there represented as possibly suffering on account of some sin he had committed, the forgiveness of which should be conferred together with the restoration of his bodily health. " Therefore, confess your trespasses one to another, and pray·," etc. Here is a reference to the "prayer of faith." "That ye may be healed:" this is parallel to "the Lord shall raise him up;" and here, probably, we catch the clue to the solution of the difficult word ἐνεργουμένη. The prayer of faith sprung from an inward energy imparted by the Spirit of God (see below), and so St. James reminds them, as a ground why they should pray for one another, especially in times of sickness and danger of death, that the petition of a just man has much influence when it is energized or inwrought by the Spirit.

Perhaps nothing is so solacing to the troubled mind as revealing the source of sorrow to another. To impart to another the sins we have committed, the infirmities that depress us, or the painful experiences we have struggled through, relieves the heart of a sore load, and often lifts the latchet of the door of hope; and this source of spiritual edification, as is so often the case in the Romish system, has been seized upon and perverted by that church. To enforce as compulsory that which is essentially voluntary robs it of all· benefit, and indeed substitutes another rite in the place of the original. It is needless to add that the dictating, prompting, and suggesting of sin in the Romish confessional is most revolting to moral feeling and subversive of inner purity, and utterly alien to the object in view in the passage under our consideration.

ἐνεργουμένη. The interpretations of this word are manifold. They may be summarily divided into two classes: (1) those that make the participle middle, and (2) those that make it passive. The Authorized Version renders it *effectual*; it may be a matter of doubt whether this means *rendered*, or, *found to be effectual*, by its success, or simply, *energetic, forceful, fervent, earnest*. Thus the word would be equivalent to ἐνεργής, *energetic*, but this is certainly not definite enough, nor consistent with the use of the word.

Of those who regard the form as middle, some think the *energy* of the person praying, in seeking to bring about the object of his prayer, is intended; others, that *inward working* so as to influence the life, and produce the fruits of holiness, is the purport of this participle. While it is admitted that the most frequent use of this verb in the New Testament is middle, yet there is no reason why it should not be used passively, and this will certainly be the more fitting and suitable form in this place, when all the features of the context and the subject treated of are taken into consideration. The prayer in the last verse is a prayer of faith that shall receive an answer, the healing of the sick man is of a miraculous character; the general εὔχεσθε ὑπὲρ ἀλλήλων of this verse partakes of the same character, the object of healing being the same. So here the special δέησις must be classed under the same head, as a petition for miraculous interposition. But it is evident that in the exercise of miraculous gifts there was not unrestricted expenditure of power, but the Spirit who imparted to the disciples "the discernment of spirits" gave them a monition where and when to put forth the Divine gift; so the prayer or petition which accompanied the act would be a divinely inspired and energized appeal to God, so that it is best to regard this word in that light, a prayer *inwrought* by the Spirit of God. The position of the participle at the end of the clause is not intended, as some commentators of great note hold, to carry out the verb ἰσχύει as if the sentence ran, The prayer of a righteous man *has influence and is energetic*, but is rather placed there as an emphatically enunciated condition on which the prevalence of the prayer is grounded. The petition must be taught by the Holy Ghost, and when so it has prevalence. The next verse adduces an instance in which the condition here laid down was exemplified.

17 Ἠλίας ἄνθρωπος ἦν ὁμοιοπαθὴς ἡμῖν,
καὶ προσευχῇ προσηύξατο τοῦ μὴ βρέξαι·
καὶ οὐκ ἔβρεξεν ἐπὶ τῆς γῆς ἐνιαυτοὺς τρεῖς καὶ
μῆνας ἕξ.

17 Elijah was a man of like feelings as ourselves,
And in prayer he prayed that it should not rain,
And it rained not upon the land three years and
six months.

Ver. 17. Prayer when energized by the Spirit of God is effectual. Take for a well known example of this truth the prayer of Elijah, first that it should not rain, and afterwards that the drought should be removed. That prayer was taught and inspired by the Holy Spirit, and see how successful it was in the result.

ὁμοιοπαθής. Elijah was *of like passions and infirmities as ourselves*. The weak side of the prophet, the old Adam of his heart came out when, after the performance of the great miracle on mount Carmel, he fled into the wilderness from the face of Jezebel, and in the midst of bitter lamentations requested that he might die: see 1 Ki. xix.

προσευχῇ προσηύξατο, *prayed in prayer*. The well known Hebraism; compare Luke xxii. 15; Acts iv. 17: at the same time, the emphasis points to the ἐνεργουμένη above. We are not told in so many words in the Old Testament narrative that Elijah thus prayed, but the fact seems to be suggested by the preface to the drought, "There shall be no dew nor rain but according to my word," 1 Ki. xvii. 1; and still more plainly after the drought by the account given in chap. xviii. 42, that "he went to the top of Carmel, and cast himself down upon the earth, and put his face between his knees;" and his faith and expectation of an answer are evident from the following words, that he sent his servant seven times to see if the cloud were rising above the distant horizon.

Three years and six months. The period is remarkable as being the same mentioned in Rev. xi. 3-6, the space of time during which the two witnesses shall exercise their ministry, to whom "power shall be given to shut heaven that it rain not in the days of their prophecy." This is not the place to enter on the question whether Elijah will be one of these witnesses, but the coincidence is noteworthy. Some difficulty has been found in reconciling this period of three years and a half with 1 Ki. xviii. 1, where it would appear that the drought foretold by Elijah terminated in the third year of its duration. It is usual to

18 καὶ πάλιν προσηύξατο,
καὶ ὁ οὐρανὸς ὑετὸν ἔδωκε,
καὶ ἡ γῆ ἐβλάστησε τὸν καρπὸν αὐτῆς.

19 Ἀδελφοί μου, ἐάν τις ἐν ὑμῖν,
πλανηθῇ ἀπὸ τῆς ἀληθείας,
καὶ ἐπιστρέψῃ τις αὐτόν,

18 And again he prayed,
And the heaven gave rain,
And the land produced her fruit.

19 My brethren, if any one among you
Is led astray from the truth,
And any one convert him;

explain this seeming discrepancy by reckoning this date from the commencement of his sojourn with the widow of Zarephath; but it is more satisfactory and natural, as the same period is given in Luke iv. 25, and in the Jewish tract *Jalcut Simeoni*, to take the three years and a half as the period during which no rain fell, but inasmuch as a whole year would pass before the drought would produce famine in the land, the writer of 1 Kings speaks of the third year after the actual famine had set in.

If any one among you be led-astray (πλανηθῇ, the passive force is to be retained as showing pressure from without, see chap. i. 16), from the faith in Jesus as the Messiah, and so become apostate. Such is the force of this passage.

Ver. 19. τῆς ἀληθείας. Not abstract truth merely, nor even Gospel truth, but (see chap. i. 18 and note there) *the truth*, that is, the Lord Jesus Christ, who called Himself by this name, Jno. xiv. 6. He is *the Amen*, see Is. lxv. 16; Rev. iii. 14, the one and only revealer of the Father to mankind. There is a strong emphasis on this whole passage. The Jew stood in special danger of apostacy. Jews and Christians alike held the law and the prophets as a revelation from God; the Christians believed that Christ brought a further and final revelation. Under persecution for the Gospel's sake, the Jew might be tempted to retire to the common ground admitted by both parties, and reject the evangelical development; this would involve open apostacy and eternal ruin. Hence we find our Lord uttering the most solemn warnings against this grievous fall, Matt. xii. 32: see also Heb. vi. 4-6; 2 Pet. ii. 1; 1 Jno. v. 16.

20 γινωσκέτω ὅτι ὁ ἐπιστρέψας ἁμαρτωλόν
ἐκ πλάνης ὁδοῦ αὐτοῦ,
σώσει ψυχὴν ἐκ θανάτου,
καὶ καλύψει πλῆθος ἁμαρτιῶν.

ΕΠΙΣΤΟΛΗ ΙΑΚΩΒΟΥ.

20 Let him know that he that converts a sinner
From the error of his way,
Shall save a soul from death,
And shall cover a multitude of sins.

THE EPISTLE OF JAMES.

Ver. 20. γινωσκέτω, *let him know* (the Vatican MS. here reads γινώσκετε, *know ye*, but ℵ, A, Syriac, and Vulgate, support the received reading), that he that is made instrumental in bringing back the sinner from the error of his way shall save a soul from apostasy, which must end in eternal death.

And shall cover a multitude of sins. A question has arisen, whose sins shall be covered, those of the converter or of the converted? The Church of Rome holds the former; the Syriac among ancient versions, Erasmus, at the time of the Reformation, and Whitby and Hammond, and others, among writers of our Church adopt the same view. A deeper insight into the passage will, however, show that the opposite reference is the one intended; that not only shall the converter instrumentally save a soul from death, but also cover a multitude of sins which the converted had already committed, and a multitude of sins which in the future he would have committed if he had remained in his apostasy would be averted and avoided. The Hebrew thought connected with "covering sins" was that of atonement. The original passage on which this is grounded is Prov. x. 12, "Hatred stirreth up strife, but love covereth all sins;" where the antithesis between the effects of hatred and those of love proves that the sins that love covers are those of the sinner and not of the loving one. It is of course easy to deny the reference to this passage, as some have done, on quite insufficient grounds, but such a denial is no proof. There are, moreover, two passages in the New Testament which corroborate this conclusion, 1 Pet. iv. 8, where the same text from Proverbs is cited more fully than in this place, "Before all things having love towards each other intense, *for love covers a multitude of sins.*" The close similitude that exists between the Epistles of St. James and St. Peter will account for their use of the same passage, and the sense in which they employ the ancient proverb will be closely allied. In the latter there can exist no doubt that mutual love will produce mutual forbearance. Our author seems to superadd a higher thought: the greatest love you can show to a man trembling on the brink of apostacy is to wrestle with him and *turn him* from his error to the Lord, and in so doing you will hide his sins, as was represented in the Levitical blood-sprinkling, from the searching eye of God. It may be noted that both St. James and St. Peter make their quotation from the Hebrew text, and not from the LXX., which in this place is not only paraphrastic, but incorrect.

The second passage which confirms this interpretation is in St. Paul's essay on love, 1 Cor. xiii. 7, where he says that love πάντα στέγει, *covereth all things*. It is quite admitted that στέγει may have the translation *beareth* as in E.V., but it is far better to translate with Bengel, Schleusner, and others, *covereth*, as the πάντα ὑπομένει which follows fully expresses the features of forbearance and endurance. There is little doubt that St. Paul had in his mind the same fundamental passage in the Book of Proverbs. The notion of *fides formata* in the Tridentine system of justification, it is superfluous to add, is quite out of place in connection with this text, as that doctrine has no support here. The work of the teacher is to bring the sinner to Jesus, and His cross, and His finished offering will cover all the sins of the sinner. Thus the doctrine of the atonement, and not of human merit, closes this Epistle.

For the subscription see remarks in the *Introduction*.

EXCURSUS ON THE GLORY.

(Chapter II. 1.)

כבוד, δόξα, *Shechinah.* The word "glory" has a lengthy pedigree, it enlightens the dim distance of the remotest past and kindles a torch in the still remoter future. We must associate with this word some sister terms which may severally serve either as the envelope to conceal the nucleus of light, or as the vehicle of its manifestation; as the casket to conceal, or the setting to exhibit the gem. Such words as שׁכן to *dwell* or *tabernacle*, and ענן *cloud*, will readily occur, as being frequently and intimately connected with the "glory" of God. We must not permit the ethical use of this word *glory* to supplant the material sense: the glory of which we are treating is not the tribute paid to the Almighty by His creatures, as when we ascribe praise in the well known doxology of the Christian church, "Glory be to the Father, and to the Son, and to the Holy Ghost." Such an application of the term is rather the result of our apprehending the objective nature of the glory, and a reflex expression of our subjective sense of wonder and adoration; but the primary use of the word is expressive of *manifested majesty,* see Gen. xlv. 13, where it is employed in a striking type of the Messiah. In

Ex. xvi. 10, the "glory" is the revealing medium of Deity; and ever after it served as the visible token of the Divine presence in connection with the tabernacle and temple, till the period of the Babylonish captivity; and in prophetic visions, as in Is. vi. 3; Ezek. i. 28, etc., it was the recognized means of Divine manifestation. Moreover, the "glory" was so identified with the presence of God, a presence so mysteriously essential, that it seems to have been an integral off-ray of the Divine Entity, or a transubstantiation of Deity into material light, for we find the word used as a synonym of God in Ps. cvi. 20; Jer. ii. 11.

When God created man, He created him "in his own image, and after his likeness." The similitude consisting in the complex constitution of man, spirit, soul, and body, a trinity of integral parts in the unity of humanity, and thus an imaging or mirroring of the Trinity of persons in the unity of the Godhead. It is more than probable that the Creator vested this facsimile of Himself with a robe of His own glory, and when the fall ruptured the bond of the covenant between man and his Maker, the transgressors were deprived of the wedding garment that had witnessed to their union with God, and when bereft of the heavenly vestment "they knew that they were naked." We may well picture to our minds our first parents anticipating the cry of one of their sorrowing daughters, when the ark, that contained the symbol of the Divine presence, was taken captive: "Ichabod, *the glory* is departed," 1 Sam. iv. 21.

But be this as it may, the first occasion that we meet with a definite and undisputed reference to the visible glory of God is after the expulsion of Adam from the paradise of Eden, Gen. iv. 24. We read there "He made to tabernacle or dwell (וישכן rendered in our version 'He placed,') cherubim, and the flame of a sword that revolved, to guard the way of the tree of life;" this verb שכן, to tabernacle, here first found in connection with the mysterious fire, became afterwards the base of the well known word Shechinah, i.e., the tabernacling, by which the later Hebrews called the visible glory of God. The cherubim appear as the guards of the glory; and this is their office throughout the whole of the Old Testament dispensation, whether the original beings were seen in vision, or their representations were sculptured or embroidered among the symbols of the Levitical ceremonial, namely, to ward off the profane from the presence of the glory, and to guard its holiness inviolate; but when the hour of redemption is perfected, in Rev. v. 9, 10 we read, according to the testimony of the Sinaitic and Alexandrine MSS., that the "living creatures" who have kept their ward while sin separated between the sinner and God, now that sin is atoned for and restoration established, sheathe the sword unscabbarded so long, and herald, as ushers at the court of a great king, the saved into the presence of the glory. The condition of man being changed, the office of the cherubim is changed also.

The next passage that supplies matter of interest in relation to this subject is Gen. ix. 27. Noah is pronouncing prophetic blessing on his two reverential sons, Shem and Japheth, and saith, "God shall enlarge Japheth, and he shall dwell (or tabernacle, וישכן) in the tents of Shem." It is a question whether *God* or *Japheth* is the subject of the verb "shall dwell:" the popular view is doubtless the latter, that Japheth by community of religious privileges shall dwell in the tents of Shem, but most Jewish interpreters favour the former construction; thus the Targum of Onkelos renders the passage, "His Shechinah shall abide in the dwelling of Shem:" Philo Judæus comments thus: "We may now consider who it is who Noah prays may dwell in the tents of Shem, for he does not say very clearly; one may affirm that he means the Lord of the universe," etc. The *B'reshith Rabba* says: "The Shechinah dwells only in the tents of Shem." Among the fathers Theodoret followed in the same opinion, and many modern critics have endorsed the same interpretation. This is not the place to discuss the merits of the question, but the above named authorities, and others that might be added, are weighty; and we shall see, as we progress, that Scripture will furnish us with parallel passages, if not with direct references, to this prophecy thus interpreted. Electing this view of the patriarch's benediction, we have gained a further step in our inquiry, that the visible glory of God, the manifestation of Deity on earth, would find its shrine among the posterity of Shem. Consistently at least with this exposition we trace the fact that the glory-presence is limited to the Hebrew section of the race of Shem, and this high prerogative throughout the domain of revelation defines the distinction between Israel and the Gentiles: the glory of God is always spoken of as dwelling in the midst of the former, and its rays or reflected light giving shine to the latter.

The next passage which bears forcibly on our subject is Ex. iii., where a distinct revelation of the glory-presence was vouchsafed to Moses in the burning bush. The bush, סנה, is found under this name only in this place and Deut. xxxiii. 16, of which more hereafter. The usual interpretation of the mystery of that "great sight" in Horeb, supported by commentators of note, may be thus summarised : the *bush* is the common thorn or bramble, the lowliest and meanest of the trees of the wilderness, a type of Israel now in Egypt in humiliation ; the flame burning, a symbol of persecution and tribulation, such as they were then undergoing in the land of the stranger; the bush not being consumed, notwithstanding the heat of the fire, a token and earnest that the interposition of Providence should prove a preservative to the seed of Abraham in all their afflictions for evermore.

But is there not a grander truth here evidenced than even this? We must call to mind that the time of the promise was now come, that Moses was commanded to recall to their memory the almost forgotten name of Jehovah, and to explain the mystery of its meaning. The "coming one," the great Redeemer promised at the fall, whom Eve vainly hoped would be her firstborn, whose presence was covenanted in the tents of Shem, now appeared as the well-known Angel of Jehovah, and claimed to be the "I am who am," the "coming one" as well as "from everlasting." The revelation made in this vision was not the depression of Israel on the one hand, or simply their preservation in the midst of dangers on the other, but rather the proof that the glory-presence was still with Israel, and a renewal of the ancient promise that it should abide with them for ever. This will be more apparent when we examine the word *bush* סנה. It has been satisfactorily established by recent investigation that this tree was one of the acacia genus, and that *s'neh* was a Hebrew form of the Egyptian name by which it was known, *sant* or *sont*. The regular Hebrew name, found frequently in other places, was *shittah* or *shittim* tree. Now, it is remarkable as bearing on the question, that the wood of the shittim tree was used as the material to construct the framework of the tabernacle in which afterwards dwelt the glory-presence, and more especially was the inner substance of the ark of the covenant, on the lid or mercy-seat of which that glory-presence rested.

This interpretation will be the more evident when we compare Deut. xxxiii. 16: Moses, when breathing his parting blessing on the posterity of Joseph, speaks of "the good will of him that dwelt in the bush," where, as we have already observed, the only other example of this word *seneh*, is found. He uses the Egyptian word in connection with Joseph, who had been the lord of Egypt, so that the reference to the burning *bush* in Horeb is clearly established; and further, the word "dwelt" is שכני, the special word that is cognate with the glory-presence, the Shechinah, which was there revealed.

This association of the *glory* with the *bush* at once brings before our minds the subject to which we have already alluded, the tabernacle and the Divine presence that dwelt therein. The first place in Holy Writ where this sacred tent is named is worthy of notice. In Ex. xxv. 8, 9 we read, " And let them make me a sanctuary, that I may *dwell* among them, according to all that I shew thee, after the pattern of the *tabernacle*." In this passage we find the verb שכן expressing the mode of the Divine habitation among His people, and משכן, a noun from the same root, used for the tabernacle; so that if we read, "That I may *tabernacle* among them, according to all that I shew thee, after the pattern of the *tabernacle*;" the force of the original will be manifest.

This building was also called a *tent*, אהל, or *house*, בית, or *palace*, היכל, all which denote the occupation of the Divine presence. We need not expatiate on the arrangements of the sacred building: it is well known that the innermost recess, the Holy of Holies, contained an ark made of shittim wood overlaid with gold, inside this chest were deposited the tables of the law, in the Divine manuscript, and on the lid, called the *mercy-seat*, rested the glory-presence, overshadowed by the cherubim: hence arose the epithet of Deity, "thou that dwellest between the cherubim;" and the phrase found in Heb. ix. 5, "the cherubim of glory." The general name of this cathedral of the wilderness was the "tabernacle of the congregation." The impression made on the ordinary reader by this translation must almost necessarily be that this tent was the gathering place of the various tribes of Israel, who met there for worship, the congregation being composed of men and men only; but if we turn to the fundamental passage, Ex. xxix. 42, we shall find a very different account given of the purport of this erection : " the tabernacle of the congregation, where *I* will *meet* you, to speak unto thee ; and there *I will meet* with the children of Israel." When we call to mind that the words translated "congregation," מועד, and "I will meet," אועד, are cognate, kindred noun and verb, the meaning will be clear, the tabernacle of the *meeting place*, where *I will meet you*. This tent then was thus called because it was appointed to be the centre where God would meet His people.

We postpone further comment on this marvellous type till we come to consider the teaching of Jno. i. 14, and the connection of that passage with the subject before us; it will be sufficient at the present point in our argument to call the reader's attention to the fact that God had fixed a permanent settlement of the glory-presence in the midst of the Hebrew nation, to be the centre from which should issue forth His oracles, laws, and judgments to the people, where also He would meet them when they should assemble for worship, sacrifice, and service.

Intimately connected with this, and identical with the Shechinah, was the cloud, ענן, that assumed the form of a pillar or column of *nebula* and fire. It would appear from a comparison of the facts given in the sacred narrative that the glory was encased in an envelope of mist; the Divine presence was veiled in a robe of cloud, so that the light within was not always visible. This ordinance was first established when Israel left Egypt and essayed the passage of the Red Sea. It afterwards became associated with the tabernacle, when that sacred structure was erected, and in connection with it led the march of the Israelites through the mazes of the wilderness, during their pilgrimage to the land of Canaan; it served at once as a special token of God's *presence* with His people, and also pointed out the way in which they should go, when and where to halt, and when and whither to depart; for the movements of this glory-cloud were extraordinary, when the host was to set forward, it ascended like a column, and acted the part of a pioneer to the pilgrim tribes; at noon-time it would seem that its crest dilated, and formed a covering or shield like an aurora over the host; and when the time arrived to pitch camp, the shaft descended upon the tabernacle, and roofed in the sacred tent with an awning, and filled it with the light of the glory-fire: see Ex. xl. 34, 38; Num. ix. 15, 17; Ps. cv. 39.

We may now leave this earlier portion of the history of God's ancient people, merely reminding the reader that the pillar of the glory-cloud conducted the children of Israel to the end of their journeyings, to the banks of Jordan and the gates of Canaan, and that the Shechinah doubtless remained surmounting the mercy-seat till the tabernacle was merged into the temple of Solomon, when we read that the glory again filled the house of the Lord: see 1 Ki. viii. 10, 11; 2 Chron. v. 13, 14.

We may pass by various and casual references to this mode of the manifestation of Deity scattered up and down the pages of the prophets, as our purpose is only to fix upon those points in the Scripture testimony that serve as links to form the chain of evidence. The next period that presents features of interest is that of the Babylonish captivity. We may with certainty conclude that up to this time the Holy of Holies had retained the treasure of the glory-presence, seen but once a year, when the high priest entered that chamber of mystery, even if then he dared, or were permitted, to gaze upon the glory that dwelt between the cherubim. The light that shone in that otherwise dark apartment would be sufficient to convince him of its presence. But at the crisis of which we are speaking the temple of Solomon fell under the axes and hammers of Nebuchadnezzar; but what became of the ark of the covenant and its mysterious surroundings? If we are to credit the authority of the writer of the second book of Maccabees, chap. ii. 5, 6, the material ark was secreted by Jeremiah the prophet: "And when Jeremy came thither, he found a hollow cave, wherein he laid the tabernacle, and the ark, and the altar of incense, and so stopped the door. And some of those that followed him came to mark the way, but they could not find it." But what became of the glory-presence, the Shechinah? This question is answered in the book of the prophet Ezekiel. The solution of this usually thought intricate and difficult prophecy is in the removal and restoration of the Shechinah. The first chapter reminds us forcibly of the vestibule of the garden of Eden after the expulsion of Adam. There is the "fire infolding itself," or "catching itself," מתלקחת, a striking parallel to the המתהפכת of Gen. iii. 24. There are also the four living creatures, identical doubtless with the cherub-guards of paradise, whose appearance was like living coals of fire, and like the appearance of lamps; but in this place the cherubim are accompanied by a chariot with complicated wheels that seem to be inspired by an indwelling, guiding, and dynamic spirit. And for what purpose was this heavenly vehicle prepared, we may naturally enquire. The tenth chapter informs us that it was for the conveyance of the glory. In the fourth verse the glory fills the house and court, in the eighteenth verse it departs from the threshhold and stands above the cherubim, and then they lift up their wings and mount up from the earth. Thus the glory-presence departed from the *temple*.

Further, in chap. xi. 22, 23, a vision is seen of the Shechinah leaving the *city*, "Then did the cherubim lift

THE GLORY.

up their wings, and the wheels beside them; and the glory of the God of Israel was over them above. And the glory of the Lord went up from the midst of the *city*, and stood upon the mountain which is on the east side of the city." After this follows the roll written within and without with lamentations and mourning and woe, descriptive of the sufferings of Israel during the times of Gentile domination; but when the cup of deadly wine is drained, and her warfare is accomplished, we witness, in chap. xliii. 2, 7, the return of the glory-presence to the *temple*, "And, behold, the glory of the God of Israel came from the way of the east; and his voice was like the noise of many waters: and the earth shined with his glory. And it was according to the appearance of the vision which I saw, according to the vision that I saw when I came to destroy the city: and the visions were like the vision that I saw by the river Chebar; and I fell upon my face. And the glory of the Lord came into the house by the way of the gate, whose prospect is toward the east. So the spirit took me up, and brought me into the inner court; and behold the glory of the Lord filled the house. And I heard him speaking unto me out of the house: and the man stood by me. And he said unto me, Son of man, the place of my throne, and the place of the soles of my feet, where I will dwell (אשכן) in the midst of the children of Israel for ever;" and henceforth and for ever we hail the *city* as Jehovah Shammah, Jehovah is there, chap. xlviii. 35. From this testimony of Ezekiel we learn two things: firstly, that when the Gentiles desolated Jerusalem, and destroyed the "beautiful house," the glory-presence departed from Israel; first it vacated the temple, then the city; and secondly, that when the Messiah shall come to reign, and His banished ones shall be gathered to Him, then shall the glory also return, and be no more taken away from them.

A few of the prophecies that were uttered after the departure of the Shechinah may serve to show what the Jewish hopes at that period were relative to the restoration of the Shechinah.

There may be doubts entertained as to the period when Ps. lxxxv. was composed: this song of the sons of Korah may have been uttered in the time of David, when he fled before Absalom, and returned in triumph to his home; or the circumstances connected with the Egyptian invasion in the reign of Rehoboam may have furnished the subject matter of this graceful hymn; or, as perhaps is more generally held, it was composed after the Babylonish captivity in the time of Nehemiah, when the refugees bewailed their desolated land, their ruined temple, and above all the withdrawal of the glory that had had its residence in the Holy of Holies. At whatever period in the history of Israel this psalm originated, the purport of the implied prophecy in the tenth verse, "that *glory may dwell* (לשכן כבוד) in our land," is clear and unmistakable, namely, that it was the purpose of God, and the hope of His people, that in the future age the Shechinah should dwell in the midst of Israel.

In the second chapter of Haggai we have a striking prophecy of the second temple. We may well call up before our imagination the elders, who had seen the former house, weeping at the comparatively poor preparations that were being made for the erection of the new edifice, and may hear the cheering words of the prophet, as he testified by the spirit of prophecy, "I will fill this house with glory, saith Jehovah Sabaoth," *v.* 7 ; and again, "the glory of this latter house shall be greater than of the former," *v.* 9. The reference in these words must evidently be to the Shechinah which had dwelt in the ancient temple, but whose absence was so deeply regretted in the modern building; and the prediction which pointed to the coming Messiah, who should bring the glory back again, was calculated to encourage the hopes of the recently restored exiles.

One more prophecy of this class will be sufficient for our purpose.

In the second chapter of Zechariah we find a lengthy description of the advent of the Messiah, the terms of which more especially delineate the second coming and the glory that shall follow. In the fifth verse (Hebrew, *v.* 9) Jehovah declares, "I will be the glory in the midst of her;" and in the eighth verse (Hebrew, *v.* 12), "For thus saith Jehovah Sabaoth, After the glory hath he sent me unto the nations that spoiled you;" where "after the glory" when taken in connection with *v.* 5 quoted above, must mean *after the glory is come.* Again in the tenth verse (Hebrew, *v.* 15), "Lo, I come, and I will dwell (ושכנתי) in the midst of thee," a declaration repeated in the next verse. From which we gather a well defined promise that the lost Shechinah should be restored to the people of Israel again in some way, which should transcend, and even eclipse in the brilliancy of its epiphany, the glory-presence that tabernacled in the wilderness tent and the Solomonic temple.

Our next task will be to show what opinions the Jewish teachers entertained upon this subject during the period that intervened between the closing of the Old Testament canon and the coming of our Lord. It is well known that the word *Shechinah* is not found in the Old Testament Scriptures, but had its rise in the period that was subsequent to the Babylonish captivity. This was also the age in which the Targums became necessary, through the change that took place in the vernacular language of the Jews, the Hebrew giving way to the Chaldee. The Targums of Onkelos and Jonathan, which have come down to us, doubtless embody much of the ancient lore that then first began to be stored up by the members of the Great Synagogue. In these Targums it is the constant habit of the interpreters to represent the Person of the Deity by this word Shechinah. Thus, to give examples bearing on some of the passages we have had occasion to quote, Ex. xxv. 8, "Let them make me a sanctuary that I may dwell among them," is rendered in the Targum of Onkelos, "I will make my Shechinah to dwell among them." Hence it became a settled belief among the Jews, based upon the undoubted warranty of Holy Writ, and correctly explained in these documents, that Messiah should restore to Israel the long lost Shechinah, the glory-presence, whose tabernacling among them distinguished them from all other nations of the earth. To illustrate this article of their creed, it will suffice to refer to Zech. ii. 10, quoted above, which is thus paraphrased, "I will be revealed, and will make my Shechinah to dwell in the midst of thee." The hope of the Jew was the recovery of the treasure that was gone. The age to come, the time of the Messiah, was at hand. He should bring the Shechinah back again, and be the revealer of God in the midst of His people Israel for ever.

If we prosecute our inquiry at a subsequent period in Jewish history we find that the book *Sohar* even identifies the Shechinah with the Son of God, for commenting on the second psalm Simeon Ben Jochai says, "The Lord of the serving angels, the Son of the Highest, the Son of the Holy One, blessed be He, yea, the Shechinah." And again he writes, "God said, Faithful Shepherd! verily Thou art my Son, yea, the Shechinah." And Rabbi Menachem of Recanati recognizes the Angel of Jehovah in the pillar of fire and cloud: "And likewise our Rabbies of blessed memory have said, that the Shechinah of the Lord went down with them to the sea; hence it is said, The Angel, who is God, removed (Ex. xiv. 19). If this Angel is the Shechinah, then it (the Shechinah) is called *Angel*, and the Prince of the world, because the government is placed in His hands."*

We now proceed to examine what evidence the New Testament furnishes to corroborate this creed of Israel, and what fulfilment its pages reveal of the realization of their hopes. St. Luke has handed down in his Gospel certain particulars relative to the surroundings of the birth and infancy of our Lord. Among these deeply interesting notes we read, in chap. ii. 8, 9, the narrative of the appearance of the angel to the shepherds, who were keeping watch in the fields of Bethlehem on the night when Messiah was born. And it is significant that the Evangelist should record the fact that on that memorable night, when prophecy was fulfilled, and the

* See Pauli's *Great Mystery*, pp. 67, 93, 94.

covenant-oath between God and His people remembered, "the *glory* of the Lord shone round about them:" with the birth of Messiah the long absent *glory* returned. But further on in the same chapter an account is given us of the incidents that occurred when the infant Saviour was presented in the temple. Foremost in the scene we see the aged Simeon embracing the holy Babe in his arms, and hear his inspired lips pouring out his "Nunc dimittis," in which the Saviour is entitled the *Light* of the Gentiles and the *glory* of His people Israel, the Shechinah that should dwell in the midst of Israel for ever, and whose rays should beam forth and illumine all the nations of the earth.

Intimately connected with this utterance of St. Simeon is the teaching of St. John, in his Gospel, chap. i. 14, a passage notable for its definite and dogmatic teaching concerning the deity and humanity of the Messiah. We have already referred to the typical teaching of the tabernacle and the indwelling glory, it will be necessary to investigate that subject further in connection with the passage now under consideration. The holy tent was a "building made with hands," the materials were earthly, the builders men, its pillars, stakes and sockets, its curtains, and its shittim-wood and gold, all proclaimed it "an earthly house of a tabernacle." Into this receptacle the glory of God descended, and the Shechinah fixed its habitation there, so that this earthly tabernacle became the presence chamber of Jehovah; the edifice was human, but the tenant was divine. St. John, fastening on these striking characteristics of the type, expounds their mystical teaching by pointing to the antitype, and presents us with the solution of the enigma in the union of the divine and human natures in the one person of our Lord Jesus Christ. "The Word became flesh and tabernacled in us, and we gazed upon his *glory* as being that of the only begotten from the Father." The Word, we are taught, made His tent in our nature. By a noteworthy coincidence the very word for *tent* in Greek (σκηνή) contains the consonants, the true skeletons of words, which are of the same value as those which form the word *Shechinah* in Hebrew. Both came, doubtless, from some primæval word, which was the common property of mankind, before dialectical varieties arose, and the human race was broken up into families, and emigration from the ancestral home dispersed men over wider areas of the globe.

The habitation of Deity was in our humanity, "in us." The human nature of our Lord was formed in the womb of the Virgin Mary; it was Adam's nature, our nature, but without sin. With this nature the Word, the Wisdom, the Glory of God was invested and united. In the person of Jesus Christ therefore the divine and human *meet together;* the Godhead and the manhood were not confounded the one with the other, but were joined together in everlasting oneness of person, never to be severed: and thus He is the antitype of the tabernacle of the *meeting place*. Such as the glory was to the tabernacle such is the deity of Christ to His humanity, such as the tabernacle was to the glory such is His humanity to His deity; "perfect God and perfect man:" "God over all," yet "bone of our bone and flesh of our flesh;" and under the veil of that flesh we gaze upon the glory of the Father manifested in His only begotten Son incarnate. Messiah is the Shechinah!

We have seen already that in the pillar of cloud and fire that marched before the Israelitish pilgrims in the desert, the enfolded light would sometimes burst through the *nebula* which encased it, and then it was said, "the glory of the Lord appeared." So it would seem that at the transfiguration the deity of our Lord shone through the veil of His humanity, the brilliancy of the gem penetrated the envelope of the casket, and "his face did shine as the sun, and his raiment was white as the light," Matt. xvii. 2. St. Luke has preserved to us the subject of the conversation that engrossed Moses and Elijah who appeared in glory with the Lord, "they spake of his *decease*," ἔξοδον, His *exodus*, "which He was about to fulfil at Jerusalem," Luke ix. 31. The word at once identified the glory of the transfiguration with the glory of the pillar that pioneered the path of Israel out of the land of Egypt. The hearing of this word, and the sight of the symbol of the old covenant, and the return of the Shechinah, it would appear, immediately brought the history of the wilderness period to the mind of the Apostles who witnessed this epiphany, for Peter exclaimed, and the words are very significant, "Let us make here three *tabernacles*," *v.* 33, where the reference to the "tabernacle of the congregation" is unquestionable. St. Luke, moreover, in describing the transfiguration, employs a more definite word for "as the light," ὡς τὸ φῶς, of St. Matthew. He tells us that "his raiment was white and glistering," *v.* 29, ἐξαστράπτων, "flashing like lightning," a word which we cannot fail to see connects the features of the transfiguration with the "appearance of the glory" as seen in the visions of Ezekiel already referred to, and carries us forward to the glory of the second advent, which shall be "as the *lightning* which cometh out of the east and shineth even unto the west," Matt. xxiv. 27.

It is deserving our notice in connection with this word that in two out of the three narratives given us of the conversion of St. Paul, the verb περιαστράπτειν is used to describe the glory-flash that witnessed to the Divine presence: see Acts ix. 3; xxii. 6; and the subsequent blindness of the convert is attributed to the sight of the *glory*, ἀπὸ δόξης τοῦ φωτὸς ἐκείνου.

Again, at the ascension of our Lord, when He was taken up into glory, the evangelist St. Luke, who gives us a two-fold account of this magnificent winding up of the Redeemer's ministry on earth, informs us that while He was engaged in the act of blessing his disciples, "he was parted from them, and a *cloud* received him out of their sight:" see Luke xxiv. 51; Acts i. 9. Thus as the cloud had hovered round and embraced the Divine presence in the pillar that pioneered the highway in the wilderness to Canaan, so the cloud received the incarnate glory as He marched into the heavenly Canaan to point the way to His pilgrim saints, and to prepare the place for their everlasting habitation.

And as we thus see the *glory* was evidently associated with the birth at Bethlehem and the ascension at Bethany: with the entrance of the Saviour into the world and His departure from it: so we cannot fail to trace the Shechinah in the star that led the Magi to the infant King of the Jews; for no star of distant systems, or sister planet of our own, could have directed the pilgrims from their own country to Judæa, much less from Jerusalem to Bethlehem, and stand "over the place where the young child was." This hope of Israel also, the return of the Shechinah, was uppermost in the minds of the Pharisees and scribes, when they came to our Lord, apparently on more than one occasion (Matt. xii. 38; xvi. 1; see also 1 Cor. i, 22), and demanded of Him a sign from heaven; and as in their unbelief of His miracles they asked for the Shechinah as a proof of His Messiahship from the height above, He gave them a proof from the depths beneath in predicting, and afterwards fulfilling, His antitypal relation to Jonas the prophet. It was the Shechinah also that appeared on the day of Pentecost in the form of tongues of fire, which betokened the presence of the Holy Ghost; the word διαμεριζόμεναι signifying not "cloven" in themselves, but separated and distributed from a central glory-light. Acts ii. 3.

It will be beyond our purpose, however, to trace all the passages, scattered throughout the writings of the New Testament, in which "the glory," under that name or its synonyms, occurs, interesting as such a task would be, as affording corroborative testimony to the views hitherto advanced; for although it cannot be denied that the word is not unfrequently met with in its ethical sense, as a synonym for superlative honour, yet there is an abundance of instances in which the word occurs definitive of Christophany. Thus, if we compare Acts vii. 2, where St. Stephen speaks of God as "the God of the glory," ὁ Θεὸς τῆς δόξης, with Eph. i. 17, where St. Paul employs the phrase "the Father of the glory," ὁ πατὴρ τῆς δόξης, in parallel with "the God of our Lord Jesus Christ," and again, in 1 Cor. ii. 8, entitles Him whom the rulers crucified as "the Lord of the glory," τὸν Κύριον τῆς δόξης, we cannot fail to see the correspondence between the glory and the Lord; a correlation which St. James assumes almost to establish an identity between the glory and the Lord Jesus Christ, as Simeon had done at the presentation in the temple, and as St. Paul describes the Son as ἀπαύγασμα τῆς δόξης, "a ray emitted from the glory," Heb. i. 3.

The frequent use of this word in the writings of the great Apostle may probably be attributed to the impression made upon him by the glory-flash at his conversion, an impression that could never be obliterated from his memory, and of which he probably bore lasting traces in an enfeebled eyesight; a conclusion naturally suggested by his closing reminder to the members of the Galatian church, who had questioned his apostleship, "See ye with how large characters, πηλίκοις γράμμασιν, I write to you with my own hand," Gal. vi. 11; and in v. 17 he gives us the apparent reason for this necessity as well as proof of his having seen the risen Lord, "Henceforth let no man trouble me, for I bear in my body the marks (τὰ στίγματα) of the Lord Jesus," that is, the marks fixed on me when I saw His glory.

Yet this frequent use of the word by St. Paul is not confined to one period of its history, or one phase of its meaning; we find it referring to the literal Shechinah in the temple in Rom. ix. 4, where, in enumerating the special prerogatives of Israel, he includes in the catalogue "the glory," ἡ δόξα. In Heb. i. 3 this word is associated in the dignity of defining the process of the eternal generation of the Son; and it frequently presents itself as the climax of all our hopes in unfolding the everlasting condition of the saints in the kingdom that is to be revealed. In connection with this final state of blessedness we are reminded of the manifestations of the glory in the person of our Lord Jesus Christ.

We have already had our attention called to the prediction that "as the lightning cometh out of the east and shineth unto the west, so shall the coming of the Son of man be," Matt. xxiv. 27. And it is further noticeable that all the pictures which the Lord portrayed beforehand with the pencil of prophecy are lighted up with the glory, "the Son of man shall come in the glory of his Father," Matt. xvi. 27; "he shall be seated on the throne of his glory," Matt. xix. 28; xxv. 31: and believers are taught to look for "the blessed hope and epiphany of the glory, ἐπιφάνειαν τῆς δόξης, of Jesus Christ, our great God and Saviour," Tit. ii. 13. This is so familiar a truth that there is no necessity to dwell longer on the predicted fact that the Lord when He returns "the second time without sin unto salvation" will appear in glory; but this glory is held out to mankind as the great prize, which is at once the gift of Christ and yet the object in hope of which we are to struggle and suffer. Under this head we may classify such phrases as "the gospel of the glory," and "the knowledge of the glory," 2 Cor. iv. 4, 6. The glory that enlightened the face of Moses when he came down from the mount was transient, and he put a veil over his countenance that the people might not see the time of its extinguishment; but the Gospel reveals a glory that is not transient, and God shines in the hearts of His people for the purpose of shedding the light of the *knowledge of the glory* in the face of Jesus Christ. Such is the present privilege; and the future is spoken of in the same chapter, v. 17, in one of the finest examples of inspired rhetoric: "For the present lightness of our tribulation works out for us in excess unto excess an eternal *weight of glory*," where, by combining " weight " (βάρος) with "glory" (δόξης), St. Paul alludes to the double meaning of the original Hebrew word כבוד, *weight* and *glory*. Similarly in the Epistle to the Ephesians, chap. i. 18, the Apostle speaks of their being enlightened in the eyes of their heart to know what the hope is which the calling of God gives, and what the *wealth of the glory* which taking them for His inheritance imparts: see also Rom. v. 2; viii. 18.

These features of the future state naturally lead us to the consideration of the resurrection body and its surroundings, a subject at once of the deepest mystery and interest.

If the "glory" be the manifestation of God, an emanation of His essence, a necessary adjunct of His being, or a symbol of His presence, if it be a correct conclusion that Adam before the fall was clothed with this robe, the panoply that invested him with immortality, if the glory-presence were the source of preservation to Israel in the wilderness, and the assurance of divine protection while it dwelt in the temple, if when the glory departed the people were given over into the hand of the enemy, if the same glory-presence tabernacled in the Word made flesh, if at the transfiguration it shone through the vestment of the flesh of Christ, as the fire through the cloudy pillar, if the same vehicle of glory-cloud, as the chariot and horses of heaven, bore up the risen and ascending Lord to the right hand of the Father, and if the same glory is to be the sign of the Son of man coming in the clouds of heaven, flashing as lightning from the east even to the west, then we cannot fail to recognize that the *glory* has no small share in the restitution of all things; and some passages will assume a new force, such as 2 Thes. ii. 14, where we read of God's calling us by the Gospel "to the *acquisition of the glory* (εἰς περιποίησιν δόξης) of our Lord Jesus Christ," and Col. iii. 4, "when Christ shall be manifested, our life, then shall ye be manifested with him *in glory;*" and the prayer of our Lord will present a more tangible form, Jno. xvii. 22, "I have given them the *glory* which thou hast given me," and the type of the transfiguration will reveal further glimpses into the mysteries of the future state, when we regard Moses and Elijah, *who appeared in glory,* οἱ ὀφθέντες ἐν δόξῃ, Luke ix. 31, as representatives of the risen church in the resurrection state.

We turn now to the celebrated essay on the resurrection by St. Paul in 1 Cor. xv.

The first feature that strikes us in connection with our subject is the illustration of the resurrection body which he finds in the grain that is sown, and the harvest that springs from it after its death and burial in the soil. He calls the seed-corn "a bare, naked, grain," γυμνὸν κόκκον, *v.* 37, and adds "God *gives* it a body," *v.* 38. Further, in contrasting the condition of the corpse, when committed to the earth, with that of the resurrection body, he says, "It is sown in dishonour, it is raised in *glory*," *v.* 43. Without pressing the word too much in this place we pass on to the contrast between the two federal heads, Adam and Christ, "the first man is of the earth, made of clay; the second man, the Lord from heaven," *v.* 47. And further, "as we bore the image of the one of clay, we shall bear the image also of the heavenly one," *v.* 49. And in unfolding the mystery he defines its operations, "For this corruptible must put on, invest itself with, ἐνδύσασθαι, incorruptibility, and this mortal put on immortality. But when this corruptible has put on incorruptibility, and this mortal put on immortality, then shall the word that is written come to pass, Death is swallowed up in victory," *vv.* 53, 54.

The change effected by the miracle of the resurrection is described as an *investing* or *clothing upon* of the body, the arraying of it in a robe (and mark that this verb is used four times in this passage), just as the dry grain is invested with a new and glorious form, when after decay and transmutation in the soil it yields a harvest to the reaper. But this subject receives further expansion in the fifth chapter of the second Epistle to the Corinthians. The passages will be fresh in the memory which have been cited from the fourth chapter of this Epistle, that contrast the abiding glory attendant on the Gospel with the evanescent glory that accompanied the giving of the law, and the comfortable assurance that reminds us that an excessive and eternal weight of glory will more than compensate us for our present tribulations. Carrying on the thought suggested by the "glory," the Apostle continues in the fifth chapter, "For we know that if our earthly tabernacle-house were taken down, we have in the heavens a building *from* God, a house not made with hands, eternal. For also in this we groan, longing to *put on over* this (ἐπενδύσασθαι) our *dwelling-place* (οἰκητήριον) which is *from* heaven," *vv.* 1, 2; and in *v.* 3

asserts the possession of this clothing (ἐνδυσάμενοι), and that we shall not be found naked (γυμνοί), with evident reference to the *bare* or *naked* seed, γυμνὸν κόκκον of 1 Cor. xv. 37, which represented the mortal body; and in *v.* 4, "For also we who are in the tabernacle (*i.e.*, in the present body) groan, being burdened because we do not wish to put off (ἐκδύσασθαι), but to *put on over* (ἐπενδύσασθαι), that the mortal may be swallowed up by the life," where it must be noticed that the future condition of the resurrection body is described as a building *from* God, ἐκ Θεοῦ, *v.* 1, and as a dwelling-place *from* heaven, οἰκητήριον τὸ ἐξ οὐρανοῦ, *v.* 2. Moreover, it will have been noticed that the mode in which we shall be made possessors of this covering is defined twice, *vv.* 2, 4, by a yet stronger word than that used in the first Epistle, and in *v.* 3 of this chapter, the preposition ἐπί being added to the former ἐνδύσασθαι, a *clothing over and above;* the figures grouped together suggest at once a house and a garment, the former showing its permanency, the latter its nearness and intimacy and all but unity with the wearer, "the mortal shall be swallowed up by the life." How exactly all this description corresponds with the glory-robe which our first parents lost at the fall; with the vesture of Jesus, which sparkled as though embroidered with lightning on the mount of transfiguration, while the train rested on and enveloped Moses and Elijah who appeared in glory; and with the glory in which the Lord shall appear when He returns from heaven, and with which He hath promised to invest His people!

Further corroboration arises from the pages of the Apocalypse: we read, chap. xxi. 2, 3, that the holy city, the habitation of the saved, was seen descending *from* heaven, and the seer heard a voice, "Lo! the tabernacle (σκηνή) of God is with men, and he shall tabernacle (σκηνώσει) with them, and they shall be his people, and God-with-them (*i.e.*, Immanuel) himself shall be their God." Here then is the fulfilment of the promise of God and the expectation of His people, the Shechinah, the glory-presence, shall be with us for ever associated with Immanuel; and *vv.* 23, 24 afford us still clearer evidence, if possible, "And the city has no need of the sun, neither of the moon, to shine on her, for the *glory* of God enlightens her and the Lamb is her *torch*, and the nations shall walk by means of her light." *

Thus also a satisfactory explanation may be given to certain passages which seem to involve a contradiction with others that treat of kindred subjects. We are told that in this present dispensation we are the temple of God, see Jno. xiv. 17; xvii. 23; 1 Cor. iii. 16; vi. 19; 2 Cor. vi. 16; Eph. ii. 21, 22, etc.; and St. Paul writes to the Colossians, chap. i. 27, that God willed to make known what is the riches of *the glory* conferred by this mystery among the Gentiles, which is *Christ in you, the hope of the glory.* Christ dwells in believers now, our body is a temple of the Holy Ghost, but what is meant by Christ being in us *the hope of the glory?* Our blessed Lord furnished the solution in His dedication prayer; for not only did He make petition for His people, "I in them and thou in me, that they may be made perfect in one," Jno. xvii. 23, but He also prayed, "As thou, Father, art in me, and I in thee, that they

* διὰ τοῦ φωτός is the reading of א, A, etc.

may be one in us," v. 21. We have here a clear statement that not only does Christ dwell in us, but also that we dwell in Him. But the visions of the Apocalypse make this revelation still plainer: in chap. xxi., which gives a glowing sketch of the new Jerusalem, we read in v. 22, "I saw no temple therein." At first this announcement seems startling, as a city on earth without a temple would be to the believer a wilderness, even though its walls were of jasper and its pavements of gold; but this seeming deficiency is more than compensated when we learn from the next clause, "the Lord God Almighty and the Lamb are the temple of it." Here then it is plainly said that in the glorified state God and the Lamb are the temple of the saved. During this dispensation Christ finds His temple and tabernacle in us, but then we shall find our temple and tabernacle in Him for ever; and thus in this heavenly and inconceivable habitation of man with the Most High, we see the children of the resurrection, the church of the glorified, like Moses and Elijah at the transfiguration, who appeared in glory vested with the Divine manifestation, "filled up into all the fulness of God," Eph. iii. 19. At that time the assurance which St. Paul gave the Philippians, chap. iii. 20, 21, will find a literal fulfilment: "For our commonwealth subsists in heaven, from which we also await the Lord Jesus Christ as a Saviour, who shall transform the *body of our humiliation* to be conformed to the *body of His glory*." "We shall be like him, for we shall see him as he is," 1 Jno. iii. 2. The church of the saved collectively, and our resurrection bodies individually, will be arrayed with the Shechinah, and robed in the "exceeding white" raiment of transfiguration glory.

To sum up the evidence contained in Scripture concerning the "glory:" it would seem that the glory was the manifestation of the being and essence of God; that when man was created in the image of his Maker he was invested in this robe, which was at once the source of his immortality, and the panoply against all harm; that in after ages the glory betokened God's presence with His people, appeared in visions to the prophets, was withdrawn from the temple when Jerusalem fell under the king of Babylon, was expected by the Jews to return when Messiah came, and finally tabernacled in the Word made flesh. Hence that He who is described as being from all eternity the ἀπαύγασμα τῆς δόξης, Heb. i. 3, is entitled by St. James, chap. ii. 1, the Lord Jesus Christ, τῆς δόξης, the Shechinah; that at the second advent the glory which was hidden under "the veil, that is to say, his flesh," shall be manifested to all, repelling, as in the day of Israel's deliverance from Egypt, all the enemies of the Lord, and driving them into everlasting banishment from the *glory*, see 2 Thes. i. 9; but it shall be light to the saved, the vestment that shall cover the ransomed, the shield and the immortality of the resurrection body, the tissue of the Divine life woven into its fabric, the house from heaven that shall be the home of the redeemed, and the everlasting temple of the glorified.

BAGSTER'S LARGE-PRINT FACSIMILE BIBLE,
ON QUARTO PAPER FOR MS. NOTES.

This is a most handy volume, being the same thickness as the Facsimile Large-Print Polyglot, with margins one inch wide all round the page for MS. notes.

BAGSTER'S LIMP KID-LINED BIBLES.

The Miniature Polyglot Bible, price £1.
The Medium Polyglot Bible, price £1 5s.
The Facsimile Large-Print Polyglot Bible, price £1 10s.

These Bibles are enriched with the following supplementary aids.—A detailed Chronological Arrangement of the Old Testament Scriptures; Tables of Measures, Weights, and Coins; an Itinerary of the Children of Israel from Egypt to Canaan; Table of the Chronological Order of the Books of the Bible; Chronological Table of the Kings and Prophets of Judah and Israel, in parallel columns; a Summary View of the principal events of the period from the close of the sacred Canon of the Old Testament, until the times of the New Testament; an Account of the Jewish and other Sects and Factions; a Table of the principal Messianic Prophecies; a List of Passages in the Old Testament quoted or alluded to in the New Testament; the Names, Titles, and Characters of our Lord Jesus Christ; the Names, Characteristics, Privileges, and Glory of the Redeemed Family of Man, called in the Scriptures, the Church of God; a Chronological Harmony of the Four Evangelists, in parallel columns; Coloured Maps; an engraved Chronological Chart of History from B.C. 500 to A.D. 400; a condensed Scripture Index; an Index to the Psalms; and a Complete Alphabetical Index.

THE BLANK-PAGED BIBLE.

This is an edition of the Facsimile Large-Print Polyglot Bible specially printed for MS. notes on writing paper. The pages of the Bible are printed on the left hand page only, the right hand page being ruled for notes. This gives greater facility for writing as the ruled page is always on the right hand.
So many cherished Bibles, inconveniently crowded with brief records of study and instruction, have passed through the hands of the Publishers, that, while they have admired the skill and perseverance of writers in condensing so much within such confined limits, they have longed to provide a Bible which should conveniently afford a wider scope for these Annotations.
Octavo, Cloth, £1; Turkey morocco plain, £1 13s. 6d.; Turkey morocco or russia, tooled to order, £1 17s. 6d.

Multis terricolis linguis, coelestibus una.

LONDON:
SAMUEL BAGSTER AND SONS,
15, PATERNOSTER ROW.

SAMUEL BAGSTER AND SONS, LONDON.

BAGSTER'S TEACHERS' BIBLE.
Comprising the English Version of the Polyglot Series; Cruden's Concordance; and 4,000 Questions with Answers, on the Historical books of the Old and New Testaments. With Indexes, Maps, Tables of Weights and Measures, and a mass of useful information to aid the Teacher, and with 24 pp. of ruled paper for MS. notes. Foolscap octavo. Roan, 18s.; Plain morocco, 23s. 6d.; Kid-lined, 30s.

The ILLUSTRATED POCKET BIBLE,
For the Young. Containing forty-eight Historical Pictures, with 4,000 suggestive Questions, coloured Maps, and a complete Index of Subjects. In attractive Morocco binding, 12s.

FOUR THOUSAND QUESTIONS,
Intended to open up the Scriptures to the Young. 16mo., price 6d.

CONCISE ANSWERS,
To the Four Thousand Scripture Questions of the Illustrated Pocket Bible. For the use of Parents and Teachers. Foolscap octavo. Paper wrapper, 2s. Cloth, 2s. 6d.

QUESTIONS on the NEW TESTAMENT,
For the use of Schools, price 2d.

QUESTIONS and ANSWERS,
On the Historical books of the New Testament, being a Key to "Questions on the New Testament," price 6d.

DAILY LIGHT on the DAILY PATH.
A Devotional Text Book for every day in the year, Morning and Evening; in the very words of Scripture. Two Volumes.

Large type edition, 16mo. Extra Cloth. Each Volume, 2s. 6d. Small edition, 32mo. Extra Cloth. Each Volume, 1s. 6d.

The AUTOGRAPH TEXT BOOK:
Containing a Text of Scripture, and a Verse of Poetry, together with a space for the insertion of Births, Marriages, and Deaths, under every Day in the Year. Cloth extra, gilt edges, price 2s. 6d.

The TREASURY OF SCRIPTURE KNOWLEDGE.
A selection of more than 500,000 Scripture References and Parallel Passages methodically arranged to suit all editions of the Holy Scriptures. With numerous illustrative Notes; a Harmony of the Four Evangelists, Chronologically arranged; and a copious Alphabetical Index. 821 pp. Foolscap octavo, Cloth, 7s. 6d.; Turkey morocco plain, 14s.; Turkey morocco tooled, 18s.

Preparing for publication, an edition of the above, Demy 8vo., to interleave with the Large Type Polyglot Bible.

The TREASURY BIBLE.
This is an edition of the above, interleaved with the Medium Polyglot Bible. Foolscap octavo, Cloth. 16s.; Turkey morocco plain, £1 5s.; Turkey morocco tooled, £1 10s.

BAGSTER'S POLYGLOT BIBLES,

In Pocket Volumes. The various languages, as separate Volumes, are complete in all respects, and adapted for study *per se,* but they also afford their possessor the assistance of the costly Polyglot editions of the libraries. An individual, for instance, purchases a single language of this series, and proceeds to study it—be it Greek, French, English, or what it may; he then desires to compare the object of his study with another translation, or with the Original, and, possessing himself of it, he finds, to his inexpressible comfort, that he has only to refer to the same page, and part of the page, to obtain the desired comparison. He afterwards adds another and another Version to his Library, and finds the same principle carried through the whole; and he obtains a Bible of two, three, four, or more languages, not only convenient for comparison with one another, but adapted to the various uses of single pocket volumes. This arrangement affords the purchaser also the opportunity of providing himself only with those languages he may require; and supplies his wants in the most convenient, elegant, as well as inexpensive manner.

The STUDENT'S ANALYTICAL GREEK TESTAMENT;

Presenting at one view the Text of Scholz and a Grammatical Analysis of the Verbs, in which every occurring Inflexion of Verb or Participle is minutely described and traced to its proper Root. With the Readings, Textual and Marginal, of Griesbach; and the Variations of Stephens, 1550; Beza, 1598; The Elzevir, 1633. Square 16mo. Cloth, 12s.

The GREEK STUDENT'S MANUAL.

Containing a Practical Guide to the Greek Testament, designed for those who have no knowledge of the Greek language; the New Testament, Greek and English; and a Greek and English Lexicon to the New Testament. Foolscap octavo, Cloth, 10s.

A SPUR AND ENCOURAGEMENT TO THE STUDY OF THE

GREEK TESTAMENT: being some Suggestions for Learners, by a LEARNER. 2nd Edition, Revised. Crown octavo, price 6d.; by post, 7d.

A PRACTICAL GUIDE TO THE STUDY OF THE GREEK

NEW TESTAMENT. Foolscap octavo, price 2s.

HOW TO LEARN TO READ THE HEBREW BIBLE,

Without Points, in Twelve Lessons. Compiled from various sources by WILLIAM PENN. New and Revised Edition. Foolscap octavo. Price 1s. 6d.

The BIBLE AND PRAYER BOOK PSALMS.

The two versions of the Psalms, in Parallel Columns, with Notes, critical and explanatory. 230 pp. By SIR LANCELOT CHARLES LEE BRENTON, Bart. 16mo., Cloth, red edges, 3s.

BAGSTER'S DEVOTIONAL HAND-BOOKS.

The Psalms, 2s. 6d.; Proverbs, 1s. 8d.; St. John's Gospel, 1s. 8d.; Romans, 1s. 4d.; Hebrews, 1s. 4d., illustrated verse by verse with suitable passages from other parts of Scripture. 32mo., Roan.

The DIVINE PROMISES contained in the Scriptures illustrated in the same manner. 32mo., Roan. 1s. 4d.

SAMUEL BAGSTER AND SONS, LONDON.

RECORDS OF THE PAST. Edited by S. BIRCH, LLD.

VOL. V.—By H. F. Talbot, F.R.S.:—Legend of the Infancy of Sargina I. Inscription of Nabonidus. Inscription of Darius, at Nakshi Rustam. War of the Seven Evil Spirits against Heaven. By Sir H. Rawlinson, K.C.B., D.C.L., etc.:—Inscription of Tiglath Pileser I. By the Rev. A. H. Sayce, M.A.:— Black Obelisk Inscription of Shalmaneser II. Accadian Hymn to Istar. Tables of Omens. By the Rev. J. M. Rodwell, M.A.:—Tiglath Pileser II. Inscription of Nebuchadnezzar. Inscription of Neriglissar. By George Smith:—Early History of Babylonia, Part II. List of Further Texts. Crown octavo, Cloth, 3s. 6d.

VOL. VI.—By S. Birch, LL.D.:—Sepulchral Inscription of Ameni. The Conquests in Asia. Egyptian Magical Text. By Professor Eisenlohr and S. Birch, LL.D.:—Great Harris Papyrus, Part I. By P. Le Page Renouf:— Inscription of Aahmes, son of Abana. By C. W. Goodwin, M.A.:—Letter of Panbesa. Hymns to Amen. The Story of Saneha. By G. Maspero:—Stele of the Coronation. Stele of King Horsiatef. By Paul Pierret:—The Inscription of the Governor Nes-hor. By Édouard Naville:—Inscription of the Destruction of Mankind. By Ludwig Stern:—The Song of the Harper. By François Chabas:—The Tale of the Garden of Flowers. List of Further Texts.

Vols. 1-6 *Now ready*. Vols. 7 and 8 *in the Press*.

THE ASSYRIAN EPONYM CANON;

Containing translations of the Documents, and an account of the evidence, on the Comparative Chronology of the Assyrian and Jewish kingdoms, from the death of Solomon to Nebuchadnezzar. By GEORGE SMITH. Octavo, Cloth extra, 9s.

ARCHAIC CLASSICS:

ASSYRIAN GRAMMAR.—An Elementary Grammar and Reading Book of the Assyrian Language, in the Cuneiform Character: containing the most complete Syllabary yet extant, and which will serve also as a Vocabulary of both Accadian and Assyrian. By Rev. A. H. SAYCE, M.A. Quarto, Cloth, 7s. 6d.

EGYPTIAN GRAMMAR. — An Elementary Manual of the Egyptian Language: with an interlineary Reading Book: in the Hieroglyphic Character. By P. LE PAGE RENOUF, F.R.S.L. In two Parts. Part I. Grammar. Cloth extra, 7s. 6d.

Part II. Reading Book. *Will shortly follow.*

AN ARCHAIC DICTIONARY,

Historical and Mythological, from the Egyptian, Assyrian, and Etruscan Monuments and Papyri. By W. R. COOPER, F.R.A.S., M.R.A.S. *In the Press.*

ANCIENT CHALDEAN MAGIC.

Translated from the French of M. FRANÇOIS LENORMANT, with Notes and References by the English Editor. *In the Press.*

THE UTRECHT PSALTER.

The History, Art, and Palæography of the Manuscript commonly styled the Utrecht Psalter. By WALTER DE GRAY BIRCH, F.R.S.L., Senior Assistant of the Department of Manuscripts in the British Museum; Honorary Secretary to the British Archæological Association, etc. *In the Press.*

LONDON:
SAMUEL BAGSTER AND SONS,
15, PATERNOSTER ROW.

WORKS BY THE

REV. FRANCIS TILNEY BASSETT, M.A.

(May be had of the Author.)

THE BOOK OF

THE PROPHET HOSEA,

LITERALLY TRANSLATED;

WITH

INTRODUCTION,

AND

NOTES CRITICAL AND EXPLANATORY.

Price 5s.

"SEARCH AND SEE;"

AN EXAMINATION

OF

CERTAIN DISPUTED MESSIANIC TEXTS;

WITH

REFERENCE TO CONTROVERSIES ANCIENT AND MODERN.

Price 3s. 6d.

WORKS BY THE
REV. FRANCIS TILNEY BASSETT, M.A.

(May be had of the Author.)

ADVENT SERMONS.

CHRIST IN ETERNITY AND TIME.

Price 2s. 6d.

"THINGS THAT MUST BE."

Price 2s. 6d.

THE TEACHERS' TEXT BOOK.

A FAMILIAR EXPLANATION

OF

DIFFICULT PASSAGES IN THE FOUR GOSPELS.

Price 2s.

SACRED ALLEGORIES,

AND

THEIR LESSONS, IN VERSE.

Price 2s. 6d.

SELECTIONS FROM
Messrs. S. BAGSTER and SONS' CATALOGUE.

AIDS TO THE STUDY

OF THE

OLD TESTAMENT SCRIPTURES.

The Hebrew Student's Manual.   £ *s. d.*
> CONTENTS:—Preface, 6 *pp.* Recommendations to the Learner, 2 *pp.* I. A Hebrew Grammar, 125 *pp.* II. A series of Hebrew Reading Lessons, analysed, 70 *pp.* III. The Book of Psalms, with interlineary translation; the construction of every Hebrew word being clearly indicated, and the root of each distinguished by the use of hollow and other types, 240 *pp.* IV. A Hebrew and English Lexicon, containing all the Hebrew and Chaldee words in the Old Testament Scriptures, 287 *pp.*
>
> Foolscap octavo, Cloth 0 10 0

A Revision of the Hebrew Text of the Old Testament.
> CONTENTS: — Introduction, 12 *pp.* Synopsis of Readings revised from critical sources; being an attempt to present a purer and more correct Text than the 'Received' one of Van der Hooght, by the aid of the best existing materials: with the principal Various Readings found in MSS., ancient Versions, Jewish Books and Writers, Parallels, Quotations, etc., 222 *pp.*
> By Samuel Davidson, D.D.
>
> Octavo, Cloth 0 10 6

The Analytical Hebrew Lexicon.
> The Words of the entire Hebrew Scriptures are arranged just as they are found in the Sacred Text, Alphabetically, and are Grammatically explained. The student of the original has only to turn from his Bible to this Lexicon for the solution of every etymological difficulty that may obstruct his progress, and he will find, without trouble or loss of time, a complete analysis of every word, with an account of its peculiarities, and a reference to the conjugation or declension to which it may belong, or if it be irregular, to its exceptional class. Every word is also referred to its root (where its various *significations* will be found), and with the root is given a conspectus of all the words which owe their derivation to its source. This feature of the work is of considerable value, because it affords the opportunity of studying the language from another point of view; for, by turning from root to root (the roots are distinguished in the

For Specimen Pages, see the Illustrated Supplement. By post, free.

alphabetical order by larger types), the student may see at a glance in what way the various nouns, adjectives, and other parts of speech are developed from the radical forms. Another feature of interest is the Grammatical Introduction, which is chiefly devoted to the study of the irregularities of the language. Here will be found, it is believed, every single exceptional word, with a concise explanation of its peculiarities. The words which, in particular forms, occur but once in the Scriptures, possess a peculiar interest, and they are very numerous. They have all been distinguished by a small letter, which refers to the passage of occurrence at the foot of the page. Among other minor advantages afforded by this Lexicon, may be mentioned, the indication, in all cases, of the *Kamets-Chatuph*, which requires some familiarity with the language to distinguish.

The ANALYTICAL LEXICON is thus:—I. A Lexicon in the ordinary sense of supplying the various meanings of the various roots ;—II. A Dictionary of every derivative and modification of every root, in alphabetical order, with analysis;—III. A storehouse of the anomalies of the language, carefully arranged and referred to from all parts of the work;—IV. A Concordance of the least easily understood words.

"It is the *ultimatum* of Hebrew Lexicography, and will leave the Theologian, who still remains ignorant of the Sacred tongue, absolutely without excuse."— *Churchman's Monthly Review*.

By Professor B. Davidson.
Quarto, Cloth   ..   .. | 1 5 0

Gesenius's Hebrew Grammar.

Enlarged and improved by Professor E. Rödiger. With a Hebrew Reading Book, 275 pp.
Quarto, Cloth   ..   .. | 0 7 6
With Lloyd's Analysis of Gen. I.-XI. (See page 31.) | 0 10 6

Gesenius's Hebrew Lexicon.

CONTENTS:—Preface, 4 *pp*. Address to the Student, 4 *pp*. Table of Alphabets, 2 *pp*. The Lexicon, 884 *pp*. English-Hebrew Index, 35 *pp*.
By S. P. Tregelles, LL.D.
Quarto, Cloth   ..   .. | 1 1 0

Gesenius's Hebrew Lexicon. Abridged Edition.

Small Quarto. *(In the Press.)*

Hebrew Reading Lessons.

CONTENTS:—Introductory Notice, 6 *pp*. The first four chapters of the Book of Genesis, and the eighth

For Specimen Pages, see the Illustrated Supplement. By post, free.

Aids to the Study of the Old Testament Scriptures.

	£	s.	d.
chapter of the Proverbs, with a Grammatical Praxis, and an Interlineary Translation, 70 pp. By S. P. Tregelles, LL.D. Foolscap octavo, Cloth	0	3	6

The Heads of Hebrew Grammar.

CONTENTS:—Preface, 8 pp. The Heads of Hebrew Grammar, containing all the Principles needed by a Learner, 126 pp.; with a Series of Hebrew Paradigms. By S. P. Tregelles, LL.D.

Foolscap octavo, Cloth	0	3	0

A Methodization of the Hebrew Verbs.

CONTENTS:—This original plan includes the verbs, regular and irregular, 32 pp. By the Rev. Tresham D. Gregg, D.D.

Octavo, Boards	0	2	6

A Practical Hebrew Grammar.

CONTENTS:—Preface and Introduction, 10 pp. The Grammar with progressive constructive Exercises to every Rule; and a Reading Book, 204 pp. By Dr. J. Robert Wolfe.

Post octavo, Cloth	0	6	0

A Pocket Hebrew-English Lexicon.

CONTENTS:—Preface, 5 pp. The Lexicon containing all the Hebrew and Chaldee words in the Old Testament Scriptures, with their meanings in English, and combining the alphabetical with the radical arrangement of the words, 287 pp.

Foolscap octavo, Cloth	0	4	6

The Hebrew Bible of the Polyglot Series.

CONTENTS:—The Hebrew Text after Van der Hooght, with the *Keri* and *Chetib*, 585 pp. The Various Readings of the Samaritan Pentateuch, 50 pp.

Foolscap octavo, Cloth	0	10	0

Hebrew and English Old Testament, interpaged.

Foolscap octavo, Cloth	0	18	0
With GREEK and ENGLISH NEW TESTAMENT, extra	0	6	0

For Specimen Pages, see the Illustrated Supplement. By post, free.

Aids to the Study of the Old Testament Scriptures.

	£	s.	d.
Hebrew Bible, interpaged with the Greek Septuagint.			
Foolscap octavo, Cloth	1	0	0
Hebrew and Latin Vulgate Old Testament, interpaged.			
Foolscap octavo, Cloth	0	14	6
Hebrew and German Old Testament, interpaged.			
Foolscap octavo, Cloth	0	14	6
Hebrew and French Old Testament, interpaged.			
Foolscap octavo, Cloth	0	14	6
Hebrew and Italian Old Testament, interpaged.			
Foolscap octavo, Cloth	0	14	6
Hebrew and Spanish Old Testament, interpaged.			
Foolscap octavo, Cloth	0	14	6
Hebrew and Portuguese Old Testament, interpaged.			
Foolscap octavo, Cloth	0	14	6
The Hebrew Pentateuch.			
CONTENTS:— The five Books of Moses in Hebrew, with points, 149 *pp.*			
Foolscap octavo, Cloth	0	2	6
The Prophecy of Joel.			
The Hebrew Text of Joel printed metrically, with a new English Translation and Critical Notes. By the Rev. Joseph Hughes, B.A.			
Foolscap octavo	0	2	6
The Apocrypha, Greek and English. In Parallel Columns.			
Quarto, Cloth	0	6	0
The Hexaplar Psalter.			
CONTENTS:—The Book of Psalms in Hebrew; the Greek of the LXX.; the Vulgate Latin; Jerome's Hebrew-Latin; the English Liturgical Version; and the English Authorised Version: in six Parallel Columns, 267 *pp.*			
Quarto, Cloth	0	15	0

For Specimen Pages see the Illustrated Supplement. By post, free.

Aids to the Study of the Old Testament Scriptures.

	£	s.	d.
An Interlineary Hebrew-English Psalter. CONTENTS :—The Book of Psalms in Hebrew, printed so as to distinguish the servile letters from the radical; with a closely literal English Translation under each word. 240 *pp.* Foolscap octavo, Cloth	0	5	0
Hebrew Psalms, without points. Foolscap octavo	0	1	0
Hebrew and English Psalms. The Hebrew Text is that of Van der Hooght, carefully reprinted from the edition, A.D. 1705. The English Version is the Authorised Translation according to the edition of A.D. 1611. Arranged in Parallel Columns, 190 *pp.* Foolscap octavo, Cloth	0	4	0
An Analysis of the first eleven Chapters of Genesis: with copious References to Gesenius's Hebrew Grammar. By the Rev. John Lloyd, M.A. Quarto, Boards	0	3	6
With Gesenius's Hebrew Grammar	0	10	6
An Analysis of the Book of Ecclesiastes: with reference to the Hebrew Grammar of Gesenius, and with Notes critical and explanatory. To which is added the Book of Ecclesiastes, in Hebrew and English, in parallel columns. By the Rev. John Lloyd, M.A. Quarto, Cloth	0	7	6
With Gesenius's Hebrew Grammar	0	15	0
A new Hebrew Concordance. A Concordance of the Hebrew and Chaldee Scriptures. Revised and corrected by B. Davidson. Royal octavo, Cloth	3	3	0
Turkey morocco plain	4	4	0
The Study of the Hebrew Vowel Points. Parts I.–II. A Series of Exercises in very large Hebrew type, printed upon writing-paper, with space between the lines for the addition in manuscript of the Vowel Points and Accents. Quarto. Nos. 1 and 2 .. .. each	0	0	4

For Specimen Pages, see the Illustrated Supplement. By post, free.

Aids to the Study of the Old Testament Scriptures.

	£ s. d.
The Septuagint. CONTENTS:—An Historical Account of the Septuagint Version, and of the principal Texts in which it is current, 16 *pp*. The Septuagint Version of the Old Testament, according to the Vatican edition; together with the real Septuagint Version of Daniel and the Apocrypha, including the fourth Book of Maccabees, 942 *pp*. Octavo, Cloth	0 18 0
The Septuagint of the Pocket Polyglot Series. CONTENTS:—Tables of the Various Readings of the Alexandrine Text, 104 *pp*. The Septuagint according to the Vatican Text, 585 *pp*. Foolscap octavo, Cloth	0 10 0
The Septuagint and Greek New Testament. Foolscap octavo, Cloth	0 13 6
An English Translation of the Septuagint. CONTENTS:—Preface, 5 *pp*. Chronological Table, 3 *pp*. The Translation of the Septuagint Version of the Old Testament, according to the Vatican Text, into English, with Critical Notes, and the principal Various Readings of the Alexandrine Copy, 920 *pp*. By Sir Lancelot Charles Lee Brenton, Bart. Octavo. Two volumes, Cloth	1 1 0
The Septuagint, interpaged with the Hebrew Text. Foolscap octavo, Cloth	1 0 0
The Septuagint and English, interpaged. Foolscap octavo, Cloth	0 18 0
The Septuagint and Latin, interpaged. Foolscap octavo, Cloth	0 14 6
The Septuagint and German, interpaged. Foolscap octavo, Cloth	0 14 6

For Specimen Pages, see the Illustrated Supplement. By post, free.

Aids to the Study of the Old Testament Scriptures.

	£ s. d.
The Septuagint and French, interpaged. Foolscap octavo, Cloth	0 14 6
The Septuagint and Italian, interpaged. Foolscap octavo, Cloth	0 14 6
The Septuagint and Spanish, interpaged. Foolscap octavo, Cloth	0 14 6
The Septuagint and Portuguese, interpaged. Foolscap octavo, Cloth	0 14 6

Arabic Reading Lessons.
CONTENTS:— Extracts from the Koran and other sources, grammatically analysed and translated; with the Elements of Arabic Grammar, 134 *pp*.
Post octavo, Cloth 0 3 6

Chaldee Reading Lessons.
CONTENTS:—Preface, 2 *pp*. The whole of the Biblical Chaldee, with a Grammatical Praxis and an Interlineary Translation, 140 *pp*. A series of Chaldee Paradigms.
Foolscap octavo, Cloth 0 3 6

The Proper Names of the Old Testament, expounded and illustrated.
CONTENTS:—A Dictionary of all the Proper Names occurring in the Old Testament Scriptures, in which these names are etymologically and hermeneutically investigated, 382 *pp*.
By the Rev. Alfred Jones.
Quarto, Cloth 0 15 0

The Hebrew Language.
CONTENTS:—Preface, 6 *pp*. The History and Characteristics of the Hebrew Language, including improved renderings of select passages in our Authorised Translation of the Old Testament, 187 *pp*.
By Henry Craik.
Crown octavo, Cloth 0 3 6

For Specimen Pages, see the Illustrated Supplement. By post, free.

Aids to the Study of the Old Testament Scriptures.

	£ s. d.
Principia Hebraica. CONTENTS:—Preface, 2 pp. The Principles of Hebrew Grammar, 7 pp. An easy Introduction to the Hebrew Language, in twenty-four large folio Tables, which contain the Interpretation of all the Hebrew and Chaldee words, both Primitives and Derivatives, contained in the Old Testament Scriptures. By Henry Craik. Folio, Cloth	0 10 6
The Englishman's Hebrew and Chaldee Concordance of the Old Testament: Being an attempt at a Verbal Connection between the Original and the English Translation; with Indexes, a List of the Proper Names, and their occurrences, etc. Third Edition. Two volumes. Royal octavo, Cloth	3 13 6
The Hebraist's Vade Mecum: A first attempt at a Complete Verbal Index to the Contents of the Hebrew and Chaldee Scriptures. Arranged according to Grammar: the occurrences in full. Demy octavo	0 15 0
How to Learn to Read the Hebrew Bible, Without Points, in Twelve Lessons. Compiled from various sources. New and revised Edition. By William Penn, F.R.A.S. Foolscap octavo	0 1 6
The Book of Jonah : The Text Analyzed, Translated, and the Accents named; being an easy introduction to the Hebrew language. By the Rev. Alexander Mitchell, M.A. Octavo	0 5 0
Old Testament History. By Andrew Thomson. Crown octavo, Cloth	0 4 6

For Specimen Pages, see the Illustrated Supplement. By post, free.

AIDS TO THE STUDY
OF THE
NEW TESTAMENT SCRIPTURES.

The English Hexapla.   £ s. d.

    CONTENTS:—The Six principal English Versions of the New Testament, in Parallel Columns, beneath the Greek Original Text. The advantages of this arrangement are obvious. The meaning of the Original is reflected from the renderings of six independent Translations on the same page.
One very handsome volume.

Quarto, Cloth	2	2	0
Turkey morocco plain	3	4	0
*** A few large-paper copies, Cloth	3	3	0

The Greek Student's Manual.

    CONTENTS:—I. A Practical Guide to the Greek Testament, designed for those who have no knowledge of the Greek language, 92 pp. II. The New Testament, Greek and English, 376 pp. III. A Greek and English Lexicon to the New Testament, 208 pp.

    Foolscap octavo, Cloth 0 10 0

A Practical Guide to the Greek New Testament.

    Designed for those who have no knowledge of the Greek language, but who desire to read the New Testament in the original. 92 pp.

    Foolscap octavo, Cloth 0 2 0

A Grammar of the New Testament Dialect.

    CONTENTS:—Introduction, 8 pp. A Treatise on the Grammar of the New Testament; embracing observations on the literal interpretation of numerous passages, 238 pp. Index of passages particularly noticed, 6 pp. By the Rev. T. S. Green, M.A.

    Crown octavo, Cloth 0 7 0

Critical Notes on the New Testament.

    CONTENTS:—These Notes are mainly grammatical, but their plan embraces observations on the meaning of particular terms, especially synonyms. The arrangement of sentences is treated as a matter of material importance to exact interpretation. 200 pp. By the Rev. T. S. Green, M.A.

    Crown octavo, Cloth 0 7 0

The Analytical Greek Lexicon to the New Testament.

    CONTENTS:—Tables of the Declensions and Conjugations, with explanatory grammatical remarks, 46 pp.

For Specimen Pages, see the Illustrated Supplement. By post, free.

Aids to the Study of the New Testament Scriptures.

	£	s.	d.
A Dictionary, consisting of an Alphabetical arrangement of every occurring inflexion of every word contained in the Greek New Testament Scriptures, with a grammatical analysis of each word, and copious Lexicography, 444 *pp*. The Student of the Greek New Testament has only to turn to this Lexicon for the solution of every etymological difficulty that may obstruct his progress; and he will find, without trouble or loss of time, a complete analysis of every word, with an account of its peculiarities, and a reference to the conjugation or declension to which it may belong, or if it be irregular to its exceptional class. Quarto, Cloth	0	12	0
Developed Criticism of the New Testament.			
Contents:—Introduction, 10 *pp.* A series of complete critical discussions on those passages of the New Testament which are materially affected by Various Readings, 192 *pp.* By the Rev. T. S. Green, M.A. Octavo, Cloth	0	7	0
A Pocket Greek-English Lexicon to the New Testament.			
By the Rev. T. S. Green, M.A. Foolscap octavo, Cloth	0	3	6
A Greek Concordance to the New Testament.			
Contents:—Address to the Reader, 3 *pp.* Preface. A Concordance of the words of the Greek New Testament, with their context, 280 *pp.* By Erasmus Schmidt.			
Foolscap octavo, Cloth	0	3	6
32mo., Cloth	0	3	6
Greenfield's Greek Lexicon to the New Testament.			
Contents:—Engraved Tables of Greek Numerals, and of the Ligatures or Abbreviations in Ancient Greek MSS. and Editions. The Lexicon, in which the various senses of the words are distinctly explained in English, and authorised by references to passages of Scripture, 98 *pp.* Foolscap octavo, Cloth	0	2	6
Ditto. 32mo., Cloth	0	2	6
The New Testament, Greek and English.			
In Parallel Columns. With Various Readings. Quarto, Cloth	0	7	0

For Specimen Pages, see the Illustrated Supplement. By post, free.

Aids to the Study of the New Testament Scriptures.

	£ s. d.
The Greek New Testament. Edited from Ancient Authorities (with the Latin Version of Jerome, from the Codex Amiatinus). By S. P. Tregelles, LL.D. Quarto, Cloth	3 13 6

A Large Print Greek New Testament.

CONTENTS:—In selecting a Text to be used in this edition, *Mill's* has been preferred, as being that which is most current in this country.

The margin contains certain of the readings which have been adopted by Griesbach, Scholz, Lachmann, or Tischendorf: the abbreviations of the names of these critics (Gb. Sch. Ln. Tf.) are subjoined to the readings which they adopt.

A selection of references to parallel passages has also been placed in thè margin: these have not been chosen without careful examination, so that they will be found, it is believed, really illustrative of the Sacred Text.

In the four Gospels the numbers of the Ammonian Sections and the references to the Eusebian Canons have been placed in the margin: for the convenience, however, of the reader, the Greek numerals have been changed into those in common use,—the Ammonian Sections being indicated by Arabic numerals, and the Eusebian Canons by Roman. 512 *pp.*

Octavo, Cloth	0 12 0

An Etymological Vocabulary of all the Words in the Greek New Testament.

CONTENTS:—Part I. Roots. The Nouns, Adjectives, Verbs. The Hebrew words, Latin words, and roots of compound words. Part II. Derivatives and Compounds. The Substantives, Adjectives, Verbs, Pronouns, Prepositions, Conjunctions, Adverbs, and Interjections, 224 *pp.*

Foolscap octavo, Cloth	0 2 6

The Englishman's Greek Concordance of The New Testament:

Being an attempt at a Verbal connection between the Greek and the English Texts; including a Concordance to the Proper Names; with Indexes, Greek-English and English-Greek.

Sixth Edition.

Royal octavo, Cloth	2 2 0

For Specimen Pages, see the Illustrated Supplement. By post, free.

The Twofold New Testament.

  CONTENTS:—A newly-formed Greek Text, with an accompanying new Translation into English. In Parallel Columns, 466 pp.

  By the Rev. T. S. Green, M.A.

  "I have taken some pains to produce, as far as possible, a strict uniformity of the rendering of terms; so that the mere English reader may have presented to him the sameness and difference of expression which are found in the Original, as far as this can be fairly done." (Preface.)

   Quarto, Cloth .. ..   **£ 1 1 0**

A Collation of the Critical Texts of Griesbach, Scholz,

 Lachmann, and Tischendorf, with the Received Text, 96 pp.

 By S. P. Tregelles, LL.D.

   Octavo, Sewed **0 3 0**

Pocket Critical Greek and English New Testament.

  CONTENTS:—The Greek Text of Scholz, with the Readings, both textual and marginal, of Griesbach; and the variations of the editions of Stephens, 1550; Beza, 1598; and the Elzevir, 1633: with the English Authorised Version, and its marginal renderings, 624 pp.

   16mo., Cloth **0 6 0**

   With GREEK-ENGLISH LEXICON, extra **0 3 6**

A Greek and English New Testament for MS. Notes.

  This is an edition of the last, printed upon writing-paper, with broad margins for Annotations.

   Quarto, Cloth **0 7 6**

The Traveller's New Testament.

  The object of this volume is to provide the Christian Student with the greatest possible help in the most portable form.

  CONTENTS:—The New Testament Scriptures, in Greek and English, with Various Readings, a complete Lexicon, and a Manual Concordance of the New Testament.

  Pocket volume, Bound in the best morocco, limp and flexible, with projecting edges and a protecting flap, secured with an elastic band **1 0 0**

For Specimen Pages, see the Illustrated Supplement. By post, free.

Aids to the Study of the New Testament Scriptures.

	£ s. d.
The Students' Analytical Greek Testament: Presenting at one view the Text of Scholz and a Grammatical Analysis of the Verbs, in which every occurring inflection of Verb or Participle is minutely described and traced to its proper Root. With the Readings Textual and Marginal of Griesbach; and the variations of Stephens, 1550; Beza, 1598; the Elzevir, 1633. Square 16mo.	0 12 0
The Polymicrian Greek New Testament. CONTENTS:—The Received Greek Text, with Various Readings, Parallel References, indication of the Roots, Maps, engraved Tables, etc., 565 pp. 32mo., Cloth	0 3 6
A Thin Pocket Greek New Testament. CONTENTS:—Preface, 2 pp. Griesbach's Various Readings, 22 pp. The Greek New Testament according to Mill's edition of the Received Text, 188 pp. Foolscap octavo, Cloth	0 3 6
With this edition of the New Testament may be bound up a Greek Lexicon and a Greek Concordance.	
The Narrow Greek New Testament. CONTENTS:—The Text of Scholz, with the Readings, both textual and marginal, of Griesbach; and the variations of the editions of Stephens, 1550; Beza, 1598; the Elzevir, 1633, 656 pp. 32mo., Cloth	0 4 6
Greek and English New Testament, interpaged. Foolscap octavo, Cloth	0 6 0
Greek and Latin New Testament, interpaged. Foolscap octavo, Cloth	0 6 0
Greek and German New Testament, interpaged. Foolscap octavo, Cloth	0 6 0
Greek and Italian New Testament, interpaged. Foolscap octavo, Cloth	0 6 0
Greek and Spanish New Testament, interpaged. Foolscap octavo, Cloth	0 6 0
Greek and French New Testament, interpaged. Foolscap octavo, Cloth	0 6 0
Greek and Portuguese New Testament, interpaged. Foolscap octavo, Cloth	0 6 0

For Specimen Pages, see the Illustrated Supplement. By post, free.

Aids to the Study of the New Testament Scriptures.

	£	s.	d.
Greek and Hebrew New Testament, interpaged. Foolscap octavo, Cloth	0	7	0

A Hebrew Version of the New Testament.
By William Greenfield.
    Octavo, Cloth ..   0 6 0

Ditto.
    Foolscap octavo, Cloth ..   0 3 6

The Acts, Greek and English, for MS. Notes.
    Small quarto, Cloth ..   0 1 6

St. John's Gospel, Epistles, and Prophecy.
    CONTENTS :—The complete Writings of the Apostle John, printed in Greek and English on opposite pages, 187 pp.
    Foolscap octavo, Cloth ..   0 5 0

The Codex Montfortianus.
    CONTENTS:—Preface, 20 pp. Introduction, 64 pp. A Collation of this celebrated MS. throughout the Gospels and Acts, with the Greek Text of Wetstein, and with certain MSS. in the University of Oxford, 196 pp.
    By Orlando T. Dobbin, LL.D.
    Octavo, Antique cloth ..   0 10 6

The Codex Zacynthius.
    " Even on a cursory examination, the value of the MS. appeared to be great; but as in many parts it was illegible, except in a very good light, and as it would take a considerable time to decipher the Biblical portion, I made application to the Committee, through the Rev. John Mee, one of the Secretaries, for permission to use the MS. at my own abode. This was kindly granted me, and thus I have been able to collate the MS., and to prepare the portion containing the text of St. Luke for publication, with a facsimile of the entire page, text and Catena.

    " I do not know of any MS. of equal antiquity accompanied by a Catena; in many respects this most valuable palimpsest is worthy of special attention: it is remarkable that it had remained in this country for nearly forty years unread and unused."
    By S. P. Tregelles, LL.D.
    Folio, Half-russia ..   1 1 0

For Specimen Pages, see the Illustrated Supplement. By post, free.

Aids to the Study of the New Testament Scriptures.

	£ s. d.
An Account of the Printed Text of the Greek N.T. With Remarks on its Revision upon Critical principles. CONTENTS:—Preface, 4 pp. Index of passages the reading of which is discussed or noticed, 2 pp. An account of the Complutensian edition:—the editions of Erasmus:—the editions of Stephens, Beza, and the Elzevirs:—Walton's Polyglot, and Bishop Fell's Greek Testament:—Mill's Greek Testament:—Bentley's proposed edition:—Bengel, Wetstein, Griesbach, Scholz, Lachmann's editions—Tischendorf's editions:—an Estimate of MS. Authorities:—Collations and Critical Studies of S. P. Tregelles:—Principles of Textual Criticism:—Passages of Dogmatic importance:—Conclusion, 274 pp. A Collation of the Critical Texts of Griesbach, Scholz, Lachmann, and Tischendorf, with that in common use, 94 pp. By S. P. Tregelles, LL.D. Octavo, Cloth	0 10 6
Syriac Reading Lessons. CONTENTS:—Extracts from the Peschito Version of the Old and New Testaments; and the Crusade of Richard I., from the Chronicles of Bar Hebræus; grammatically analysed and translated: with the Elements of Syriac Grammar, 123 pp. Post octavo, Cloth	0 3 6
Syriac New Testament, with a Literal English Translation. Small Quarto. *(In the Press.)*	
The Syriac New Testament. Post octavo, Cloth	0 8 0
Turkey morocco plain	0 16 0
A Syriac Lexicon to the New Testament. By E. Henderson, Ph. D. Post octavo, Cloth	0 2 6
A Samaritan Grammar. CONTENTS:—Introduction, 13 pp. The Grammar of the Samaritan Language, with Extracts and Vocabulary, 138 pp. By G. F. Nicholls. Post octavo, Cloth	0 6 0

For Specimen Pages, see the Illustrated Supplement. By post, free.
** **

Aids to the Study of the New Testament Scriptures.

	£ s. d.
The Seven Epistles and Revelation. CONTENTS:— Introduction, 18 pp. An Original Translation of the Epistles of James, Peter, John, and Jude; and the Book of Revelation; with Critical Notes, 66 pp. By Joseph Turnbull, Ph.D. Octavo, Cloth	0 4 6
The Epistles of Paul the Apostle. CONTENTS:—Introduction, 35 pp. An Original Translation, with Critical Notes, 146 pp. By Joseph Turnbull, Ph.D. Octavo, Cloth	0 7 0
The Revelation, from Ancient Authorities. CONTENTS:—Preface, 6 pp. Address to the Reader, 23 pp. The Book of Revelation, translated from the Greek Text, according to the Ancient Authorities; so that there is not a single word which is not guaranteed by MS. authority of at least 1200 years old, 44 pp. Prospectus of a Critical Edition of the Greek New Testament, with an Historical Sketch of the Printed Text, 33 pp. Description of a Palimpsest MS. hitherto unused, 4 pp. By S. P. Tregelles, LL.D. Foolscap octavo, Limp cloth	0 2 0
An amended Translation of the Hebrews. CONTENTS:—Preface, 4 pp. The Epistle to the Hebrews, 22 pp. Notes explanatory of the altered renderings, 10 pp. By Henry Craik. Foolscap octavo, Sewed	0 0 6
The Gospel of Matthew in Arabic. Printed with all the vowels, on a new and simpler plan, with an Introduction explanatory of the method of printing the Arabic vowels, both mechanically and philologically. By the Rev. Jules Ferrette, Missionary at Damascus. Foolscap octavo, Cloth	0 3 0

For Specimen Pages, see the Illustrated Supplement. By post, free.

Aids to the Study of the New Testament Scriptures.

	£	s.	d.

The Narrow Gospels.

CONTENTS :—The four Gospels, according to the Authorised Version, printed in a narrow shape to secure the utmost portability.

    32mo. Roan 0 2 6

    Turkey morocco limp 0 5 0

The Narrow Epistles.

CONTENTS :—The Epistles, according to the Authorised Version, printed in a narrow shape to secure the utmost portability.

    32mo., Limp roan 0 2 6

    Turkey morocco limp 0 5 0

Historic Evidence of the New Testament.

CONTENTS :—Introduction, 16 pp. A Lecture on the Historic Evidence of the Authorship and Transmission of the Books of the New Testament, 96 pp. Appendix, No. 1. On the Text of the New Testament. No. II. Some of the results of the genuineness of the New Testament, 34 pp.

By S. P. Tregelles, LL.D.

    Post octavo, Cloth 0 3 0

Improved Renderings of the New Testament.

CONTENTS :— Preface, 4 pp. Introduction, 8 pp. Hints to Students, 2 pp. Improved Renderings of those passages of the New Testament which are capable of being more correctly translated, 46 pp.

By Henry Craik.

    Crown octavo, Cloth 0 1 0

Textual Criticism of the New Testament, for English Bible Students.,

(Second Edition, Revised and Corrected.)

CONTENTS :—A succinct comparison of the Authorised Version of the New Testament with the critical Texts of Griesbach, Scholz, Lachmann, Tischendorf, Tregelles, and Alford, and the Uncial MSS.

By C. E. Stuart, Esq.

    Foolscap octavo, Cloth 0 5 0

For Specimen Pages, see the Illustrated Supplement. By post, free.

Aids to the Study of the New Testament Scriptures.

A Revised New Testament.   £ *s. d.*

    CONTENTS:—Preface, 8 *pp*. A Revised Translation of the New Testament, with a notice of the principal Various Readings in the Greek Text, 532 *pp*. By the Rev. H. Highton, M.A.

    Octavo, Cloth .. .. | 0 10 6

A Critical English New Testament,

    presenting at one view the Authorised Version and the Results of the latest criticism of the Original Text.

    The Authorised Version is printed unaltered, but in those passages in which it will be necessary in adapting the Translation to a restored Greek Text to *omit* certain words, such words are inclosed between brackets. In all cases where it will be necessary to *add* anything to the Authorised Version, such additions are given between brackets, and in italic type. And wherever the restoration of the Original necessitates an alteration of the expression, the fact is brought under the reader's notice by very simple and obvious typographical arrangements.

    It has been thought desirable in a matter of such solemn importance as the attempted rectification of the New Testament Scriptures, to adduce in every instance the critical authority upon which every proposed alteration rests. When the remarkable agreement in judgment of the Editors whose recensions have been adopted as the basis of this Critical English New Testament (although they have arrived at their results by slightly different principles), is observed, there is abundant ground for confidence that the Greek Text to which we now happily have access, really represents in a high degree of exactitude the veritable Word of God. Second Edition.

    Octavo, Cloth .. .. | 0 3 6

The New Testament,

    According to the Authorised Version; with Analysis, Notes, etc.

    Designed to put the English reader in possession of the accuracies and perfections of the Inspired Original.

    In paragraphs; with the subject of each paragraph given in the margin: and with suggestions for improved renderings, with proofs. Altered tenses of verbs restored.

For Specimen Pages, see the Illustrated Supplement. By post, free.

Indications of the presence or absence of the Greek article. Emphatic pronouns marked. Revised references; and other features.
By Thomas Newberry.

	£	s.	d.
Cloth boards	0	10	6
Extra Cloth	0	12	6

The Emphasised New Testament :

Newly translated, from the Text of Tregelles, and critically emphasised according to the logical idiom of the original by means of underscored lines. With an Introduction and occasional Notes.

"THE EMPHASISED NEW TESTAMENT" is marked by the following features:—

1. It distinguishes all emphatic words.
2. It shows every recurrence of the Greek Article, whether translated or not.
3. It pays special heed to the Moods and Tenses.
4. It endeavours to render theological and ecclesiastical terms according to their simple meaning.
5. It is an entirely Independent Translation, formed directly from the Greek, and is in no sense a mere Revision.
6. It has been faithfully executed from the Text of Tregelles.
7. It contains an Introduction treating of Emphasis, the Greek Article, and the Tenses.
8. It has occasional brief suggestive Notes.

"Designed for the private use of studious readers, this Translation, of set purpose, adheres more closely to the idiom of the original than a Version intended for public use could have done with propriety. Especially in respect of EMPHASIS has an endeavour been made to enable the English reader to perceive the point and energy which are everywhere, in the Greek, revealed simply by the arrangement of words and clauses. Not only is the emphatic *effect* of that arrangement uniformly marked in this Translation by careful UNDERSCORING, but as much of the emphatic *idiom itself* is reproduced as seemed likely to meet with thoughtful appreciation." The Introduction discusses, not only the Laws of "Emphasis," but also "The Power of the Greek Article," and "The Forces of the various Tenses," —to all of which careful regard has been paid by the Translator. The Notes, though occasional and brief, are suggestive, and it is hoped will incite the reader to discover for himself many valuable hints conveyed by the Emphasised Text
By Joseph B. Rotherham.
Octavo, Cloth 0 7 6

For Specimen Pages, see the Illustrated Supplement. By post, free.

Aids to the Study of the New Testament Scriptures.

	£	s.	d.

The Vulgate New Testament,
    Compared with the Douay Version of 1582. In Parallel Columns.
    Small Quarto, Cloth   0   6   0

A Spur and Encouragement.
    CONTENTS :—An incentive to the Study of the Greek Testament, with some practical Suggestions for Learners.
    (New and Revised Edition.)
    Octavo. Sewed   0   0   6

The Reason Why all Christians should read God's written Word in Greek : and demonstration afforded of the ease with which an accurate knowledge thereof may be gained by those who have not had a classical education.
    Octavo. Sewed   0   0   6

How to Learn to Read the Greek New Testament.
    Compiled from various sources. *(Second Edition Revised.)*
    By William Penn, F.R.A.S.
    (In the Press.)

The Gospel according to St. Matthew, Greek and English, for MS. Notes.
    Printed upon writing-paper, with broad margins for Annotations.
    Quarto, Cloth   0   1   6

New Testament History.
    By Andrew Thomson.
    Crown octavo, Cloth   0   3   6

The Epistle of St. James.
    A revised Text with Translation, and Notes Critical and Exegetical.
    By Francis Tilney Bassett, M.A.
    Quarto. *(In the Press.)*

Fruits of the New Testament Revision.
    By S. J. B. Bloxsidge..   0   0   6

For Specimen Pages, see the Illustrated Supplement. By post, free.

MISCELLANEOUS.

	£	s.	d.

Archaic Classics. Assyrian Grammar.

    An Elementary Grammar and Reading Book of the Assyrian Language, in the Cuneiform Character: containing the most complete Syllabary yet extant, and which will serve also as a Vocabulary of both Accadian and Assyrian. By Rev. A. H. Sayce, M.A.
    Quarto, Cloth   0   7   6

Archaic Classics. Egyptian Grammar.

    An Elementary Manual of the Egyptian Language: with an interlineary Reading Book: in the Hieroglyphic Character. In two Parts.
    Part I. Grammar.
    By P. le Page Renouf, F.R.S.L.
    Quarto, Cloth   0   7   6
    Part II. Reading Book. *Shortly to follow.*

Archaic Classics. Exercise Sheets.

    These Sheets have been prepared to enable the Student to test his progress, by translating a short passage from some well-known Text. In Sheet No. 1 of each series, Assyrian and Egyptian, will be given an interlineated Text, with space left between the lines for the translation. And the succeeding Sheets will contain another portion of Text, for translation, and also the correct rendering of the passage given in the preceding Sheet.
    On Writing Paper .. .. each   0   0   2

Records of the Past. Vols. I.–VI. Being English Translations of the Assyrian and Egyptian Monuments. Published under the sanction of the Society of Biblical Archæology. Edited by S. Birch, LL.D.

Records of the Past. Vol. I. Assyrian Texts, 1.

CONTENTS:—
    Inscription of Rimmon-Nirari; Monolith Inscription of Samas-Rimmon; Babylonian Exorcisms; Private Will of Sennacherib; Assyrian Private Contract Tablets; Assyrian Astronomical Tablets; Assyrian Calendar; Tables of Assyrian Weights and Measures. By Rev. A. H. Sayce, M.A.

For Specimen Pages, see the Illustrated Supplement. By post free.

	£ s. d.

Inscription of Khammurabi; Bellino's Cylinder of Sennacherib; Taylor's Cylinder of Sennacherib; Legend of the Descent of Ishtar. By H. Fox Talbot, F.R.S.
Annals of Assurbanipal (Cylinder A). By George Smith.
Behistun Inscription of Darius. By Sir Henry Rawlinson, K.C.B., D.C.L.
Lists of further Texts, Assyrian and Egyptian. Selected by George Smith and P. Le Page Renouf.
Crown octavo, Cloth 0 3 6

Records of the Past. Vol. II. Egyptian Texts, 1.

CONTENTS:—
Inscription of Una; Statistical Tablet; Tablet of Thothmes III.; Battle of Megiddo; Inscription of of Amen-em-heb. By S. Birch, LL.D.
Instructions of Amenemhat. By G. Maspero.
The Wars of Rameses II. with the Khita. By Prof. E. L. Lushington.
Inscription of Pianchi Mer-Amon. By Rev. F. C. Cook, M.A., Canon of Exeter.
Tablet of Newer-Hotep. By Paul Pierret.
Travels of an Egyptian. By François Chabas.
The Lamentations of Isis and Nephthys. By P. J. De Horrack.
Hymn to Amen-Ra; The Tale of the Doomed Prince. By C. W. Goodwin, M.A.
The Tale of the Two Brothers. By P. Le Page Renouf.
Egyptian Calendar; Table of Dynasties; Egyptian Measures and Weights.
Lists of further Texts, Assyrian and Egyptian. Selected by George Smith and P. Le Page Renouf.
Crown octavo, Cloth 0 3 6

Records of the Past. Vol. III. Assyrian Texts, 2.

CONTENTS:—
Early History of Babylonia. By George Smith.
Tablet of Ancient Accadian Laws; Synchronous History of Assyria and Babylonia; Kurkh Inscription of Shalmaneser; An Accadian Liturgy; Babylonian Charms. By Rev. A. H. Sayce, M.A.
Annals of Assur-nasir-pal. By Rev. J. M. Rodwell, M.A.
Inscription of Esarhaddon; Second Inscription of Esarhaddon; Sacred Assyrian Poetry. By H. F. Talbot, F.R.S.
List of further Texts.
Crown octavo, Cloth 0 3 6

For Specimen Pages, see the Illustrated Supplement. By post, free.

Miscellaneous.

	£	s.	d.

Records of the Past. Vol. IV. Egyptian Texts, 2.

CONTENTS:—
Inscription of Anebni; Inscription of Aahmes; Obelisk of the Lateran; Tablet of 400 years; Invasion of Egypt by the Greeks in the Reign of Menephtah; Dirge of Menephtah; Possessed Princess; Rosetta Stone. By S. Birch, LL.D.
Obelisk of Rameses II.; Hymn to Osiris. By François Chabas.
Treaty of Peace between Rameses II. and the Hittites; Neapolitan Stele; Festal Dirge of the Egyptians. By C. W. Goodwin, M.A.
Tablet of Ahmes; Inscription of Queen Madsenen. By Paul Pierret.
Stele of the Dream; Stele of the Excommunication. By G. Maspero.
Hymn to the Nile. By Rev. F. C. Cook.
Book of Respirations. By P. J. De Horrack.
Tale of Setnau. By P. Le Page Renouf.
List of further Texts.
Crown Octavo, Cloth .. .. | 0 | 3 | 6 |

Records of the Past. Vol. V. Assyrian Texts, 3.

CONTENTS:—
Legend of the infancy of Sargina I.; Inscription of Nabonidus; Inscription of Darius at Nakshi-Rustam; War of the Seven Evil Spirits against Heaven. By H. F. Talbot, F.R.S.
Inscription of Tiglath-Pileser I. By Sir Henry Rawlinson, K.C.B., D.C.L., etc.
Black Obelisk Inscription of Shalmaneser II.; Accadian Hymn to Istar; Tables of Omens. By Rev. A. H. Sayce, M.A.
Inscription of Tiglath-Pileser II.; Inscription of Nebuchadnezzar; Inscription of Neriglissar. By Rev. J. M. Rodwell, M.A.
Early History of Babylonia, Part II. By George Smith.
List of further Texts.
Crown octavo, Cloth .. .. | 0 | 3 | 6 |

Records of the Past. Vol. VI. Egyptian Texts, 3.

CONTENTS:—
Sepulchral Inscription of Ameni; The Conquests in Asia; Egyptian Magical Text. By S. Birch, LL.D.
Great Harris Papyrus, Part I. By Professor Eisenlohr and S. Birch, LL.D.
Inscription of Aahmes, son of Abana. By P. Le Page Renouf.

For Specimen Pages, see the Illustrated Supplement. By post, free.

Miscellaneous.

	£	s.	d.
Letter of Panbesa; Hymns to Amen; The Story of Saneha. By C. W. Goodwin, M.A. Stele of the Coronation; Stele of King Horsiatef. By G. Maspero. The Inscription of the Governor Nes-hor. By Paul Pierret. Inscription of the Destruction of Mankind. By Edouard Naville. The Song of the Harper. By Ludwig Stern. The Tale of the Garden of Flowers. By François Chabas. List of further Texts. Crown octavo, Cloth	0	3	6

Vols. VII. and VIII. *In the Press.*

The Assyrian Eponym Canon:

Containing Translations of the Documents, and an Account of the Evidence, on the Comparative Chronology of the Assyrian and Jewish Kingdoms, from the Death of Solomon to Nebuchadnezzar. By George Smith, of the Department of Oriental Antiquities, British Museum. Octavo, Cloth extra	0	9	0

The Resurrection of Assyria.

A Lecture delivered in Renfield Presbyterian Church, Glasgow, on January 31, 1875. By W. R. Cooper, F.R.A.S., M.R.A.S., Secretary of the Society of Biblical Archæology. Paper Wrapper	0	1	6

The Heroines of the Past.

A Lecture delivered at the Working Mens' Institute, Leighton Buzzard, on February, 23, 1875. By W. R. Cooper, F.R.A.S., M.R.A.S., Secretary of the Society of Biblical Archæology. Paper Wrapper	0	1	6

Egypt and the Pentateuch.

An Address to the Members of the Open Air Mission. By W. R. Cooper, F.R.A.S., M.R.A.S., Secretary of the Society of Biblical Archæology. Octavo, Paper wrapper	0	2	0

An Archaic Dictionary,

Historical and Mythological, from the Egyptian, Assyrian, and Etruscan Monuments, and Papyri. By W. R. Cooper, F.R.A.S., M.R.A.S. *In the Press.*

For Specimen Pages, see the Illustrated Supplement. By post, free.

Miscellaneous.

	£ s. d.
Ancient Chaldean Magic. Translated from the French of M. François Lenormant, with Notes and References by the English Editor. *In the Press.*	
The Utrecht Psalter. The History, Art, and Palæography, of the Manuscript commonly styled the Utrecht Psalter. By Walter de Gray Birch, F.R.S.L., Senior Assistant of the Department of Manuscripts in the British Museum; Honorary Secretary to the British Archæological Association, etc. *In the Press.*	
The Autograph Text Book: Containing a Text of Scripture, and a Verse of Poetry, together with a space for the insertion of Births, Marriages, and Deaths, under every Day in the year.	
Cloth extra, gilt edges	0 2 6
Turkey morocco, limp	0 8 6
„ „ plain	0 9 0
Daily Light on the Daily Path. *Large Edition.* CONTENTS:—A devotional Text-book for every day in the Year, Morning and Evening; in the very words of Scripture. Large-print edition, 16mo. Two Volumes.	
Extra cloth, gilt edges. Each vol.	0 2 6
Bound in calf. Each vol.	0 6 0
Bound in morocco. Each vol.	0 7 0
ditto, turkey, tooled	0 8 6
ditto, with flaps	0 10 6
Daily Light on the Daily Path. *Small Edition.* 32mo. Two Volumes.	
Extra cloth, gilt edges. Each vol.	0 1 6
Bound in calf. Each vol.	0 4 6
Bound in morocco. Each vol.	0 5 0
ditto, turkey tooled	0 6 6
ditto, with flaps	0 7 0
The Illustrated Pocket Bible, For the Young. Containing forty-eight Historical Pictures, with 4,000 suggestive Questions, coloured Maps, and a complete Index of Subjects.	
In attractive Morocco binding	0 12 0
Four Thousand Questions, intended to open up the Scriptures to the Young. 16mo.	0 0 6

For Specimen Pages, see the Illustrated Supplement. By post, free.

Miscellaneous.

	£	s.	d.
Concise Answers To the Four Thousand Scripture Questions of the Illustrated Pocket Bible. For the use of Parents and Teachers.			
Foolscap octavo. Paper wrapper	0	2	0
Cloth	0	2	6
Questions on the New Testament, For the use of Schools	0	0	2
Questions and Answers On the Historical books of the New Testament, being a Key to "Questions on the New Testament"	0	0	6
A French Reading Book, For Schools and Families. Being the Historical Books of the New Testament, in pure modern French. By Jonas Vuitel.			
Octavo, Cloth	0	3	0
Prayers and Devotional Meditations, From the Psalms of David. By Elihu Burritt.			
Octavo	0	2	0
The Children of the Bible. By Elihu Burritt.			
32mo.	0	0	6
An Order for Morning and Evening Prayer, Being an abridgement of the forms in the Common Prayer Book. To be used by Lay Readers in Mission Rooms, Hospitals, etc.			
Sewed	0	0	2
The Poetry of the Hebrew Pentateuch. Being Four Essays on Moses and the Mosaic Age. By the Rev. M. Margoliouth, M.A., LL.D., Ph.D., etc.			
Octavo	0	3	6
The Oracles of God, and their Vindication. Being a Sermon preached at St. Saviour's Church, Forest Hill. By the Rev. M. Margoliouth, LL.D., Ph.D., etc.			
Octavo	0	1	0

For Specimen Pages, see the Illustrated Supplement. By post, free.

Practical religion. PHILIPPIANS, III. *Confidence in Christ alone.*

11 And *that* every tongue should confess that Jesus Christ *is* Lord,[a] to the glory of God the Father.

12 Wherefore, my beloved, as ye have always obeyed, not as in my presence only, but now much more in my absence, work[d] out your own salvation with fear[e] and trembling:

13 For it is God[f] which worketh in you both to will and to do of *his* good pleasure.

14 Do all things without murmurings[h] and disputings;[i]

15 That ye may be blameless and [β]harmless, the sons[m] of God, without

A. D. 64.

a John 13.13. Ro. 14. 9. b Ac. 23. 6. c Ac. 22. 3, 4. Ga. 1.13,14. d Pr. 10. 16. Jno.6.27..29 He. 4. 11. 2 Pe.1.5..10. e Ep. 6. 5. f Lu. 1. 6. g He. 13. 21. h Mat. 13.44. i Is. 53. 11.

that he hath whereof he might trust in the flesh, I more:

5 Circumcised the eighth day, of the stock of Israel, *of* the tribe of Benjamin, an Hebrew of the Hebrews; as touching the law, a Pharisee;[b]

6 Concerning zeal,[c] persecuting the church; touching the righteousness which is in the law, blameless.[f]

7 But what things were gain to me, those I counted loss[h] for Christ.

8 Yea, doubtless, and I count all things *but* loss, for[i] the excellency of the knowledge of Christ Jesus my Lord: for whom I have[m] suffered the loss of all things, dung, that I may

n him, not having
ss, which is of the
through the faith
ness[r] which is of

m, and the power
d the[s] fellowship
ade conformable

s I might[v] attain
he dead.
d already attain-
y perfect:[z] but I
I may apprehend
m apprehended of

unt not myself to
t *this* one thing *I*
things which are
forth unto those

the mark for the
calling of God in

s many as be per-
ed: and if in any
minded, God shall

ereto we have al-
walk by the same
me thing.
wers[i] together of
ch walk so as ye

, of whom I have
now tell you even
e the enemies[l] of

estruction, whose
nd *whose* glory[o] is
earthly things.)
n[p] is in heaven;
look[q] for the Sa-
Christ;
ge[r] our vile body,
ned like unto his
g to the working[s]
en[u] to subdue all

R IV.
y brethren, dearly
d for, my joy and
st in the Lord, *my*

and beseech Syn-
the same mind in

ee also, true yoke-
n which laboured
ith Clement also,
labourers whose
life.

II.

Practical religion. PHILIPPIANS, III. *Confidence in Christ alone.*

11 And *that* every tongue should confess that Jesus Christ *is* Lord,[a] to the glory of God the Father.

12 Wherefore, my beloved, as ye have always obeyed, not as in my presence only, but now much more in my absence, work[c] out your own salvation with [d]fear

A. D. 64.

a Jn°. 13. 13. Ro. 14. 9. b Ac. 23. 6. c Jn°. 6. 27.. 29.

that he hath whereof he might trust in the flesh, I more:

5 Circumcised the eighth day, of the stock of Israel, *of* the tribe of Benjamin, an Hebrew of the Hebrews; as touching the law, a Pharisee;[b]

6 Concerning zeal,[c] persecuting the

ess which
in to me,
all things
he know-
for whom
ll things,
hat I may
ot having
h is of the
the faith
hich is of
he power
ellowship
formable
tain unto
attained,
t I follow
that for
of Christ
f to have
I do, for-
e behind,
so things
k for the
in Christ
ns be per-
if in any
od [d]shall
o have al-
the same
gother of
so as ye
have told
weeping,
cross of
hose God
s in their
gs.)
heaven;
r the Sa-
vile body,
unto his
working
ubdue all
early be-
d crown,
my dearly
eech Syn-
mind in
rue yoke-
laboured
aent also,
rs, whose

I.

Practical religion. PHILIPPIANS, III. *Confidence in Christ alone.*

11 And *that* every tongue should confess that Jesus Christ *is* Lord, [a]to the glory of God the Father.

12 Wherefore, my beloved, as ye have always obeyed, not as in my presence, only, but now much more in my absence, work [d]out your own salvation with fear[e] and trembling;

13 For it is God [f] which worketh in you both to will and to do of *his* good pleasure.

14 Do all things without murmurings[h] and disputings;[i]

15 That ye may be blameless and [β] harmless, the sons [m] of God, without rebuke, in the midst of a crooked[n] and perverse nation, among whom [γ] ye shine as lights [p] in the world;

16 Holding forth the word of life; that I may rejoice in the day of Christ, that I have not run in vain, [l] neither laboured in vain.

17 Yea, and if I be [δ] offered [t] upon the sacrifice and service of your faith, I joy, and rejoice with you all.

18 For the same cause also do ye joy, and rejoice with me.

19 [ζ] But I trust in the Lord Jesus to send Timotheus [w] shortly unto you, that I also may be of good comfort, when I know your state.

20 For I have no man [η] like-minded, who will naturally care for your state.

21 For all seek their own, [y] not the things which are Jesus Christ's.

22 But ye know the proof of him, that, as a son with the father, he hath served with me in the gospel.

23 Him therefore I hope to send presently, so soon as I shall see how it will go with me.

24 But [c] I trust in the Lord that I also myself shall come shortly.

25 Yet I supposed it necessary to send to you Epaphroditus, [f] my brother, and companion in labour, and fellow-soldier,[g] but your messenger, and he that ministered to my wants.

26 For he longed after you all, and was full of heaviness, because that ye had heard that he had been sick.

27 For indeed he was sick nigh unto death: but God had mercy on him; and not on him only, but on me also, lest I should have sorrow upon sorrow.

28 I sent him therefore the more carefully, that, when ye see him again, ye may rejoice, and that I may be the less sorrowful.

29 Receive him therefore in the Lord with all gladness: and [θ]hold such in reputation:

30 Because for the work of Christ he was nigh unto death, not regarding his life, [t] to supply your lack of service toward me.

CHAP. III.

FINALLY, my brethren, rejoice [u]in the Lord. To write the same [w] things to you, to me indeed *is* not grievous, but for you *it is* safe.

2 Beware of dogs, [x] beware of [y] evil workers, beware of the [z] concision.

3 For we are [a] the circumcision, which worship God in the spirit, and rejoice in Christ Jesus, and have no confidence in the flesh:

4 Though I might also have confidence in the flesh. If any other man thinketh

A. D. 64.

a Jon. 13. 13. Ro. 14. 9. b Ac. 23. 6. c Ac. 22. 3, 4. Ga. 1. 13, 14. d Pr. 10. 16. Jn. 6. 27.. 29. He. 4. 11. 2 Pe. 1. 5.. 10. e Ep. 6. 5. f Lu. 1. 6. g He. 13. 21. Mat. 13. 44. i Is. 53. 11. Je. 9. 23, 24. Jno. 17. 3. 1 Co. 2. 2. k 1 Co. 10. 10. l Ro. 14. 1. m 2 Co. 11. 23.. 27. β or, sincere. n Mat. 5. 45. Ep. 5. 1. o De. 32. 5. γ or, shine ye. p Mat. 5. 14, 16. q Ro. 10. 3, 5. r He. 1. 17. 3. 21, 22. s 1 Co. 9. 26. δ poured forth. t 2 Ti. 4. 6. u 1 Pe. 4. 13. v Ac. 26. 7. ζ moreover. w 1 Th. 3. 2. x He. 12. 23. η or, so dear unto me. y 2 Ti. 3. 2. z Ps. 45. 10. He. 6. 1. a 1 Co. 9. 24. He. 12. 1. b He. 3. 1. c ch. 1. 25. d 1 Co. 2. 6. e Ga. 5. 10. f ch. 4. 18. g Phile. 2. h Ga. 6. 16. i 1 Th. 1. 6. k 1 Pe. 5. 3. l Ga. 1. 7. 6. 12. m 2 Co. 11. 15. 2 Pe. 2. 1. n 1 Ti. 6. 5. o He. 4. 7. p Ep. 2. 6, 19. q He. 9. 28. θ or, honour such. 1 Co. 16. 18. r 1 Co. 15. 43, &c. 1 Jno. 3. 2. s Ep. 1. 19. t 1 Co. 16. 17. u 1 Co. 15. 26, 27. v 1 Th. 5. 16. w 2 Pe. 1. 12.. 15. x Is. 56. 10, 11. Re. 22. 15. y Ps. 119. 115. z Ga. 5. 1.. 3. a Re. 2. 28, 29.

that he hath whereof he might trust in the flesh, I more:

5 Circumcised the eighth day, of the stock of Israel, *of* the tribe of Benjamin, an Hebrew of the Hebrews; as touching the law, a Pharisee;[b]

6 Concerning zeal, [c] persecuting the church; touching the righteousness which is in the law, blameless. [f]

7 But what things were gain to me, those I counted loss [h] for Christ.

8 Yea, doubtless, and I count all things *but* loss, for [i] the excellency of the knowledge of Christ Jesus my Lord; for whom I have [m] suffered the loss of all things, and do count them *but* dung, that I may win Christ,

9 And be found in him, not having mine own [q] righteousness, which is of the law, but that which is through the faith of Christ, the righteousness [r] which is of God by faith:

10 That I may know him, and the power of his resurrection, and the [s] fellowship of his sufferings, being made conformable unto his death;

11 If by any means I might [v] attain unto the resurrection of the dead.

12 Not as though I had already attained, either were already perfect: [z] but I follow after, if that I may apprehend that for which also I am apprehended of Christ Jesus.

13 Brethren, I count not myself to have apprehended: but *this* one thing *I do*, forgetting [a] those things which are behind, and reaching forth unto those things which are before,

14 I press [a] toward the mark for the prize of the high [b] calling of God in Christ Jesus.

15 Let us therefore, as many as be perfect, [d] be thus [e] minded: and if in any thing ye be otherwise minded, God shall reveal even this unto you.

16 Nevertheless, whereto we have already attained, let us walk by the same rule, [h] let us mind the same thing.

17 Brethren, be followers [i] together of me, and mark them which walk so as ye have us [k] for an ensample.

18 (For many walk, of whom I have told you often, and now tell you even weeping, *that they are* the enemies [l] of the cross of Christ;

19 Whose end [m] *is* destruction, whose God [n] *is their* belly, and *whose* glory [o] *is* in their shame, who mind earthly things.)

20 For our conversation [p] is in heaven; from whence also we look [q] for the Saviour, the Lord Jesus Christ;

21 Who shall change [r] our vile body, that it may be fashioned like unto his glorious body, according to the working[s] whereby he is able even [u] to subdue all things unto himself.

CHAP. IV.

THEREFORE, my brethren dearly beloved and longed for, my joy and crown, so stand fast in the Lord, *my* dearly beloved.

2 I beseech Euodias, and beseech Syntyche, that they be of the same mind in the Lord.

3 And I entreat thee also, true yokefellow, help those women which laboured with me in the gospel, with Clement also, and *with* other my fellow-labourers, whose names *are* in the book of life.

BAGSTER'S POLYGLOT BIBLES.

THE FACSIMILE SERIES:
- No. I., The MINIATURE Edition, 16mo.
- No. II., The MEDIUM Edition, Foolscap octavo.
- No. III., The LARGE PRINT Edition, Octavo.

THESE three Editions correspond page for page, and line for line, to afford to those who use more than one Edition of the Series the inestimable help of local memory. "It has been some advantage for this reason to accustom one's self to books of the same Edition : and it has been of constant and special use to Divines and private Christians, to be furnished with several Bibles of the same Edition, that, wheresoever they are, whether in their chamber, parlour, or study, in the younger or elder years of life, they may find the chapters and verses standing in the same parts of the page."—*Art of Improving the Memory*.

BAGSTER'S POLYGLOT BIBLES.

These Bibles are enriched with the following supplementary aids:—A detailed Chronological Arrangement of the Old Testament Scriptures; Tables of Measures, Weights, and Coins; an Itinerary of the Children of Israel from Egypt to Canaan; Table of the Chronological Order of the Books of the Bible; Chronological Table of the Kings and Prophets of Judah and Israel, in Parallel Columns; a Summary View of the principal events of the period from the close of the sacred Canon of the Old Testament, until the times of the New Testament; an Account of the Jewish and other Sects and Factions; a Table of the principal Messianic Prophecies; a List of Passages in the Old Testament quoted or alluded to in the New Testament; the Names, Titles, and Characters of our Lord Jesus Christ; a Chronological Harmony of the Four Evangelists, in Parallel Columns; Coloured Maps; an engraved Chronological Chart of History from B.C. 500 to A.D. 400; a condensed Scripture Index ; an Alphabetical Index to the Psalms; and the Names, Characteristics, Privileges and Glory of the Church of God.

Another not unimportant advantage is secured by printing these Bibles on the facsimile principle; they not only correspond one with another, but with the whole Polyglot series of Hebrew, Greek, Latin, German, and other languages, which are all arranged on the same convenient plan. See Index, under Polyglot Bibles.

Polyglot Bibles.

	Seconds mor. blocked, gilt edges.	Turkey mor. plain.	Best flexible morocco, hand tooled.	Antique mor. tooled, gold on red edges.	Antique mor. plain gold on red edges.	Plain antique morocco, plain gold on red edges.	Limp Turkey morocco, with projecting flaps.	Levant mor. lined calf, new perfectly supple style.
I. The Miniature Polyglot Bible, 16mo.	0 9 0	0 0 12	0 0 15	0 1 2	0 0 17	0 0 17	0 0 17	0 1 0
Do. with the Book of Common Prayer	0 11 0	0 0 14	0 0 17	0 1 4	0 0 19	0 0 19	0 0 19	0 1 2
Do. with the Psalms of the Church of Scotland	0 9 0	0 0 13	0 0 15	0 1 2	0 0 17	0 0 17	0 0 18	0 1 0
Do. with Wesley's Hymns	0 13 6	0 0 17	6 1 0	0 1 7	6 0 2	0 1 2	0 1 2	0 1 5
Do. with Greek and English Test.	0 14 0	0 0 18	6 1 1	0 1 7	6 0 2	0 1 2	0 1 5	0 1 5
Do. with 108 Pictorial Illustrations	0 17 0	0 1 0	6 1 3	0 1 10	6 0 5	0 1 5	0 1 5	0 1 8
II. The Medium Polyglot Bible. Fcp.8vo.	0 12 0	0 0 16	6 1 0	0 1 6	6 0 2	0 1 2	0 1 2	0 1 5
Do. with the Book of Common Prayer	0 14 0	0 0 18	6 1 2	0 1 8	6 0 4	0 1 4	0 1 4	0 1 7
Do. with the Apocrypha	0 14 0	0 0 18	6 1 2	0 1 8	6 0 4	0 1 4	0 1 4	0 1 7
Do. with Cruden's Concordance	0 16 0	0 1 0	6 1 4	0 1 10	6 0 6	0 1 6	0 1 6	0 1 9
Do. with the Psalms of the Church of Scotland	0 12 0	0 0 17	0 1 0	0 1 7	0 0 2	0 1 2	0 1 3	0 1 5
Do. with Wesley's Hymns	0 18 0	0 1 2	6 1 6	0 1 12	6 0 8	0 1 8	0 1 8	0 1 11
Do. with Greek New Testament	0 17 0	0 1 1	6 1 5	0 1 11	6 0 7	0 1 7	0 1 7	0 1 10
Do. with 108 Pictorial Illustrations	1 0 0	0 1 4	6 1 8	0 1 14	6 0 10	0 1 10	0 1 10	0 1 13
III. The Large-print Polyglot Bible. 8vo.	0 14 0	0 1 1	0 1 5	0 1 18	0 0 7	0 1 7	0 1 7	0 1 10
Do. with the Book of Common Prayer	0 16 0	0 1 3	6 1 7	6 2 0	6 0 9	6 1 9	0 1 10	0 1 12
Do. with the Apocrypha	0 17 0	0 1 4	0 1 8	0 2 1	0 0 10	0 1 10	0 1 10	0 1 13
Do. with the Psalms of the Church of Scotland	0 15 0	0 1 2	0 1 6	0 1 19	0 0 8	0 1 8	0 1 8	0 1 11
Do. with Greek and English Test.	1 0 0	0 1 7	6 1 11	0 2 4	6 0 13	6 1 13	6 1 14	0 1 16
Do. with Cruden's Concordance	0 18 0	0 1 5	6 1 9	0 2 2	6 0 11	0 1 11	0 1 12	0 1 14

∗∗ The Book of Common Prayer, the Scripture Index, the Psalms of the Church of Scotland, the Apocrypha, etc., may be bound up with these Bibles in any desired combination.

www.ingramcontent.com/pod-product-compliance
Lightning Source LLC
Chambersburg PA
CBHW020814230426
43666CB00007B/1005